MANY RIVERS, ONE SEA

T0333531

JOSEPH ALLCHIN

Many Rivers, One Sea

*Bangladesh and the Challenge of
Islamist Militancy*

HURST & COMPANY, LONDON

First published in the United Kingdom in 2019 by
C. Hurst & Co. (Publishers) Ltd.,
41 Great Russell Street, London, WC1B 3PL

Printed in India

Distributed in the United States, Canada and Latin America by
Oxford University Press, 198 Madison Avenue, New York, NY 10016,
United States of America.

A Cataloguing-in-Publication data record for this book
is available from the British Library.

ISBN: 9781849048743

www.hurstpublishers.com

CONTENTS

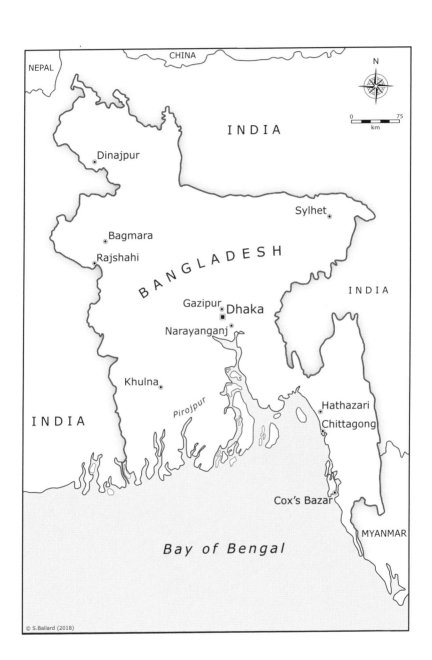

INTRODUCTION

This book was conceived in the rubble of a hostage crisis. The crisis shook Bangladesh and drew international attention to the country, for all the wrong reasons. But it also happened at a strange time globally. I was not far away in Dhaka when the attack by five young men on the Holey Artisan Bakery took place on the evening of 1 July 2016. I had left the UK for Bangladesh only a few days before, on 24 June, the morning after that country, my country of birth, was convulsed by its shock vote to leave the European Union, in the so-called Brexit referendum. In hindsight, the mornings of 24 June and 2 July 2016 were strangely similar. When morning light returned to the corpse of a body politic, it seemed to reveal a hitherto less-than-well-understood anger—seemingly populist and organic, but at the same time, at least in certain ways, deeply intertwined with the machinations of sections of the political classes. The relationship between these two types of force, the popular and the political, forms the basis of the analysis in this book.

I started out trying simply to tell the story of a sequence of events in Bangladesh that spawned the modern phenomenon of militancy in the country. In doing so, through snapshots of, on occasion, disparate times, events and actors, I also delve into how historical movements and ideologies forged anxieties and the grounds on which militancy has arisen. Extremism and subsequent terrorism or militancy are intensely social activities. They cannot simply be understood through grand political or historical acts or formal organisations. This is particularly the case in Bangladesh, where politics and mobilisation are characterised by great informality, in a society comparatively un-governed by formal institutions. This informality is vital to understanding Bangladesh—a 'young' country, where through the vicissitudes of recent centuries the land and people have so often been viewed as subordinate or peripheral. Here, societal structure, institutions and behaviours seem to be deeply 'traditional' and ingrained, but are in reality dynamic, contested and fluctuating. Bangladesh, for example, adheres little to traditional social constructs such as caste. With centuries of foreign domination, institutions of sovereign statehood are also newer and less rigid. As a result, they are less durable and effective.

In many analyses of contemporary Bangladesh, this informality is most often seen as a 'challenge'—at best—and otherwise as a crippling Achilles heel. But the view of this phenomenon as necessarily negative is mistaken. It could be argued that it has helped encourage some of the improvements that Bangladesh has made in human development—the country did well in meeting most of the UN Millennium Development Goals, for instance, through greater inclusion of women in the economy and women's empowerment more broadly. While this book does not set out to examine these issues per se, it is also worth noting that these characteristics of informality and dynamism make Bangladesh important and worthy of greater consideration from scholars and the global public.

The phenomenon of modern-day extremism, whether with Islamic characteristics or not, is imbued with the fragmented informality that globalisation, increased connectivity and the post-Cold War global political economy have created. Thus, while most analyses of development and politics would suggest that Bangladesh is converging or attempting to converge with the world, through the endeavours of the state and attendant stakeholders, it could be argued that the world is in fact converging with Bangladesh. In a world of intense economic competition and growing ecological fears, small states are often felt to be failing their citizens. Bangladesh's informality means that it has lived through and faced many of the world's emerging challenges.

Bangladesh is increasingly described as 'emerging', and it is in a sense doing so from unimaginable tribulations in recent centuries—from colonialism to famines to genocides and more. Once seen as being at the 'wrong end' of the Gangetic plain, Bangladesh now sits at a fulcrum point between the world's two most populous nations—India and China—in the middle of a region that is ever growing in importance. It could be argued that young people in Bangladesh are living a more quintessentially twenty-first-century existence than any group of people anywhere else, emerging rapidly from 'traditional' agrarian existences into more interconnected and more deeply competitive, yet informal and crowded, urban lives. Their reality will come to be the norm for people all over the world. While the world's attention is drawn to the denizens of cities such as New York or Singapore, the reality of our collective future as a species is far more tangibly exemplified by the young people of Gazipur or Mohammadpur. The anxieties, cultures and movements that are thrown up by the paradigms of those communities will affect far more people than those of the aforementioned bastions of wealth and magnets of global attention.

It is no doubt a challenge writing a book such as this as an 'outsider'—neither a Bangladeshi citizen, nor a Muslim, nor even a scholar of that great world religion. Islam has so shaped the region, governed its people's behaviours, and given faith and guidance to multitudes through hard and less hard times. Of this I was very aware when writing, researching and thinking about this book. But here and in other writing, I hope that the perspective of a relative outsider, invested only as a passive observer to tell stories of political significance, can add something to telling the story of the region. However, as the great thinker Edward Said observed in the introduction to his seminal work *Orientalism*:

> No one has ever devised a method for detaching the scholar from the circumstances of life ... These continue to bear on what he does professionally, even though naturally enough his research and its fruits do attempt to reach a level of relative freedom from the inhibitions and the restrictions of brute, everyday reality.[1]

Indeed, detaching oneself from the 'brute, everyday reality' of Bangladeshi politics can be particularly difficult. The country's informality creates what is commonly referred to as a culture of zero-sum politics. It is deeply confrontational, and, by necessity and

3

definition, one in which a winner-takes-all paradigm must prevail. It can thus be hard to freely analyse and engage with multiple perspectives on issues that arise in this book: power, identity, religion, state and society. It is difficult to escape from the convenient labels that are used to rapidly ascribe 'friend' or 'foe' in the fraught debates that rage on social media, on the street, in offices of state, and beyond. Veracity can often be the victim, from official government denials of fact to tropes that circulate on social media.

Having said that, Bangladesh can also be an incredibly frank and open place, with many stakeholders and actors keen, and gracious enough, to spend their time and energy conveying their side of a story to a foreign journalist. Perhaps more valuable still, the enthusiasm and hunger for discussion and debate that are found up and down the country are a boon for the curious and for the exchange of ideas and study.

As this book was being written, and periodically throughout Bangladesh's history, those traditions of debate and expression have come under withering attack. Those who seek to limit expression commonly do so on the pretext of creating order, instilling discipline in those considered loose of tongue or lacking in respect for authority. Again, this is an area in which Bangladesh has starkly modern characteristics. It is a place where, in lived experience, a linguistic-cultural identity forged a nation, built on almost entirely new grounds and in response to a direct political project by Pakistan to restrict expression and identities and impose 'discipline' on a population. In Bangladesh, religious identities are also changing rapidly, but have long balanced globalised or transnational ones with fiercely local ones. These great cleavages make the anxieties that Bangladesh has struggled with in the course of its journey very relevant globally. The informality and 'newness' of Bangladeshi identities, and thus the great conflicts that go with them, prefigure many of those that are felt today in once 'stable' nations, where economic and societal changes have forced peoples to re-examine their identities and truths.

The title of the book came from an investigator for Bangladesh's International Crimes Tribunal (ICT). This team of police was tasked with poring over the country's history to attempt to correct decades of impunity and challenge ideologies that have existed in the mainstream whilst being drastically at odds with the country's founding principles.

The convergence of the ICT and militancy was apparent, and I recall asking one of these investigators about the extent to which the new militant attacks were linked to the kind of politics that the accused had been involved with in the 1970s. Perhaps according to script, the officer used a very apposite Bangladeshi analogy: many rivers, leading to one sea. The strands of associations and networks that made up the Islamist political world were many, like the rivers that make up the Ganges delta, but they all led or aspired to lead to the same sea. This seemed a fitting analogy in a geographic sense, but also in that it conveyed the complex disorder that organisations and ideology had in the Bangladeshi theatre. More importantly, it also conveyed that zero-sum quality to politics in Bangladesh. There was no stagnant resting for this water; all actors invariably rushed towards the sea, and to change politics irrevocably through the creation of some deep and other-worldly new political body. I reflected that in this sense, every act—whether in the investigation of war crimes committed over four decades ago or in the passage of more mundane politics—was part of that lively conflict to define the state and society that Bangladesh is, and will be.

This work has relied on a good many government or official sources. It is their job to combat, contain and on occasions inform journalists of the nuances of these phenomena. This presents obvious challenges. Combined with the zero-sum political game intertwined with the issues at the centre of this work, the reliance on limited sources means that there are unanswered questions and that great efforts have had to be made to disentangle propaganda and slander from genuine fact. Added to this are the simple facts of how information and accusation are spread in a context such as Bangladesh, where government resources are so limited. This is especially the case in the judicial and law enforcement arenas. Even without political malpractice, these pillars of state are massively overburdened. The ability to investigate and then establish coherent narratives based on truth and justice, for citizens to have faith in, is limited. This has been a particular challenge in producing this book, for in many cases discussed, finality has been elusive.

On the morning of 2 July 2016, it was hard to process what was happening down a leafy Dhaka lane, enrobed in monsoon humidity and crowded with military personnel bristling with weaponry. Like most there, I was exhausted—it had been a long night. Heavily armed members of many branches of the security services slumped in vehicles trying to get some rest. Most were eager to bat away questions: What had driven this audacious attack, on such a gilded restaurant and symbol of wealth? How did the attack fit into the context of Bangladeshi militancy and politics? How, moreover, did it fit into trends and movements of international jihadism? This book attempts to answer these questions and provide some nuance to many of the knee-jerk, lazy or intentionally inaccurate reports on the phenomenon. I try to look beneath the surface, and to orient Bangladeshi militancy beyond what are often binary debates.

1

THE IDEA

In the name of 'God and a united Pakistan,' Dacca is today a crushed and frightened city.[1]
—Simon Dring, *The Daily Telegraph*, 30 March 1971

In a packed courthouse in Dhaka, fire and brimstone erupted. The preacher stood tall, spewing curses and promising revenge on the 'atheistic' judges and assembled crowds—myself included. Shaking his finger in a well-worn routine, dramatised by his deep crimson beard and black eyeliner, Delwar Hossain Sayeedi, televangelist, politician and, henceforth, convicted war criminal, was sentenced to death. This judgement, passed in February 2013 at Bangladesh's International Crimes Tribunal (ICT), crystallised the deep schisms dividing the country. It ushered in days of violence, acting like a clarion call at the beginning of one of the bloodiest years for Bangladeshi politics since Sayeedi's blood-soaked year of infamy in 1971, which had prompted this very trial. The ruling was, in several ways, a trigger moment, presaging a period of political conflict that seemed to herald the arrival of a very modern form of international jihadism in the country.

The Sayeedi case represents the confluence of several vital questions in Bangladeshi politics. It is the embodiment of the country's Islamist issue as well as the resistance the movement provokes—a neat characterisation of a deep fissure in contemporary Bangladeshi

7

politics and society. It also highlights the anxieties amongst practising Bangladeshi Muslims to reconcile religious convictions with politics in a state nominally governed by a secular constitution. Born in British-ruled East Bengal in 1940, Sayeedi was significant not only for having played an active role in the country's largest Islamist political party, Jamaat-e-Islami (commonly known as Jamaat), but also for straddling the divide between religious preacher and politician. He was perhaps the vanguard that Jamaat's founder and ideologue Maulana Maududi himself had envisaged. This relationship between personal religiosity and public activism and agitation is essential to understanding extremism and militant discord in Bangladesh today. It is this conflict that is shaping and encouraging new religious practices and fertilising the growth of radicalisation in Bangladesh. In some ways, these tensions have helped non-indigenous, pan-Islamic identities in modern Bangladesh to flourish.

The Jamaat party was founded in pre-Partition British India in 1941 by Syed Abul A'la Maududi, an Islamist preacher, journalist and anti-colonial thinker. Maududi's importance is comparable to that of Islamist theorist and intellectual of Egypt's Muslim Brotherhood, Sayyid Qutb, whom he influenced deeply. Both men sought to put forth the case for political Islam as an answer to the twentieth century's otherwise binary, Western-focused, right–left debates and conflicts. They sought to rectify what they saw as the subordination of the Muslim world and its return to a pre-Islamic state of *jahiliyyah*—ignorance or foolishness. They believed that the propagation of political Islam, 'focused almost exclusively on the preservation of doctrinal purity', was the only way to challenge and overcome Western hegemony.[2]

This revivalist movement to 'purify' the faith is often known as Salafism, in reference to its attempts to follow the supposed practices of the Prophet Muhammad's very first followers, the *salaf*. While the movement emerged in late nineteenth-century Egypt, with a precursor in eighteenth-century Saudi Wahhabism, it has always looked far back to the Islam of the seventh and eighth centuries as a golden age of piety and Muslim pre-eminence. Much like Western far-right movements, it seeks to reconstruct a glorious past, following 'a philosophy that believes in progression through regression.'[3] To Maududi and Qutb, Muslims had since strayed from the path of Islam and been subjugated by disbelieving colonial powers—the answer was to resurrect the Islamic society and to create 'an environment of separation and confrontation' between the West and the Muslim world.[4]

Thus, by ridding the religion of what they viewed as 'innovations' or corruptions, the Muslims would be able to galvanise and re-strengthen their faith into a unifying, coherent political movement. It seemed a guarantee of winning God's favour, which they knew had been bestowed on the early Islamic empires, surely as a reward for belief and piety. The task ahead was formidable—for in the case of Bangladesh, as with much of the Muslim world, it was not merely modern 'Western' infringements that had muddied the waters of Islamic practice in the eyes of these purists. Over the course of its history Bengali Islam had moulded itself around and merged with unique local customs and traditions to best suit the needs of its practitioners and their everyday lives. For Islamist reformers, these heterodox religious practices were considered heretical innovations, and, perhaps more importantly, were seen to pull societal morals away from the pulpit towards the dreaded realm of secular rulings, rulers, thinkers and institutions.

The trap of Western secularism 'epitomised the modern *jahiliyyah* because it amounted to a rebellion against God's rule.'[5] There should be little surprise that, like many such movements, Jamaat and Maududi's work and thinking arose at a time of angst and turmoil, as British colonialism was concluding its ignominious adventure in South Asia and new futures had to be contemplated for the subcontinent's various religious communities. For Maududi, this amounted to trying to see off the idea of a secular state, which was and still is often viewed as a quintessentially Western political construct, even in South Asia, where it has a long political legacy.

Divine Impunity

I stood but a few feet from Maududi's heir, the crimson-bearded Sayeedi, in that Dhaka courtroom in February 2013 as he was sentenced. The whitewashed colonial-era courthouse was packed, as indeed it was for most sentencing sessions of the ICT. Journalists pushed for entry against weighty doors and reluctant police officers. Once in, we stood sweating, shuffling in the aisle, chatting and pressed up against one another, while the almost inaudible drone of the judgements and officialdom wore on, in poorly amplified legalese, to its inevitably dramatic conclusion. Sayeedi could have been expected to rant and rave. The septuagenarian had not only enjoyed decades of impunity but had built himself into one of Bangladesh's most prominent and popular preachers, supposedly one of the 500 most influential Muslims globally.[6] His fame was built on both a 'distinctly different style of rhetoric and a belligerent style of presentation', as well as on an embrace of feasible, people-friendly and modern delivery methods.[7] Inspired by the Islamic revolution in Iran, Sayeedi had used easily disseminated tapes to spread his message throughout the country, as rural masses, denied much electronic entertainment, could easily sit around a cheap tape deck and listen to his uncompromising message. Tapes of his sermons or *waz mahfils* could help while away the hours spent on tiring bus journeys, stuck in traffic or on ponderous rural roads, and countered secular alternatives such as Bollywood film music, local pop music or indigenous folk music.[8]

Sayeedi's impunity had lasted partly for this reason. Despite spending much of 1971 aiding the Pakistan military as it sought to 'purify' then East Pakistan of supposed 'deviants', such as Hindus and non-Muslims, by killing, raping and forcibly converting them—all in order to prevent the birth of Bangladesh—he had served two terms as an MP, had amassed wealth, and had the liberty to travel and preach, advancing his version of Islam and nationalism. His life and work had experienced a revival that forty-one years earlier, at the birth of Bangladesh, would have looked extremely unlikely.

Language and Identity

Bangladesh had been formed out of the conflict fought by men such as Sayeedi. Almost since the initial inception of Pakistan in 1947, when the British fled India leaving behind a deadly mess, Bengalis had been concerned about the usurping of their identity within the new state. Pakistan was founded by a secular Shia Muslim Western-educated lawyer, Muhammad Ali Jinnah. However, the new nation quickly started to evolve into a theocratic 'tyranny of the majority', whereby Sunni Islam, and an attendant identity formed in West Pakistan, would come, as it still does, to dominate, harass and devastate all others. A 'triumphant Islamic orthodoxy defined the country's identity', as former Pakistani politician Farahnaz Ispahani has it.[9]

Bengali anxieties over identity were first formally and politically expressed in February 1948 in Pakistan's National Assembly. A Bengali Hindu named Dhirendranath Datta raised the absurdity of the fact that, despite being the most common mother tongue in all of united Pakistan, Bengali was not considered an official state language; only Urdu and English were. Urdu, the national language of Pakistan, evolved after the Persian language was introduced and indigenised in the west of the Indian subcontinent; it remains the lingua franca for Muslim South Asians and harks back to the great Muslim dynasties, which invaded and ruled swathes of the subcontinent for some 800 years. It is, however, to this day the mother tongue of only around 7.57 per cent of Pakistanis.[10] Meanwhile, as is the case today in India, English was a colonial relic of officialdom that had morphed, unsurprisingly, into the language of business, connectivity and status.

Datta's highly rational request was met with dismissal and fury from West Pakistani officials. Jinnah visited East Pakistan for the first time in March 1948, where he made clear:

> that the state language of Pakistan is going to be Urdu and no other language. Anyone who tries to mislead you is really the enemy of Pakistan. Without one state language, no nation can remain tied up solidly together and function. Look at the history of other countries. Therefore, so far as the state language is concerned, Pakistan's shall be Urdu.[11]

And so the germ of an idea was planted in the East Pakistan delta, over a thousand miles from its overlords in Karachi on the other side of India.

The existence of East Pakistan hadn't always been a certainty. It was an absurdity of cartography, born of toxic communalism that simmered as India's 'tryst with destiny'—its independence—dawned.[12] Many historians and commentators to this day believe that the British intentionally divided the two major religious groups in India, and in particular in Bengal, to maintain order over a swathe of humanity far larger than their own population at home, let alone the tiny coterie of British officials and soldiers actually stationed in the subcontinent.

As Salil Tripathi writes, 'encouraging groups to assert their narrower [religious] identity became a priority.'[13] Just one year after the partition of Bengal by the British, the All India Muslim League, which went on to lead the movement for an independent Muslim-majority nation-state in the subcontinent, was formed in Dhaka on 27 December 1906, in the city's Shahbag area where Dhaka University stands today.

The backlash against the imposition of Urdu as Pakistan's state language simmered from the National Assembly meeting in 1948 until 21 February 1952, when, despite a ban on protests, students gathered to demonstrate at Dhaka University. They were soon surrounded by armed police, who fired tear gas shells and bullets at the protestors, killing several people. The protests spread across East Pakistan, building up to the eventual climax of war and Bangladeshi independence in 1971.

The Bengali Language Movement had deep and far-reaching antecedents, but it was here at Dhaka University on 'Language Movement Day' or 'Language Martyrs' Day' that the defining and fairly unique notion—regionally speaking—of a cultural or linguistic nationalism crystallised, an idea that to this day is perpetually confronted by Islamism.[14] In 1999, UNESCO declared 21 February International Mother Language Day. The date is commemorated annually as a public holiday in Bangladesh with parades and speeches, and a Bengali-language book fair is held in Dhaka's Ramna Park, just over the road from where the police opened fire on the students at Dhaka University—a site that remains a perpetual starting point for protest today.

A Troublesome Past

Over forty years after the brutal civil war that led to Bangladeshi independence, Sayeedi was convicted for crimes against humanity during that conflict at the International Crimes Tribunal—a court that was not really 'international'. Rather, the trials were held in realisation of a manifesto pledge from the Awami League, a centre-left secular nationalist party led by Sheikh Hasina, daughter of Bangladesh's first president and founding father, Sheikh Mujibur Rahman. The Awami League won the 2008 elections in Bangladesh with a huge majority, and in 2009 began enacting its pledge to try leading figures accused of crimes during the war of independence in 1971.

These trials were harshly criticised, not only by members of Jamaat, who in 1971 had unequivocally supported a unified Pakistan (despite Maududi's initial opposition to the creation of Pakistan in the 1940s), but also by influential members of the so-called international community. There was not only the issue of ruffling the feathers of the accused and their influential friends and supporters, but also the justified fears that the trials would expose deep divisions in society, that they would be politicised, and, moreover, that they would be incompetently run. It is difficult to envisage a war crimes trial that is not politicised, especially in a case such as this one, in which so many of the accused had, like Delwar Hossain Sayeedi, been profoundly rehabilitated by the political system. In fact, since independence Jamaat's creed had not only been rehabilitated but also actively utilised for the allure and credence that zealous and absolutist beliefs so often hold for politicians. There are, after all, many clichés about war and politics being the same entities in different guises.

There are suggestions that Bangladesh did initially seek to make the trials 'international' with the help of the United Nations, but, as revealed by a Wikileaks cable from 12 May 2009, this was lobbied against by Pakistan. Pakistan's then high commissioner to Bangladesh, Alamgir Babar, was 'particularly annoyed' about potential UN involvement in the trials: 'Alamgir said the GOP [government of Pakistan] saw the war crimes issue as political and feared it would open up other issues (such as the question of genocide) which would be a problem for the GOP.' Meanwhile, the French ambassador to Bangladesh, Charley Causeret, told his American counterpart that the government of France 'was disinclined to do anything that would cause additional problems for Pakistan'. The US ambassador, James F. Moriarty, noted that 'the concerns expressed by Pakistan and France appear legitimate.'[15]

It must be noted that Pakistan was a cause to be coddled for Western powers in 2009, as it was in the early 1970s. At the time of the ICT, Western powers were leaning heavily on Pakistan as a launch pad and supply route to Afghanistan and to securing that country after its liberation from the Taliban, some seven years before. In the 1970s the United States, and in particular President Richard Nixon, not only got on well with Pakistan's generals but also relied on them to reach out to China. The White House was ready to preserve its historic rapprochement with China at any cost, and as Washington buried their heads in the sands of realpolitik, the hundreds of thousands of civilians who died in Bangladesh's independence struggle paid the price of their neglect.

While Nixon and US Secretary of State Henry Kissinger were busy making a deal with China to isolate the USSR, Sayeedi was selling groceries in Pirojpur, in the southwest of what was then East Pakistan. Pirojpur sits right in the jaws of the Ganges delta, meeting the Bay of Bengal next to the world's largest contiguous mangrove forest, the Sundarbans—Bengali for 'beautiful forests'—which straddles Pirojpur's southern reaches. Sayeedi was educated solely in *madrasas* (Muslim seminaries), and by 1970 was a local small businessman selling groceries and, by some accounts, Islamic amulets and ceremonial garb—while preaching on the side. His father had similarly been an Islamic preacher. Sayeedi was not wealthy and was hardly involved in party politics.

A Great Cleavage

By 1971 the Language Movement had spread, seeking to put Bengali cultural and linguistic identity in a more central national position. Men like Sayeedi and members of Jamaat fretted that this would eclipse Pakistan's Muslim identity and the project of creating a purely Islamic state, concerned that their notions of Islam would be overwhelmed by reverence for more heterodox, locally relevant traditions. They worried that their national character, based entirely on belief in the oneness of God, would be usurped by a different, linguistically grounded and distinctively Bengali identity.

This project had evolved and grown since Pakistani independence in 1947, with the tides of blood from Partition and later war with India combining ominously with military rule to steadily foster the growth of a new nationalist fervour. Sayeedi soon became involved in militia groups and movements to stop the division of Pakistan and the birth of the new Bangladeshi state. For as Bengali nationalist fervour swept the country, among people of all religions, so too rose a counterinsurgency movement and narrative, imposed by the Pakistani authorities. Collaborators in every district spied and informed on the local population's secular feelings and anxieties.

This counterinsurgency movement was founded on the need to protect the 'pure' Islamic nation-state. The loyalist paramilitary forces in East Pakistan became known as Razakars, or 'volunteers' in Urdu; Razakar today has come to mean 'traitor' or 'Judas' in Bengali. Like the Hyderabadi Razakars before them, who fought in opposition to the integration of the Muslim-ruled princely state of Hyderabad into the new Indian nation, the East Pakistani unionists rallied around the sincere desire not to be ruled by unbelievers, despite huge popular opinion against them and no rational odds of succeeding. Thus a cleavage emerged in post-colonial South Asia, about statehood and national character. Many Muslims fretted about being subsumed by hostile ideologues.

The Earthquake Plebiscite

In December 1970 unified Pakistan held its first general elections. The result would shake the western wing of Pakistan, its generals and Zulfikar Ali Bhutto, who aspired to be the country's first democratically elected civilian ruler, and who founded the left-wing Pakistan People's Party in 1967. Highlighting the deep divisions running through the supposedly united nation, the more populous eastern wing of the country voted almost unanimously for the Awami League, led by the energetic leader Sheikh Mujibur Rahman, who had grown up in the tough world of Bengali student politics and had found a voice in the region's Language Movement.

Pakistan's powers that be, from its then ruling president, General Yahya Khan, to Bhutto, rejected the Awami League's thumping triumph in the elections, which saw Sheikh Mujib's party win a majority of seats in the National Assembly. The Awami League and its six-point demands were dismissed as secessionist and an attempt to dismantle the unified state, primarily because of calls for greater rights and autonomy for East Pakistan.[16] For by the late 1960s Bengalis felt not only that their linguistic and cultural rights were being ignored, but also that they were being economically exploited. A tiny proportion of the national

15

budget was spent in the country's eastern wing, which Pakistan's rulers viewed and treated as little more than a colony. While fractious politics and state creation no doubt kept the country's rulers busy in the west, there was also a persistent theme of racism that West Pakistanis expressed towards Bengalis in the east. As Salil Tripathi notes, Bengalis 'hated being called short, dark, rice-eating peasants.'[17]

The callous rule of Pakistan's generals was brought into stark relief when, as campaigning for the year's election was in full swing, the deadliest cyclone in recorded history made landfall in East Pakistan and the Indian state of West Bengal on the evening of 12 November 1970. When Cyclone Bhola struck with 185-kilometre-per-hour winds, pushing a 6-metre tidal surge through the low-lying coastal floodplain, around half a million Bengalis are believed to have perished. The scale of devastation and loss of life shocked those who witnessed it. Meg Blood, wife of the American consul-general, 'had the image of a huge chocolate pudding dotted with raisins. As she got closer, she realized with horror that the dots were actually human corpses.'[18] This was, as the history of deadly storms demonstrates, such an appalling event largely because of the callous attitude of Pakistan's policymakers and their subsequent lack of planning and poor disaster response, which many East Pakistanis saw as 'unconscionably tardy and inadequate.'[19] The storm itself was nowhere near record-breaking in terms of its physical magnitude.

The US consul-general in Dhaka at the time, Archer Blood, telegrammed Washington on 21 November 1970 noting that 'alleged deficiencies of [government of Pakistan] in responding to disaster may rekindle acute sense of neglect on part of East Pakistanis... there appears to be a growing undercurrent of dissatisfaction with central government's role in relief efforts.'[20] He was, of course, correct, as were the citizens of then East Pakistan. Bangladesh is a regular victim of massive storms and cyclones. Its governments since 1971 have recognised the threat, and, by taking measures to install resources such as basic shelters and warning systems, have been extremely successful in preserving life.

In 1970 when the cyclone struck, Pakistan's President Yahya Khan was returning from Beijing. In China, the British-trained general was building an important, and to this day enduring, relationship with the Chinese Communist Party. He was also there in part on behalf of Nixon's White House. At the time 'the single most important fact about world politics' was that 'Nixon and Kissinger were secretly planning an opening to China.'[21] Nixon's trip to China in 1972 was the first in history by a serving US president, and was seen as a triumph for America, opening up that country and assisting in prising it further from the USSR. In some ways, however, the visit was even more important for China than it was for the United States. It was arguably this rapprochement that began China's surge in international importance and economic clout in the years since. The meeting did not yield an end to Chinese support for the North Vietnamese, who would defeat the United States and her allies by 1975 and unify that country under communist leadership, at the cost of as many as 2 million civilian lives and despite vast American expenditure. Meanwhile American indifference to the ramifications of blind support for Pakistan's rulers would arguably contribute to similarly seismic and devastating, if less reported, events in South Asia.

Yahya flew over East Pakistan to see the devastation of Cyclone Bhola from above, but only visited fleetingly. Arnold Zeitlin, the Associated Press correspondent in Pakistan at the time, remembered that as Yahya flew back, Henry Kissinger in far-away Washington 'warned Nixon that the deep antagonism of Bengalis for the central Pakistani government was now much worse.'[22] The cyclone was a further lightning rod, if any were needed, for Bengali nationalist sentiment in the east that had started on more ideological or identity-based grounds. American diplomats, including the consul-general, Archer Blood, began cabling home, noting that Bengali politicians like the 'venerable leftist firebrand' Maulana Bhashani were calling for Yahya to resign as a result of the appalling loss of life from the cyclone and the government's uncaring response.[23] While an official West Pakistani relief effort was absent or deeply inadequate, foreign aid poured in and Mujib's centre-left Bengali nationalist Awami League party, its leaders, and activists were out in force, assisting the hundreds of thousands affected by the cyclone.

Sheikh Mujib was by this point already a towering figure in East Pakistan. The 'charismatic leader of the moderate left Awami League dominates the political arena in East Pakistan,' noted the CIA in August

1970. 'Extremely popular throughout the province, 50-year-old Mujib has become the acknowledged spokesman of the East Pakistani autonomy movement and a hero to "sons-of-the-soil" Bengalis for his relentless championing of their cause.'[24] American Consul-General Archer Blood agreed with his surreptitious colleagues, recalling that Mujib was 'ever more eloquent (and extreme)' in his criticism of the government response to the cyclone. As Mujib railed, the West Pakistani leaders were 'guilty of almost cold-blooded murder. They deserve the most severe punishment ... the textile millionaires have not given a yard of cloth for our shrouds. They have a huge army, but it is left to British marines to bury our dead.'[25]

The CIA correctly predicted that a regional confrontation was imminent, 'because the East Pakistanis appear no longer willing to accept what they regard as second-class citizenship.'[26] The sense of being second-class citizens had now become pervasive, not just with regards to the Language Movement.

On 7 December 1970, less than a month after the cyclone, Pakistanis went to the polls. The result was crushing for the West Pakistani establishment, and in particular for military ruler Yahya Khan. Out of 162 seats contested in the east, the Awami League won 160. This gave Sheikh Mujib and the League a majority in both wings, leaving the Pakistani establishment in a bind. Civilian politicians, like runner-up Bhutto, could not accept Bengali leadership or a Bengali party ruling over the united country. Sheikh Mujib and his party knew this. And so, without formally calling for independence, they pushed for their democratic rights.

Yahya and the military had completely misread how the elections would go, and were left scrabbling for answers. Their explanations of the results included that the League's victory 'was attributable to the Hindu community and "its sinister purposes."'[27] On 27 February the Pakistani authorities delayed the sitting of the National Assembly, which had been scheduled for March and would herald the transfer of power to a civilian government made up of the victorious Awami League. West Pakistani statesmen were worried that if the Assembly were convened, 'Bengalis, not Punjabis, would call the shots.'[28] Not only would this signal the relinquishing of their state power; West Pakistanis were also concerned that with the Awami League in charge, the Islamic foundations of the Pakistani state would be undermined and eroded. Sheikh Mujib, after all, 'was publicly committed to reducing the role of religion in government by advancing the causes of secularism and federalism.'[29]

Mujib's commitment to secularism is recalled by his grandson, Radwan Siddiq, who was gracious enough to take me on a tour of his grandfather's house, which is now a museum in the Dhanmondi neighbourhood of Dhaka. Radwan, who is Prime Minister Sheikh Hasina's nephew, described the 'shouting match' that his grandfather had had with Saudi Arabia's King Faisal, at an Organisation of Islamic States conference in 1973. Faisal, Radwan told me, had offered Bangladesh and Mujib a 'blank cheque' to induce the ruler of the new state to insert Islam into the nation's constitution and de-secularise the nation. 'But my grandfather refused,' Radwan claimed, as we stood in the faded 1970s reception room of his grandfather's former house and headquarters, peering at the fascinating collection of black-and-white photos of the independence hero pictured with various international leaders.

The stakes of Mujib's predicament in those early days of the Bangladeshi nation prefigured the orientation that the country would later take, if or when those with the democratic mandate were given the freedom to do so. The Awami League—theoretically—occupies a centre-left position, and is challenged most prominently in the political arena not only by Jamaat on the far right but also, more notably, by the centre-right Bangladesh Nationalist Party or BNP. The latter only emerged as a political entity in 1978, taking in a coalition of disparate, largely anti-League parties.

With negotiation and brinkmanship ongoing, on 1 March 1971, Yahya Khan announced the indefinite postponement of the National Assembly, which had been due to sit on the third, citing the refusal of Bhutto's losing Pakistan People's Party to sit in a Bengali-dominated house as his reason. The general fell back on the predictable, communally inspired 'blame India' card, claiming that the 'situation of tension created by India has further complicated the whole position'.[30] Some commentators have suggested that had the Pakistani military not been in the driving seat, Bhutto and Mujib might have been able to resolve the situation through peaceful dialogue; both leaders in fact had a fair amount in common. However, this is a point of contention. Recalling 'the most horrible month of my life', Archer Blood observed that 'once again the interests of East Pakistan were to be sacrificed before the altar of West Pakistani concerns'.[31]

Vindicated by their electoral mandate, and left with little alternative after its denial, the Awami League called for agitation. On 2 March, the government announced the imposition of a curfew and the League called for a *hartal*, or strike, in the capital and, the following day, in the whole province, to last until 6 March. Frustration, anxiety and paralysis gripped the country. On 7 March, Mujib addressed a vast rally in Ramna Park, a former racecourse next to Dhaka University. His speech that day was both shrewd and hugely inspiring. 'The history of the last twenty-three years is the history of the wailing of dying men and women,' he declared. 'The history of Bangla is the history of staining the streets with the blood of the people of this country.' He spoke of broken West Pakistani promises and the disgraceful reaction of the state to peaceful protests and demonstrations with armed violence and killings. He famously concluded with a crescendo, 'The struggle this time is a struggle for our emancipation, the struggle this time is the struggle for independence. *Joy Bangla* [victory to Bengal]!'[32] This last phrase is one that is now ubiquitous for the Awami League, a sort of nationalist mantra or salute that bookends official speeches or oratory at conferences, political rallies and beyond.

The agitation that began at the beginning of 1971 would induce a ferocious backlash from the Pakistani authorities: a response that was officially known as Operation Searchlight. Already on the drawing board in February, it was this Pakistani military operation that would result in genocide and the war that would culminate in the independence of the country. Operation Searchlight was launched on 25 March and aimed to entirely debilitate the Awami League and secessionist elements within the province. These 'elements' were broadly defined to include anyone sympathetic to the party, which extended to secularists, intellectuals, leftists, and Hindus—the latter were all viewed as fifth columnists because of their faith and/or their inquisitive, secessionist minds.

'The political narrative that Hindus were conspiring against Pakistan had been widely promulgated since the days of the Ayub dictatorship [1958–69],' writes Farahnaz Ispahani. She adds that populist propaganda of the day in Pakistan scapegoated the minority Hindu population, blaming them for the economic woes of the province, in a manner not dissimilar to that of the German Third Reich's scapegoating of Jews. 'The Hindus were accused of smuggling rice, jute, and steel from East Pakistan to India so that the Muslims would not advance economically.'[33] This is a common theme, which intentionally sought to use communalism to hide the utter exploitation of the east by the west. It harks back to historical caste systems and their attendant resentments, as higher-caste Hindus had often served as *zamindars*, or landlords, and in higher clerical roles, under both the Mughals and the British, but particularly since the British Permanent Act of Settlement in 1793. The vast majority of Bengali Muslims, meanwhile, were cultivator peasants.

The echoes of this historical resentment are still felt today. During the build-up to the 2014 elections, Bangladesh's western border district of Satkhira was one of the most violent areas of the country. The area is remote from Dhaka, cut off by the vast, as yet unbridged Padma River. As the crow flies Satkhira is closer to Kolkata, in the neighbouring Indian state of West Bengal, than to Bangladesh's capital, but the international state border means it is now removed from there too. The area has a large Hindu minority, making up about a quarter of the population in the district, but there is also strong support for Islamist parties, such as Jamaat.

In the weeks after the 2014 elections, I met Subhash Ghosh, then sixty-three years old, in his once-idyllic ancestral home overlooking lush paddy fields and a typically Bengali pond. The previous December, the day after Jamaat leader Abdul Quader Molla was hanged for war crimes he had committed in 1971, a mob of about seventy Islamists had specifically targeted Ghosh's family home. The walls were still charred and debris scattered the floor, a pile of burnt-out motorbikes and household objects still scarring the driveway in front of the house, weeks after the attack. The home's Hindu shrine had been smashed to pieces. Ghosh suspected that the issue of land had been important to the attackers, in conjunction with his religion. The mob, he suspected, was filled with resentful landless young men. As we gazed at his tranquil pond, he noted with sadness and pain that if he fled his burnt-out house and land, out of fear of a fresh attack, the mob would grab his land.[34] 'I cannot leave the country like a coward, and I cannot become a rickshaw puller in India, because I have land and property here,' he told me. While Ghosh and his family were not wealthy, they owned and leased out small but fertile plots of land. Many of the landless citizens of the region, in contrast, had seen their employment opportunities shrink as agricultural land was taken over by shrimp farming for export—a business that was more profitable for the owners but, locals noted, employed far fewer people.

Reporting a Massacre

25 March 1971 was the beginning of the end for united East and West Pakistan. Central to this day of terror that would mark the starting gun for the war of independence and the attendant genocide were military actions at Dhaka University. There, in the day's early hours, Pakistani troops went from dorm to dorm, murdering students and specific teachers who were known to support Bengali nationalism or secularism. 'The first target as the tanks rolled into Dacca on the night of the 25th was the students,' reported Simon Dring in *The Daily Telegraph*.[35] Dring was one of very few foreign journalists able to report on this event:

> one column of troops sped to Dacca University shortly after midnight. Troops took over the British Council library and its grounds, and used it as a fire-base to shell nearby dormitory areas.
>
> Caught completely by surprise, some 200 students were killed in Iqbal Hall, headquarters of the militantly anti-government students' union, as shells slammed into the building and their rooms were sprayed with machine-gun fire.
>
> Two days later bodies were still smouldering in their burnt-out rooms, others were scattered outside and more floated in a nearby lake.[36]

Pakistani soldiers forced surviving students to drag out the corpses of their slain classmates the next morning. At gunpoint they were made to dig their friends' graves, before facing the same fate. An army major speaking to *The New York Times* justified the assault by claiming that, 'The new generation must be brought up according to strict Islamic principles, with a return to the old ways. Too many people forget that the sole reason for the existence of Pakistan is as a home for Moslems. When we lose sight of that idea, we become corrupt.'[37]

Most foreign journalists in Dhaka at the time were confined to the InterContinental Hotel, a few hundred metres from the Dhaka University campus, on what has become known as 'Black Night': 25 March. The following day the Pakistan authorities rounded up most of the 200 odd members of the foreign press and took them directly to the airport to be flown out, hoping to avoid details of the military's 'cleansing operations' leaking internationally.

A handful of journalists escaped the dragnet. Arnold Zeitlin of the Associated Press (AP) vividly recalls how he happened to be out of the hotel at dinner at a friend's house in Gulshan, a relatively leafy suburb to the north of Dhaka. When the crackdown began that night, he told me, he had tried to go back but 'there was a tree across the road and some very funny looking people behind the tree, so we decided to go back to the house in Gulshan and spend the night there.' He remembered going up to the roof to watch the 'fireworks'. 'There was firing and shooting and what looked like anti-aircraft fire. And the radio was playing martial music already.' Zeitlin stayed indoors through the following day's curfew—'there was no way to get out.' On 27 March, it was announced that the curfew would be suspended for a few hours, and so he drove into the city. 'People were streaming out of Dhaka, very much in distress,' he recalled. 'We passed the University of Dhaka and there were bodies in front of one hall.'

Simon Dring of *The Daily Telegraph* was at the InterContinental Hotel, but hid from the authorities on the roof and in the laundry room for thirty-six hours. The two correspondents, Zeitlin and Dring, and AP photographer Michel Laurent, who had also managed to stay in Dhaka, were some of the only foreign journalists to witness the scale of devastation on the twenty-seventh. Laurent would even return to shoot Pulitzer Prize-winning photos of the war's aftermath. He died tragically in one of the last battles of the Vietnam War in 1975.[38]

The three were forced to fly out of Dhaka that afternoon. Zeitlin proudly recalled how he was the first eyewitness to bring news of the Pakistani army's vicious crackdown and its brutality to the world. 'We went through a very extensive search at the airport [when leaving]—

they took all our notes, they took as many films from Michel as they could find.' He chuckled as he remembered the authorities discovering racy photos buried deep in Dring's bag. Zeitlin landed in Sri Lanka, where the flight made a stopover en route to Karachi. There he was able to call the local AP stringer and dictate a story, which he said was 'the first story out from someone in Dhaka who had been there when the crackdown had happened.'

Pakistani troops had targeted Hindu communities in central Dhaka, as well as students, during the crackdown. Shankaria Bazar in Old Dhaka—today one of the world's most densely populated areas—was targeted particularly savagely. This part of the city is an ancient, tightly packed warren of alleys and people living on top of one another. It would have been hard to specifically target anyone in particular in this cramped neighbourhood. Instead, according to Dring, 'the soldiers made people come out of their houses and then just shot them in groups.'[39] The area was eventually razed.

Old Dhaka is, as its name suggests, the city's most historic area. Here was one of the first places where Europeans became infatuated with the exotic arts and craftsmanship of this great subcontinent. The city under the Mughals had been a trading centre where Hindu and Muslim artisans and traders lived side by side. An early Portuguese visitor, Fray Sebastien Manrique, described it as a 'Gangetic emporium' possessing 'stupefying' wealth when he travelled to the city in 1640 during the rule of Mughal emperor Shah Jahan.[40] Out of the port in this part of Dhaka poured the finest cotton textile in the world: muslin.

Archer Blood recalled spending much of the night of 25–26 March 1971 sheltering on the floor of his residence, 'watching with horror the constant flash of tracer bullets across the dark sky and listening to the more ominous clatter of machine gun fire and heavy clump of tank guns.'[41] Days later he would cable Washington describing news gathered from his sources, including the method of 'cleansing' Hindu houses: 'the Army's technique was to set houses afire and then gun down people as they left their homes.'[42]

The following day, President Yahya banned the Awami League. The nation woke in shock at the crackdown, staring at the violent struggle for self-determination that lay ahead. Yahya again addressed his 'fellow countrymen'—West Pakistanis. East Pakistanis were not included, being deemed solely culpable for the impasse that now gripped Pakistan: 'no West Pakistani leader or party was judged responsible either wholly or in part.'[43] Sheikh Mujib was blamed for 'obstinacy, obduracy and absolute refusal to talk sense'; the winners of the popular vote—the party and its leader—were thus branded enemies of Pakistan.[44]

By June, Pakistani reporter Anthony Mascarenhas, in a hard-hitting front-page story in *The Sunday Times*, noted being 'repeatedly told by senior military and civil officers in Dacca and Comilla' that 'we are determined to cleanse East Pakistan once and for all of the threat of secession, even if it means killing off two million people and ruling the province as a colony for 30 years.'[45] The story had a simple, one-word headline: 'Genocide'. Essential to this 'cleansing' operation were local collaborators—the small minority of the population for whom their Islamic identity was more important than their cultural Bengali one, and who therefore wished to remain part of a united Pakistan.

Enduring Divisions

More than forty-two years later, convict Sayeedi's supporters responded to his sentencing in much the same way as their West Pakistani comrades and Sayeedi himself had reacted to the elections of December 1970. Jamaat supporters and cadre, particularly from its student wing, the Islami Chhatra Shibir (commonly known as Shibir), took to the streets in violent protests across the country. Mobs attacked police stations, government buildings and, inevitably, Hindu homes and places of worship. In one of the worst bouts of political violence that the country had suffered since 1971, around seventy people were killed in a few days. Press pictures showed young men beating a police officer lying crumpled on the street. In the northern district of Gaibandha, thousands-strong mobs attacked police, beating three officers to death. A state of emergency was declared in four districts. Protesters armed with improvised grenades and sticks fell by the dozen as the security forces responded with live ammunition. The trials and the confrontation with Bangladesh's painful history had opened the wounds that had so scarred the country over four decades earlier. This clash and agitation, as we shall see, would be instrumental in mobilising a new generation of Islamist militancy. It would galvanise violent opposition and engender a deadly pattern of attacks and killings.

In strikingly contemporary fashion, the apparent sighting of Sayeedi's face on the moon further inspired his supporters. The rumours spread, as had Sayeedi's sermons, over the most populist of channels—Facebook—driven by Shibir's propaganda wing, Basherkella. *The Daily Star* published the photo with a translation of its caption: 'From late Friday night to early Saturday, people from Bangladesh to Saudi Arabia saw Sayedee's face (in the moon). Such an image is God's sign that true devotees are honoured in different ways.' The paper added that, 'To draw attention of the people who do not use internet, announcements were made through loudspeakers of mosques about the picture.'[46]

Not far away from where Sayeedi was sentenced and where Bangladesh's history was being pored over by lawyers and judges, an entirely different set of protesters were attempting to make their voices heard.

The Shahbag Protests

While the ICT's verdict on Sayeedi had sparked violent street protests, clashes with police, and the targeting of Hindus by the preacher's conservative supporters, the earlier sentencing of Abdul Quader Molla had been met with fury from supposedly liberal or secular proponents of the trials. It was hard for many foreign observers to wrap their heads around the ubiquitous chanted slogan of their huge, spontaneous protest: '*Fashi chai!*'—'We want a hanging!'

Abdul Quader Molla's sentence was pronounced three weeks before Sayeedi's, and had prompted just as profound a response. On 5 February 2013, the man who had become known as the 'butcher of Mirpur'—after a suburb in north-west Dhaka—walked out of the white colonial-era courthouse that housed the tribunals, flashing a 'V for victory' sign at the assembled reporters, cameramen, police and sundry onlookers. Molla's initial sentence, which was the first to be passed at the tribunal, consigned him to life imprisonment, but not to death. He had been convicted of multiple counts of murder, abetting murder, and rape during the nation's war of independence over four decades earlier.

Molla was infamous. In many ways, like for other war crimes suspects, to many Bangladeshis his guilt or innocence had already been conferred before the tribunal's verdict was announced. Many years had passed since the war but its brutal realities had not yet been reckoned with, making it 'all but impossible to differentiate individual criminal accountability from a more collective opprobrium.'[47] Moreover, many conceived of the trials as 'a judgement for one philosophy against another philosophy, the Bangladesh philosophy', as secular blogger and activist Maruf Rosul put it to me. As we shall see, the notion of a secular state reflecting indigenous Bengali culture, which was gained at such a great cost in lives in 1971, has not been a closed case. With stakes high, Molla's escape of the death penalty provoked outrage. His 'V for victory' gesture was seen as the height of chutzpah, the gall of exemption for a man and a movement associated not only with putting religion first, but also with impunity before the law despite committing mortal crimes against a people.

Bangladeshi 'liberals', or at least the majority of the country's population who backed the trials, smelt the whiff of impunity. In keeping with contemporary activism and conspiracy, the demonstrations began online. As pictures of Molla and his 'V for victory' gesture circulated online on news websites and blogs, secular bloggers like Maruf rallied people to protest at the Shahbag junction near Dhaka University. Soon the usually incessant traffic had been replaced with a sea of people. This was not long after the Arab Spring erupted in 2010–11. In some ways, the movements bear comparison. Bangladesh had seldom witnessed anything like this, possibly not since the demonstrations to depose the country's second military dictator, Hussain Muhammad Ershad, in the late 1980s.

At the time, I described the Shahbag protests as 'a liberal street festival with a morbid demand'.[48] Those in attendance varied in age and in gender. Rather than the usual rent-a-mob of bored young males who are usually mustered for opportunist political marches and gatherings, the throngs of men this time were joined by women of all ages. This superficially liberal character soon came to be celebrated by attendees and by the country's urban commentariat. Long into the night, imaginatively costumed protesters mingled with men and women singing and acting in ways that, for many, seemed antithetical to the norms of Bangladeshi life.

The crowds did not die down. People stayed at the junction overnight, and those who couldn't came back nightly after work. A carnivalesque atmosphere prevailed; very quickly trinket sellers appeared to provide everything from snacks and cigarettes to macabre T-shirts with pictures of nooses on them. Parents bought their children along to enjoy the convivial atmosphere and, almost inadvertently, to demand capital punishment for a handful of Bangladeshis who had been part of a movement that had tormented their grandparents.

The Party Political Reckoning

Both of Bangladesh's major political parties were forced to offer some kind of public support for the protests. While the natural advocates of the war crimes trials and the Shahbag protests would come from the ruling Awami League, the more right-leaning BNP was also compelled to proclaim its tacit support, on the condition that the government not 'draw political mileage from the movement.'[49] The caveat was important, not least because appropriating public emotion was the Awami League's usual modus operandi. In fact, both parties, almost regardless of ideology, could naturally be expected to attempt either to destroy or to co-opt any movement that drew such support, crowds and publicity. The BNP was thus keenly aware that its political opponents would capitalise on the opportunity. For here were thousands of people on the streets, in theory showing their support for the Awami League and its promised trials, as well as for death sentences for the accused men, almost all of whom had been politicians in Jamaat, which had been in an electoral alliance with the BNP since 1999.

It is indicative of both the cynicism and structure of Bangladeshi politics that even an issue as sensitive and important as war crimes does not muster political consensus. If one party supports something, or draws 'mileage' from it, it often follows that the other must oppose it vehemently. The BNP has often played the 'anything or anyone but the Awami League' card, for a host of reasons—many of which are genuine grievances, but still more of which are contrived—simply to try to grab power from the League, which for the moment seems to hold a monopoly on both political and historical legitimacy.

It must be remembered that the Awami League had won a landslide victory in the 2008 elections. Its success was partly attained on the back of a pledge to try war criminals, as well as on the electorate's usual anti-incumbent tendency, again highlighting the cynicism of the 'theatre'. Repeated polling shows broad public support for the trials and for seeking justice or retribution for the crimes of 1971. Yet, reflecting the lack of faith the populace has in the justice system, a majority in April 2013 were in agreement with countless human rights groups that the trials were not 'fair'. Despite this, even more people supported the trials, and many approved of the government because of them.[50] Ultimately, however, actors who did not hail from either of the two main parties would be the ones to cast a dark shadow over the protest movement and set off a trend that would escalate well beyond the buzz of liberal chatter on the streets of Shahbag that spring.

The Killing of a Blogger

Ten days into the still-cacophonous protests, on Friday, 15 February 2013 (the first day of the Bangladeshi weekend), at around 9 p.m., 31-year-old Ahmed Rajib Haider was leaving the home he shared with his brother in Mirpur. The street was not lit, and out of the darkness the young architect was set upon and attacked by at least two men with machetes. Press reports suggest that Rajib was first struck on the head and shoulder, causing him to fall to the ground, at which point his assailants slit his throat. It was later claimed by police that his killers had acted in two groups. One group had surveilled Rajib and his neighbourhood by playing cricket outside his house. The other had been the kill team.

Rajib, who used to blog under the pseudonym Thaba Baba, hoping to protect himself by concealing his identity, was the first blogger associated with the Shahbag protests to be murdered. He would be the only one whom the government expressed any real sympathy for, and his death was the only one to lead to significant convictions—most prominently of two middle-class students, who were sentenced to death in December 2015. The pair was found to be part of a network emanating from private universities in the capital, most notably from North South University in northwest Dhaka. One of the men,

Redwanul Azad Rana, was only arrested in 2017, having absconded to Malaysia and lived there as a fugitive. The other, Faisal Bin Nayeem, was arrested shortly after the attack. Rana was said to have been the group's ringleader and, according to Nayeem's court testimony, had told his co-conspirators that, 'Being a believer, it is your duty to kill [Thaba Baba].'[51] The killers had reportedly identified Rajib by scouring photos of the Shahbag protests on Facebook. Their group was known as Ansar al Islam, and as we shall see, it would become one of the major streams of Islamist terror operating in Bangladesh.

Rajib's laptop and two bloodstained machetes were found near his mangled body, which reports suggest was barely recognisable as a result of the attack. Rajib had been a fairly well-known atheist blogger, and had been instrumental in rallying the Shahbag protests. The exact motivations behind his murder are hard to disentangle. Had he been targeted and killed because of his role in organising the protests? Or had he been attacked simply because of his outspoken atheism online? Only a month before Rajib's death, Asif Mohiuddin, another similarly outspoken atheist blogger, had been assaulted in much the same manner by fanatical Islamists, and had narrowly survived. But even if Rajib's murder had not been directly prompted by his association with the protests, his death was weaponised as a way to brand the entire Shahbag movement as atheistic. Moreover, it was only thanks to the intensely political nature of the trials and subsequent protests that Rajib and his fellow protesters had become so prominent in the first place.

While Rajib and many of the other online voices that supported the protests most fervently were undoubtedly atheists—after all, the protests did take place beside Dhaka University, not unnatural terrain for questioning minds—the majority of the protesters were ordinary Dhaka dwellers, whom one might assume to be 'God-fearing' Muslims. It is impossible to know what percentage of Bangladeshis are atheists or doubt the existence of God because of the real threat of attack, cultural taboo and general intolerance. Still, the targeting of atheists to delegitimise the Shahbag protests gives us a glimpse into the nature of political control in Bangladesh, and the claiming of political space and discourse.

Controlling Popular Dissent

Rajib's brutal demise was quickly set upon by opposition political parties, and by the BNP and Jamaat in particular. In late February 2013, Jamaat made the absurd claim that 'the main objective of the Shahbagh protesters is to root out Islam from the country.'[52] The implication was that by calling for the deaths of the war criminals, the Shahbag protesters were working against Bangladesh's identity, which the accused personified through their long-cultivated veneer of piety. An Islamist madrassa network called Hefazat-e-Islam (Defenders of Islam) took out half-page adverts in three newspapers condemning the Shahbag protests as 'anti-Islam'.[53] By March, BNP leader Khaleda Zia was railing that:

> Shahbagh Square is an atheists' square. There are [50 million] youths in the country and less than a percent of them are in Shahbagh. … These youths scream 'death penalty for war criminals' … they sing and dance and do many evil deeds there … The government is putting mosques under lock and key while providing security to [Shahbagh protesters].[54]

With a further conspiratorial jab, she claimed that the government had 'staged the drama to divert people's attention from its corruption', and drew attention to the fact that the ongoing war crimes trials had failed to meet international standards. Khaleda had made a complete turnaround from coming out in support of the protests only a month earlier.

After the sentencing of Delwar Hossain Sayeedi on 28 February, thousands of his supporters or cadre from the BNP's electoral ally, Jamaat, and from Jamaat's student wing, Shibir, had attacked Hindu homes and places of worship. When she made her anti-Shahbag speech, Khaleda was visiting some of the affected communities. Much like populist leaders elsewhere, she could not let minorities get in the way of her agenda, which relies heavily on blaming Bangladesh's problems on Hindu India and its political ally, the Awami League, to score points and secure support. This was especially the case when the perpetrators of the violence were supporters of a coalition partner, as Jamaat was. Of course, pointing the finger is not exclusively a BNP tactic—the Awami League also spends most of its time and energy trying to blame all and sundry on its political opponents.

While Khaleda Zia used her public platform to rail against Shahbag, the *Amar Desh* newspaper went even further. Since 2008, the paper has been owned and run by Mahmudur Rahman, a businessman and BNP advisor. In response to Shahbag, *Amar Desh* went into overdrive, publishing the names and personal details of bloggers who had committed 'contempt of religion'. Such charges would lead to lists of bloggers, academics and secularists being circulated by Islamic websites and, as we shall see, seemingly encouraged a spate of killings that would come to scar Bangladesh.

Rahman had already been targeted by the authorities for publishing leaked transcripts of conversations between an ICT judge and an acquaintance in Belgium. These were most probably procured for a price to discredit the tribunal and air the court's shaky practices. In any case, Rahman was viewed as a wily ideologue and would spend years in jail on often-flimsy charges. It is not an unfair comparison to describe him as Bangladesh's answer to the American businessman turned gutter-media editor and one-time presidential advisor Stephen Bannon. Much like in America, Bangladesh's media landscape is generally populated by relatively liberal, university-educated urbanites—the same class of people who attended the Shahbag protests. *Amar Desh*, which means 'my country', offered something very different. Like Bannon's Breitbart news website it championed a pugnacious right-wing vision, distrustful of the conventional secular establishment, giving both voice and legitimacy to the parochial, dog-whistle bigotry that simmered in many but that urban media types assiduously believed should be expunged. Like Breitbart, it worked and enjoyed a huge circulation, until the government shuttered its operations in 2013. Just as Bannon's right-wing vision was at odds with many of the more orthodox members of the Republican Party, so Rahman's was on the hard line of the BNP spectrum.

As senior counter-terror police chief Monirul Islam told me, *Amar Desh* 'stigmatised all bloggers as atheists' to the point that the Shahbag protests had to stop, 'because the whole nation, most of the Muslims, turned against this movement and finally this movement could not go further.' As Awami League politician and Sheikh Hasina's son Sajeeb Wazed Joy would later tellingly comment, 'We don't want to be seen as atheists. It doesn't change our core beliefs. We believe in secularism.'

Nonetheless, the campaign to smear the protestors as godless had been very effective, and the Awami League too was forced to step back. 'Given that our opposition party [the BNP] plays that religion card against us relentlessly,' explained Wazed, 'we can't come out strongly for [a murdered blogger]. It's about perception, not about reality.'[55]

Indeed, while the government had initially defended Rajib, the rising vitriol and accusations of atheism soon became too much to bear. While Rajib's attackers were arrested, the Awami League quickly moved on to adopt a stance of victim blaming in incidents where an atheist was killed. In March 2013, the government set up a nine-member panel to 'check comments on Islam [and the] Prophet'.[56] Prime Minister Sheikh Hasina would later go on record to claim, 'You can't attack someone else's religion. You'll have to stop doing this. It won't be tolerated if someone else's religious sentiment is hurt.'[57] The irony, of course, was that the government tolerated hurting the sensitivities of every religious group except the country's Sunni Muslim majority. Only the most populous religious cohort was granted a panel to protect its sentiments, while no one would ever be arrested for hurting the 'religious sentiment' of atheists, despite regular, public exhortations to kill them. This hypocrisy amounts to preferential treatment for the most powerful religious group over the most persecuted, from a government, state and party that claim to be secular, exposing the weakness of the notion of secularism on which the state was founded only four decades before.

2

1975—ANNUS HORRIBILIS

To understand Bangladesh today, it is worth looking at the origins of its principal opposition party, the Bangladesh Nationalist Party (BNP). The events of the party's formation and the reasons for its success are crucial indicators of the schism that cuts through contemporary Bangladeshi society and politics. The BNP's evolution is also broadly instructive for looking at the rebirth of religious politics in Bangladesh, for not only does the party represent a vast constellation of many right-wing views, but it also pulls together some ideas from the hard left. Its history dates back to 1975 and the rise of Khaleda Zia's late husband, General Ziaur Rahman, to absolute power in the country.

While Bangladesh had achieved its hard-fought independence in 1971, life as a new nation was not easy. Sheikh Mujibur Rahman, the independence hero, had struggled to keep the tenets of the constitution, democracy, socialism and prosperity alive. By 1975 Mujib's Awami League government was in crisis and faced growing popular opposition and criticism.[1] While the country held an election in 1973, which Mujib won easily, by 1974, 'only three years after independence: as many as 1.5 million people—2 percent of the total population, overwhelmingly the rural landless proletariat—died' in a famine, 'having already been starved, displaced, terrorized, and otherwise harmed during the liberation war of 1971.'[2] The trauma of the 1974 famine left profound scars in the national psyche, and in some ways went on to shape many of Bangladesh's surprising development successes in more recent years.

Many suggest that the famine was a result of poor, corrupt management and a deeply fragile state, two issues that continue to plague many aspects of governance in Bangladesh to this day, but which were then far more acute in the newly formed nation. While Mujib and his party are rightly held accountable for the famine and the poor state of governance, the state was undoubtedly hobbled and weakened by many forces beyond the government's control. It was plagued by a host of political and economic issues—indeed, in many ways the two facets were deeply entwined. Political and state weakness resulted in '[s]muggling, hoarding, profiteering and black-marketing', which very much contributed to the famine, and also indicated the severe lack of capacity possessed by the Bangladeshi state.[3]

The Struggle for an Amicable Peace

In the arena of foreign policy, Bangladesh struggled to gain an amicable peace within its neighbourhood well after the cessation of hostilities. 'Bangladesh was in no position to force its [reduced] will upon Pakistan, while India was eager for a peace deal.'[4] To force the release of Bangladeshis in Pakistani custody, Bangladesh agreed for 195 Pakistani war crimes suspects (a number that had already been cut down from over 1,000) to remain in India, while in return for Pakistan's recognition of Bangladesh as a new state, India consented to drop its pressure for war crimes trials, 'which would presumably compel Bangladesh to give up as well'.[5]

In other words, despite Bangladesh having won the war and having suffered undoubted war crimes and the suppression of its democratic rights, Pakistan gamely 'won impunity', in the words of war crimes trials expert Gary Bass. The mere act of recognition of its statehood was the most that the wounded country would receive as reparations, and even that was only achieved with pressure from the so-called 'international community'—which in practice meant Western powers and their institutions, in this case, the International Court of Justice. Bass calls this position, in which the imperative of peace and stability in a post-conflict situation is given precedence over justice, that of the realist. As he notes of the 1973 tripartite negotiations between India, Pakistan and Bangladesh, 'With every round of diplomacy, the chances for justice were fading away.'[6]

At the time, Mujib was seen to be handing over prisoners of war as a bargaining chip, which was not respected by the Pakistanis. In 1974, when Henry Kissinger visited Dhaka, Mujib told him that:

> We did our part. We released all the POWs. But then when we want to discuss a division of assets they say nothing. ... I have got 75 million people who have nothing. I have nothing from the Pakistanis; they have the planes, the ships, the reserves. ... Unfortunately many of my people are dying every day. In part because Pakistan has taken everything from me.[7]

Bangladesh was in effect at the mercy of its dysfunctional neighbourhood and unforgiving global realpolitik. Both regional hegemons, India and Pakistan, were, as they are to this day, obsessed with furthering their ancient blood feud. Each had its own hegemonic patron during the Cold War, arming them and providing moral support and the potential wielding of a UN Security Council veto. These benefactors were themselves wrapped up in their own vendettas and mendacious calculations. There was, in other words, little international interest in pressuring Pakistan, the war's losing party, into splitting the loot of the once-unified state between its two constituent parts, let alone in trying its soldiers for the vicious crimes committed in the war.

Mujib's End

Probably well aware of the political tremors and potential dangers of his decision, Mujib declared a state of emergency on 28 December 1974. Not only did Bangladesh face an uphill struggle and awful treatment in the international arena, but leftist insurgency had joined famine, corruption and lawlessness to buffet the government of a country that Kissinger notoriously described as a 'basket case'. The emergency was shortly followed by the announcement of the formation of Baksal, or the Bangladesh Krishak Sramik Awami League. This catch-all political platform effectively ended competitive politics by collapsing most parties into a single, Soviet-style political grouping. Furthermore, Mujib had a sinister personal militia known as the Jatiya Rakkhi Bahini, which was separate from the army and was accused of a litany of human rights abuses, including killings, rapes and enforced disappearances. By August, Mujib had been busy filling positions in this 'second revolution', as he termed it. That month, he had started to receive warnings that his life might be in danger, but shrugged them off.

In the early hours of 15 August 1975, a group of junior officers rallied their men in Dhaka. Some 700 men of the Bengal Lancers Armoured Division and of the 2nd Artillery Division were briefed by Major Syed Faruque Rahman, who told the men that there 'was no way to change the government except using force, otherwise the country would become subservient to India'.[8] Soldiers arrived first at the house of Mujib's brother-in-law, Abdur Rab Serniabat, on Minto Road, not far from Mujib's own house. Mujib heard of the attack on his relative's house and began frantically calling for help to come to his family home. Soon, gunfire was heard on the road outside, and panic ensued inside the property. As Mujib was desperately trying to reach help on the phone, his eldest son, 26-year-old Sheikh Kamal, ran downstairs. Explosions were heard outside, and members of the Bengal Lancers barged into the house. They shot Kamal at point blank range in a reception room near the front door. They had faced little resistance at the gates; there was minimal security in those days, Mujib's grandson explained to me, as he took me on a tour of the house. Furthermore, the security personnel who were there were reluctant to stop, question or fire upon uniformed army men. The soldiers went from room to room and killed all those inside, including Mujib's youngest child, Sheikh Russel, who was only ten years old.

In total, some forty-one members of the family were assassinated in four locations on that August night in 1975. In the downstairs hallway of Mujib's house today, the corridor is lined with portraits of those killed at the property. As the soldiers tore through the house, they killed all those they found alive, until they finally found the president upstairs and escorted him down. Soldiers Bazlul Huda and Nur Chowdhury were at the foot of the stairs when they saw their comrades leading Mujib down; they opened fire, killing him. Bullet holes scar the property to this day, gouged out of the walls and roofs of a building now preserved as a museum. It is manifest that the attack was exceptionally brutal, judging by the unsparing nature of the murders and the quantity of ammunition that was evidently used. The officers had wanted to eliminate Mujib's entire family, preventing the possibility of heirs.

Mujib's two daughters were both in Germany at the time of the attack. One of them, Sheikh Rehana, is the mother of Radwan Siddiq, who showed me around the museum, and of British politician Tulip Siddiq. The other, Sheikh Hasina, would return after years of exile and has latterly dominated politics. The assassination was a formative event in Hasina's early life, which was scarred by war, exile, fear, and undoubtedly deep resentment. Her government now lionises Mujib as the father of the nation, bestowing him with the honorific 'Bangabandhu', or friend of Bangladesh. Many institutions, buildings and bridges are named after him. But this was not always the way.

Political Reorientation

The murders had been much more than a political assassination. They were a genuine attempt to rewrite history books and irrevocably reshape the future direction of the country—a trend of deeply political nation shaping that would become a recurrent trait in Bangladesh. What followed was a chaotic mess, one that—as is so often the case in weak states—saw the army and one general in particular float to the top as victors. The motives that led a small clique to take such drastic action and the reasons that the military tolerated and even applauded the coup are important. A principal factor was India, and its role in Bangladesh's liberation and in creating the subcontinent's new political settlement.

Bangladesh's giant neighbour did not occupy the country for long in its decisive intervention in the winter of 1971. Even so, when Indian forces spearheaded the final offensive against Pakistan, taking advantage of the preparatory work of the Mukti Bahini, or Bangladeshi freedom fighters, the latter were 'marginalised … and denied … the role of victors in national liberation,' notes scholar S. Mahmud Ali.[9] The freedom fighters had often been led and staffed by mutinying East Pakistani soldiers. After the war, they went on to form the military in the new state. By contrast, Sheikh Mujib had by necessity developed a tight patron–client relationship with New Delhi. To assert his own control and wage political vendettas in the informal mess of the new state, he had created the aforementioned militia, the Jatiya Rakkhi Bahini or JRB, whom he trusted more than the conventional army. For many in the Bangladeshi army, 'Delhi's direct involvement in building up the JRB, seen by many soldiers as a rival force loyal to Mujib personally, deepened anger.'[10]

The weak state and subsequent dependence on India are perennial themes in Bangladeshi nationalist discourse. The reasons that Bangladesh and the Mujib government were so dependent on India were in part due to the broader geopolitical dynamic and freeze: Western nations, and the United States in particular, mistrusted the Indians, who had a close relationship with the Soviet Union, and as a result found it difficult to accept India's actions or its regional hegemony. The Nixon administration was bitter about its client state, Pakistan, losing the war in 1971, and seemingly being dismembered by India, a Soviet ally.

China for its part held very pro-Pakistani sentiments; a mouthpiece for Beijing described the birth of Bangladesh, in typically stilted Communist official speak, as 'India's armed occupation of Pakistan territory and the forcible imposition of the puppet "Bangla Desh" regime on the East Pakistan people so as to satiate Soviet revisionism's greed of expanding its sphere of influence in the Subcontinent and the Indian Ocean.'[11] The Chinese went as far as to compare India's 1971 military venture into East Pakistan with the behaviour of the Axis powers in the 1930s, as telling of India's 'expansionism'.[12] China itself had then only recently annexed Tibet, had fought a border war with India over territory, and would in 1979 abortively invade Vietnam. Much like Cambodia and its liberation by the Vietnamese, Bangladesh was bedevilled by the enmity of its liberator's enemies, in this case the motley anti-Soviet alliance of Pakistan, China and the United States.[13] Thus, numerous factions of the elite had links and sympathies to the various powers that be.

Mujib for his part had been stuck with the Indians, even if he had not wanted to be. This provided perfect fuel for both the opprobrium of many in the Bangladeshi army and for the birth of an altogether different and potent Bangladeshi nationalism. Many in the army had fought for and supported the Pakistan cause when, in the 1960s, India and Pakistan went to war. Many remembered the horrors of Partition, and some no doubt still harboured the feelings of communalism that led to that horror in the first place. Numerous members of the military also felt that politicians from the Awami League, including Mujib, had spent the war safely in custody, and that as soon as soldiers had secured victory, they had come back to claim the glory—and the country. They believed that the soldiers who had actually done the hard work had not been rewarded.

In any case, as soon as Mujib had been killed, along with most of his family, a former foreign minister and right-leaning 'pro-American' member of the Awami League assumed the presidency.[14] Khondaker Mushtaq Ahmed, who was the commerce minister in Mujib's government at the time of his assassination, took over as the nation's new leader and immediately rewarded the army majors who had carried out the coup, promoting them to lieutenant colonels and giving them roles as government advisors.

The Leftist Challenge

The right-wing coup plotters, who included Mushtaq himself and the army majors, were also attempting to head off a looming left-wing reaction to Mujib's crisis-wracked government. This leftist challenge was very real, and was led by men such as Colonel Abu Taher and his Jatiya Samajtantrik Dal (JSD), or National Socialist Party. The party's aim was to uphold some of the tenets of the independence struggle, principally socialism. It objected to many of the authoritarian turns of Mujib's government, and to some of its economic ones, too. Much support for the JSD was to be found among disenfranchised rank-and-file members of the military, who resented the class stratification within the army, reflecting its colonial origins.

The Mushtaq government initiated a 'shift away from the broadly Indo-centric foreign and security policy framework in place since 1972'.[15] While Mushtaq's government would not last long, this new breed of nationalism would. On 3 November 1975, Mushtaq resigned, only months after the coup that had killed Mujib and forced the Awami League out. Pro-Mujib forces led by a military officer named Khaled Mosharraf promulgated the second coup, and troops surrounded the residence of the chief of general staff of the military, General Ziaur Rahman, and placed him under arrest. Like Mujib before him, General Zia jumped on the phone to call a friend for help, probably in the belief that his life was on the line. He called his fellow war hero, the leftist Colonel Abu Taher.

While the in-fighting and disruption of the military's chain-of-command that had begun with the killing of Mujib in August continued, pro-Awami League voices celebrated, believing that the departure of Mushtaq would restore their side to power. This was hugely amplified, and the overbearing nature of India's support for Mujib exposed, when India's official press aired eulogies and glorious accounts of Mujib on the radio. They saluted Khaled Mosharraf, who was viewed as pro-Awami League, and thus, by extension, as pro-India.

The third front in this ideological battle over governance, and over the ideological future of the country, then mustered its forces and moved on 7 November. Leftists, including left-leaning soldiers, under the command of Colonel Abu Taher planned a two-pronged putsch, the first of which would free General Zia, whom they viewed as an ideal, if not entirely ideologically compliant, figurehead.[16] General Zia had been a leading military figure in 1971. During the conflict, the Mukti Bahini had divided the country into sectors. The Chittagong sector was presided over by General Zia. Chittagong was an important sector, as the city is the country's second largest metropolis, home to the country's largest port, and an important industrial centre. While Sheikh Mujib was in detention in Pakistan, having been jailed shortly after the crackdown by the Pakistani military on 25 March 1971, Zia delivered major announcements on a clandestine, pro-independence radio station, based just north of the city in Kalurghat. On 27 March, he is believed to have made the first formal declaration of independence. This act is taken to have a high symbolic value, and has been played up or diminished by supporters and political adversaries respectively ever since.[17]

In November 1975, the leftists planned to 'mount a revolutionary surge to capture organs of state authority and to establish a hierarchy of revolutionary councils with Zia as its formal leader.'[18] The insurrection was met with jubilant crowds as the lower-ranked troops revolted, confronting traditional military class hierarchies. They successfully freed Zia and looked set to promulgate yet another socialist revolution in Asia. The US embassy reported 'wild celebrations here of his [Mosharraf's] overthrow', which 'carried distinctly anti-Indian overtones.'[19] Meanwhile, Zia seemed to be cooperating with his wartime comrade, leftist leader Colonel Abu Taher, taking to the airwaves again to indicate as much and to call for stability. However, within days, Zia and other military colleagues expressed second thoughts. They were stung by the challenge to military rank that the leftists believed in and were instigating against, at times through violent revolt against senior officers whose personal servants they had previously been. Zia's objections and interventions to prevent the dethroning of officers elevated his status and enabled him to build up his following among senior members of the military. While the rebellious leftists needed him to act as a formal figurehead, he bolstered his standing in the army to 'near mythical heights' by simultaneously offering support for the more senior ranks.[20]

The US embassy already knew which way the wind would blow. As they cabled on 17 November 1975, 'Zia should be in a position to dominate the scene, particularly in light of the way in which he was restored to command of the army by the armed [leftist] rising of enlisted men in his support on November 7.' This was the firm hope of the embassy, who fretted that 'the effort of the Jatiyo Samajtantrik Dal (JSD) to manipulate and capitlaize onthe [sic] collapse of discipline in the armed forces is a most dramatic and dangerous development.'[21]

On the morning of 7 November, as the second coup was in the offing, Zia and Abu Taher met at the latter's compound in Narayanganj, a town just south of Dhaka. Zia thanked Abu Taher for saving him as the two men embraced warmly. While Zia was under house arrest, it was Abu Taher whom he had first called for help, and it was his lower-ranked troops who had eventually freed the general and elevated him to a position of supreme power. However, things quickly started to sour between the two men. By 15 November, Abu Taher's leftist JSD party 'had publicly begun to dissociate itself from Zia, after he refused to order further prisoner releases and continued a ban on political meetings.'[22] The party was busy trying to form revolutionary councils among soldiers, industrial workers and peasants, to help solidify and provide structure to their socialist revolution.

By 23 November, the US embassy's hopes and predictions had come to fruition: General Zia staged his counter-coup. That evening the conventional police arrested JSD leaders, including Hasanul Haq Inu, who would come back to serve as the information minister under the Awami League government that took power in 2009. The next day, paramilitary police went after Abu Taher and arrested him. Another crackdown began, as the turncoat General Zia, having betrayed his friend and saviour, went after JSD members and leftists of most walks of life. The exception, somewhat bizarrely, would be pro-Chinese Maoists, who found accommodation within the new nexus of power, again reflecting the adherence to and importance of foreign powers in giving legitimacy to internal groupings of elites within newly formed states. In 1976, General Zia put his former comrade Abu Taher on trial. At secret military tribunals, Abu Taher was charged with trumped-up offences such as high treason, murder and 'propagating political opinion'. The leftist war hero was hanged in June 1976.

So in November 1975 began Bangladesh's first era of military autocracy as an independent state, less than four years after the country's victory over the Pakistanis. Military rule, or military dominance under the guise of 'pseudo-civilian government', would last until 1990.[23] With General Zia at its helm, the government immediately embarked on a massive increase in military spending, to cement its own martial power and to buy favour with and appease the military, which would be both the principal support base of the new regime and its main threat to political authority. Military spending doubled in the single year between 1975 and 1976.

Anti-Indianism and Political Islam

Like the Americans, the Pakistanis and the Chinese, General Zia harboured a deep distrust of India. For the Americans, this antipathy stemmed from India's long-held neutrality in the Cold War and relatively close ties to the Soviets. For his part, Zia most likely shared a degree of Pakistan's regional, communal nationalism. At this point in the mid-1970s, Zia, the Americans and the Pakistanis all either believed or wanted to believe that the Indians would re-invade Bangladesh, to ensure that an India-friendly regime was in power in Dhaka. This is evident from cables from the American embassy, which reflect panicked drum beating with regards to potential Indian involvement. The messages sound almost like an effort to vindicate the beliefs of the White House. In a notorious conversation with Kissinger, President Nixon announced, 'The Indians need—what they need really is a—'. Kissinger interjected, 'They're such bastards.' Nixon finished his thought: 'A mass famine.'[24]

The anti-Indian mood led Zia to make a 'top secret' approach to Pakistan through Bangladesh's ambassador in neighbouring Burma, K. M. Kaiser.[25] This was done very soon after taking power, and not very long after Pakistan had promulgated genocide in Bangladesh. Pakistan's foreign ministry had been specifically instructed to keep the Americans abreast of the mission, which was chiefly concerned with drumming up fear over an imaginary, imminent Indian invasion. The American embassy appears, even before this, to have spent much time looking for Indian infiltration along the border.[26] Meanwhile, Zia continued the previous Mushtaq government's plea for arms from the Americans.

India never did invade. However, the fear and loathing of India from Zia's government and the political party that he went on to found did not fade. Large segments of Bangladesh's population as a whole, moreover, retain a deep suspicion of India, perhaps in part inspired by official fearmongering and the stoking of communal enmity.

In 1978, Zia consolidated his political movement into the Bangladesh Nationalist Party. It would come to be an institutional mainstay of the political right in Bangladesh, and comprised a wide variety of factions and interests, from religious zealots to pro-Chinese Maoists, and much in between. These groups share one unifying trait, a loathing of the Awami League and that party's chief patron, India. This antipathy or emotion is possibly the simplest yet one of the most important and defining impulses in Bangladeshi politics. It works on multiple levels: religious, communal, neighbourly, and so on.

This Cold War realignment ran concurrently with General Zia's efforts to rehabilitate political Islam. Up to that point, this dictum had been sidelined by the banning of communalist parties implicated in siding with Pakistan in 1971. Much like in post–Second World War Germany, the Awami League and most of the country's left viewed the crimes of 1971 as ideological, and believed that the eradication of these ideologies was important for overcoming the traumas and crimes of the war—as part of what is commonly referred to in the West as 'never again'. Zia, however, needed to shore up his legitimacy within the weak newly formed nation-state. Having betrayed the leftist party and rank-and-file soldiers who had saved him, he lacked a political creed. He decided to build his new creed almost entirely on being against India and pro-Islam. This married well with the Washington consensus that others, like the Pakistanis and General Pinochet in Chile, were then signing up to. Washington's outlook matched the ideals of discipline and conservatism honoured by Zia's military rule, and it fit with religiosity, which Zia saw as an easy means of gaining legitimacy.[27] His was a simple, traditionalist vision, and it resonated in army barracks.

In 1977, Zia removed secularism from the constitution as one of the country's guiding principles, replacing it with a statement of 'absolute trust and faith in Almighty Allah'. He also lifted the ban on Jamaat-e-Islami and opened the country to the party's senior figures, who had fled to Pakistan, Saudi Arabia and the UK after 1971. In 1978, the leader of Jamaat, Ghulam Azam, returned to Bangladesh. Zia also instituted a number of more subtle changes, which continue to resonate to this day. In 1977, madrassa education was given its own directorate within the ministry of education, and the following year the government established the Bangladesh Madrassa Education Board.[28] These moves would help to crystallise and institutionalise religious identity and conservative values and inculcate religiosity in millions of young Bangladeshi Muslims.

Modern Reverberations

Among those who would be part of the phenomenal rise of madrassa education from 1975 was one Mufti Muhammad Jasimuddin Rahmani, a Dhaka-based imam who was born shortly after independence in the deltaic Barguna district, not far from the birthplace of Jamaat leader and convicted war criminal Delwar Hossain Sayeedi. Rahmani was arrested in August 2013 for inspiring the killing of Ahmed Rajib Haider, the young architect and atheist blogger who had been one of many who had rallied people to the Shahbag protests in the spring of 2013.

Rahmani was an imam at the Markajul Uloom Al Islamia Madrassa in Mohammadpur in central Dhaka. Like Sayeedi, Rahmani was a popular orator and delivered musical *waz mahfils*, or sermons, that attracted a large number of students from some of Dhaka's better universities. Many of these can be found online and were also distributed on CDs.

Rahmani's sermons resembled and were inspired by the Yemeni-American preacher Anwar al-Awlaki, who was famously hunted down and killed in Yemen by an American drone in 2011, after he had joined Al-Qaeda in the Arabian Peninsula (AQAP). Awlaki's sermons were often delivered in English and were extremely popular. His peaceful, almost nerdy demeanour belied his antagonistic, hate-laden themes, his sermons carrying titles such as 'Never Trust a Non-Muslim'.[29] His speeches were a 'mix of half-understood radical theology, politics and self-help.'[30] They were witty, straightforward, clear and bilingual, gaining him an astonishing outreach. This finally led to the formation of the slick online Al-Qaeda publication *Inspire*, which would in many ways act as a template for later efforts from the Islamic State and other groups in disseminating their message.

Upon his discovery in 2002 that the FBI had learned of regular rendezvous with sex workers, Awlaki panicked and fled the United States, heading east to Yemen.[31] From the remote Shabwa mountains, southwest of the capital Sanaa, he successfully waged his cyber jihad, inspiring troubled young men around the world to commit acts of violence, including the Fort Hood attack in Texas in November 2009, in which thirteen people were killed.[32] His is a strangely modern, peripatetic tale, but it is also frighteningly indicative of a new anxiety-laden 'digital native' existence. Rahmani, bespectacled like his idol, communicated with the same demographic: young, educated men who felt lost and angry, and perhaps somewhat alone in the online world, which was becoming increasingly important to their lives as they entered adulthood. While Awlaki was actually capable of using the internet and computers, Rahmani was not, and instead had his followers upload his speeches and *waz mahfils* for him. Despite the modern, popular means being used to consume and disseminate material, these strains of thinking are not necessarily new. Much of Rahmani's support was based on the perception that secularism is an emasculating philosophy that serves to deprive the Muslim world of unity.

What is striking about Sayeedi, Awlaki and Rahmani and those that followed them is their common sense of victimhood. In the case of Sayeedi this was prompted by the existential challenge of the secular movement for independence in 1971. For Awlaki, it was seemingly the combination of severe personal anxiety regarding his extramarital behaviour and the febrile post-9/11 atmosphere. With Rahmani, it seems, the perceived aggressor was again the rise of the threat of secularism, which manifested itself most pointedly in the much-hyped Shahbag protests. The protests seemed to target and campaign against Islamism while championing and celebrating behaviours and identities deemed antithetical to orthodox Islam.

This crucial persecution complex—and in particular the belief that Muslims in Bangladesh are being victimised by the supposedly secular or unbelieving Awami League, as part of a global anti-Islam conspiracy—is a recurrent theme on social media in Bangladesh. It chimed with and would latterly be picked up or parroted by transnational jihadist groups, such as Al-Qaeda. Like many conspiracy theories, many of the themes or issues this belief touched on had bases in truth. For instance, the authoritarian, deadly or inept actions of the Awami League government were often very real, if at times exaggerated and falsely put down to a global Islamophobic scheme. References to the misfortunes of the Rohingya minority group in neighbouring Myanmar are similarly genuine and tragic, even if they somewhat ironically often mirror the difficulties faced by non-Muslim minorities in many Muslim-majority countries, including Bangladesh. Like conspiracy theories elsewhere, the narrative that Muslims in Bangladesh are being persecuted as part of a worldwide Islamophobic plot uses a mixture of half-truths, fanciful theories and scripture to join dots in ways that resemble prophecy.

In reality, even political opponents concede that Prime Minister Sheikh Hasina, the leader of the Awami League, is an extremely pious woman, with some even claiming that she is more so than her bitter rival Khaleda Zia. Hasina is said to rise at around 5 a.m. to pray. Her politics are probably driven not so much by any great secular zeal or Islamophobic impulse, but rather by a combative, survivor's paranoia, emanating principally from that August night in 1975 when almost her entire family was gunned down.

Despite this, Rahmani has prescribed what can be termed 'defensive jihad' in Bangladesh. As Shiraz Maher explains, it is 'generally accepted within both normative Islam and Salafi-Jihadi circles that only a rightful authority, such as the Caliph, can sanction [offensive jihad].'[33] Defensive jihad, on the other hand, can be approved in a situation where Muslims lack political authority or a leader but the community has come under attack by non-Muslims. Thus, the rhetorical position of characterising perceived enemies as unbelievers becomes a necessity to justify Rahmani's and other ideologues' exhortations to violence.

On Thursday, 7 March 2013, 27-year-old Sunnyur Rahman, an engineer and secular blogger who had rallied behind the Shahbag protests, stepped off a bus at the Purabi cinema in Mirpur. This was the same neighbourhood in Dhaka where Ahmed Rajib Haider had lived, and where he had died only three weeks earlier. It was around 8.30 p.m. and Sunnyur was walking home. Minutes after alighting from the bus, he was attacked by two young bearded men wearing *panjabis*, or traditional robes. The men hacked at his head and legs with machetes, as they shouted '*Allahu akbar!*'—'God is great!' Locals helped Sunnyur to hospital, and he was lucky to survive.[34]

Towards the end of that month, perhaps the most formal manifestation of the move to silence secularists and critics of those on trial came about. Two organisations, Hefazat-e-Islam and a group called Anjuman al-Bayyinat, handed a list of fifty-six individuals whom they claimed had insulted Islam to the aforementioned special panel tasked with taking action against those making 'derogatory remarks' about Islam and the Prophet.[35] The nine-member panel was stocked full of members of the 'secular' government and party, from the religious affairs ministry, the prime minister's office and the two intelligence agencies, and was headed up by the home ministry's additional secretary, Mainuddin Khondaker.

The list contained the names of the deceased Rajib Haider and of blogger Asif Mohiuddin, who at the time was recuperating from stab wounds. The idea caught on and the Jamaat student wing's online media outfit, Basherkella, soon published its own list of eighty-three names, including those from the original list.[36] The special panel narrowed down its list to ten people who they believed had been especially insulting towards Islam and the Prophet. Four of these, including Asif

Mohiuddin, who had narrowly survived a butcher's cleaver to the neck, were thrown in jail for writing published on their blogs. Those who submitted the lists would not stop there. They would instead take their demands for unbelievers to be punished even further.

3

MOBILISATION

Mobilisation of people is, of course, the rice and dahl of politics. In Bangladesh, as elsewhere in the contemporary and historical Muslim world, religion is essential to that endeavour. We have already looked at episodes in contemporary and less-than-contemporary Bangladesh that demonstrate how politics and radical Islam can fuse. We have explored the motives for the secular Shahbag protests, and seen the violent way a small cabal of ultra-conservative, urban students responded to the protests and to what they represented: a modern rendering of the very crimes that Shahbag was protesting. In fact, there were multiple levels to the blowback against the secularists.

On a muggy April day in 2013, I went down to Motijheel, the traditional, late-twentieth-century central business district of Dhaka, where the central bank and other concrete edifices protrude into the heavily polluted skies. The crowd gathering here were not the area's regulars, and I entered a sea of men, around 80 per cent of whom wore small white skullcaps, or *tupis*. To enter the crowds was tough enough, such were their size and density: perhaps half a million men, and boys, had converged on Dhaka's Shapla Square. But getting to the front was another matter altogether. This convergence of humanity was a protest—or, as the participants termed it, a 'siege' of the capital—by an organisation or network of madrassas known as Hefazat-e-Islam, meaning 'Defenders of Islam'. They carried a thirteen-point list of demands, which could be seen as a somewhat bizarre, *sharia*-inspired wish list. The individuals in the crowd were incredibly friendly to this lone male foreigner, perspiring heavily and laden with a heavy camera. Their demands, however, were less friendly. Among them were calls for no 'mingling' of men and women together in public; a ban on concrete statues of humans; a blasphemy law with the provision for capital punishment; the punishment of 'atheist bloggers'; a ban on 'alien cultures', and so on. Ironically, the throng itself was observing an overwhelmingly 'alien culture'—one from the Middle East—their *tupis* covering their heads as they emulated the Prophet.[1]

The task of navigating the crowd became easier when a couple of members of Jamaat and its student wing latched onto me and chaperoned me, leading me to the front and guiding me through the sea of bodies pressed against one another. Every five minutes or so, someone would ask fairly agreeably what my religion was, an obsession rather poisoned by the nature of the gathering, and its loud calls for unbelievers to be killed. The statement from the Hefazat chief prior to the gathering had explained their position quite clearly: 'Atheists won't be allowed in this country. Plots are being hatched to destroy Islam.'[2]

Piety for Anxiety

I was fortunate to be with Jahidur, a Jamaat supporter who lent me a *tupi*—if not for the eyes of the Almighty, then at least for the several hundred thousand men around us, supposedly eager for the deaths of non-believers, whom my *tupi* amused and reassured in equal measure. Jahidur proved a persistent friend over the following weeks; he would call incessantly from different numbers asking for my address. That April day was an important moment, for the march was a very real manifestation of the perceived or at least strategically wielded persecution complex that the 'Defenders of Islam' possessed. Religion was being weaponised by one wing of the political classes against another, and this found a welcome audience in young men like Jahidur.

Of course, there is no 'plot' against Islam in Bangladesh. In reality, religious minorities in Bangladesh have steadily and precipitously shrunk as a proportion of the population. At times they have left in torrents, for instance during the independence struggle, when around 10 million Bangladeshis fled the country to India, most of them Hindus. This was famously illustrated in photographs of Pakistani soldiers peering down men's *lunghis* to see if they were circumcised—if not, it is assumed that they would be killed. At other times, minorities have left more quietly. And of course, on many occasions, minorities have fled or been killed as a result of sporadic attacks. But in the same way that Khaleda Zia had jumped on the supposed lack of religiosity of the Awami League and the Shahbag protestors in an attempt to delegitimise and stigmatise that protest, so too were thousands of madrassa students and the acute sensitivities of the population being used here for political ends.

Just as Sayeedi, Rahmani and Awlaki called people to jihad at moments of increased anxiety, so Hefazat rose and were sponsored at a time of heightened tensions: in 2013 an election was fast approaching, scheduled for 5 January 2014. Hefazat's first protest or 'siege' of 2013—the march where I met Jahidur—took place on 6 April. Four days earlier, the Bangladesh Nationalist Party's then acting general secretary, Mirza Fakhrul Islam Alamgir, had told the press, 'we extend full moral support to [Hefazat's] valid demands.'[3] Hefazat maintained that the march was non-political.

Several months later, I was drinking with a wealthy businessman who hoped to win a seat as a BNP MP in the next elections. We were sitting in one of the embassy 'clubs' in the upmarket Dhaka suburb of Gulshan; embassy-run recreation centres are some of the very few places where one can purchase alcohol legally in Bangladesh. The aspirant MP was 'mingling' with the opposite sex, in public (if such an exclusive place could be described as such), and drinking one of the more expensive whiskies on offer. I enquired how this fit with the line of the party of which he hoped to become a representative. His answer was memorable and honest (perhaps it was the whisky talking): 'We are using them [Hefazat].'

Shaking the Truth, Questioning Legitimacy

Indeed, within a month of the April 'siege', Hefazat organised a second march. This time I did not attend, and things turned violent. On 5 May Hefazat again demanded that the government step down or accede to their thirteen-point set of demands. Throughout the day, large numbers of protesters, mostly madrassa students who had been bussed in from around the country, congregated in Dhaka. As the day progressed, the sieging 'defenders' changed their marching route. They burned down bookshops, firebombed properties, including the offices of the Communist Party of Bangladesh, and clashed with police. During the night, they camped out in central Dhaka and refused to leave. In the early hours of 6 May, security forces 'cleared' the protesters, having cut the electricity to the area and its surrounds.

I called my friend Jahidur. He claimed that 4,000 people had been killed and that their bodies were laden onto pick-up trucks and taken to India. The BNP concurred with this line from Jamaat, their electoral ally, 'hyperbolically' claiming it was 'genocide'.[4] According to Human Rights Watch, fifty-eight people including police personnel had been killed in what undoubtedly amounted to a deadly, excessively heavy-handed police operation.[5] The generally pro-BNP human rights organisation Odhikar found sixty-one people had been killed. Odhikar, which is run by Adilur Rahman Khan, a former assistant attorney general who served in the last BNP government, which was in power from 2001 to 2006, ran into a serious and unsavoury clash with the government over these figures. When Odhikar refused to hand over its list of casualties, the government vindictively hounded the group, and has ever since, preventing its fundraising and therefore its activities.[6]

Opponents of the government jumped on the affair. As pressure on the government to acknowledge the casualties of the police crackdown mounted, the figures became increasingly exaggerated. The issue even reached the UK and was picked up by a number of left-leaning politicians, chief amongst them George Galloway. Speaking at a Hefazat UK meeting, the then MP for Bradford West called the killings of protesters a 'massacre of thousands' that had been 'worse than 9/11'.[7] Revealing what the controversy was really all about, Galloway called for a revolution to depose Prime Minister Sheikh Hasina—'from the streets'. No doubt the MP did not have time to read about the details of the issue and Hefazat's thirteen-point list of demands, or to note the arson attack on the Communist Party of Bangladesh, an organisation that he might have had some sympathy for. Led by Galloway, British MPs went on to file an 'early day motion' in parliament on 15 May 2013:

this House notes the reports currently circulating on the electronic media about a massacre of peaceful demonstrators in Shapla Square, Dhaka, Bangladesh by security forces on 6 May 2013; further notes that the lowest estimates of the number of deaths runs to thousands; further notes there has been a news blackout about this massacre in Bangladesh…

Arriving at the crucial point about agitation and protest in Bangladesh, the motion's sponsor 'further believes these latest events mean that free and fair elections in Bangladesh will be extremely problematic.'[8] This hyperbole-laden motion was co-signed by the MP for Islington North, Jeremy Corbyn, who would later become the leader of Britain's Labour Party.

The early day motion reveals much about agitation and the recurring political modus operandi in Bangladesh (as well as the strange position of many on the left in the UK, when it comes to Islamists). Mayhem and chaos are used to question the government's ability to run the country and thereby to bring about regime change. Exaggerated allegations against a government can be used to make pre-emptive judgements about the future course of politics and foul play. The Awami League used these precise tactics in 2006 by calling strikes, which were generally less violent in nature than the BNP's anti-government protests in 2013–2015 but which contributed to bringing about a military coup at the beginning of 2007. The aim of this type of agitation is to question the capacity and therefore the legitimacy of a government, which is the principal Achilles' heel of party politics in Bangladesh. It is an accusation that Western missions routinely level at governments in Bangladesh, and elsewhere, whenever they find their actions distasteful—that this young country, carved out of failed Western cartography and design and founded at the cost of its own countrymen's blood, lacks the institutions to legitimately govern itself.

Election Fever

In 2013, the most important focus for the opposition alliance was the upcoming 2014 election and how to unseat the Awami League. For the Awami League, it was how to stay in power and avoid again being on the back foot in often messy, vindictive party political feuding.

In the 2008 elections, the Awami League had won a huge mandate, winning a whopping 263 in 300 seats, compared to the BNP's 30. As a result, the BNP virtually ignored the country's parliament. The BNP leader, Khaleda Zia, only attended the striking Louis Khan-designed parliament building on six occasions in the three years from 2009 to 2012.[9] This sore-loser syndrome is part of what commentators call Bangladesh's zero-sum politics.

The ruling Awami League duly and ruthlessly took advantage of its mandate and the free hand it had been given politically. It removed a provision in the electoral rules that called for a caretaker government to oversee polls and run the country during the election period. The League was able to make this change unchallenged, partly because the opposition lacked a mandate and partly because instead of using its weak political hand, the BNP decided simply to combat the measure through strikes, protests, vitriol and worse. Bangladeshi voters traditionally have severe anti-incumbency tendencies and Bangladeshi democracy to this date has consisted of the two main parties taking it in turns to rule the country for five-year stretches. These periods afford the respective party hierarchies a few years in which to 'capture state resources' and to trade access to these resources for fealty.[10]

When the Awami League declared that the ruling government would run the elections, the BNP announced that it would boycott the process. Election boycotts had occurred before, the idea being to highlight a lack of legitimacy in the outcome: a belief certainly shared by the American embassy and other Western missions. The opposition's reasoning was that the political environment and pressure would somehow force the government from office. However, the Awami League government proved both resilient and wily; it 'used reverse psychology', recalled Shamsher Mobin Chowdhury, then a senior member of the BNP and former foreign minister. The BNP was effectively and pre-emptively saying that the democratic government could not hold a free and fair election and would cheat, which may very well have been the case, but it was no more than a hypothetical. Furthermore, opposition chief Khaleda Zia liked to project an image of herself as an uncompromising leader. And so the government pushed ahead and offered a compromise, knowing that Khaleda would not go along with it and correctly assuming that the

BNP would instead try to bring about a change of power through destabilising acts of protest and violence, to try to induce a coup of some sort. In effect, the BNP would try to cause so much disruption and chaos that the aching sense of a legitimacy deficit would induce the military to intervene.

For this, the opposition needed manpower and allies. Through its relationship with Hefazat, the BNP already looked to the clerical madrassa network for legitimacy, and sometimes, the two groups shared personnel. On one rain-sodden afternoon in September 2013, I travelled to the town of Narsingdi, several hours northeast of Dhaka. Despite the rain, a vast crowd had packed into a field. In distant, half-constructed buildings, people could be discerned, perched a few floors up and observing the excitable gathering. They were all there for a BNP rally at which Khaleda Zia and much of the party's top brass were in attendance. I was fortunate to make it onto the stage where a wooden throne awaited Khaleda, the prime ministerial hopeful, while a small throng of speakers and influential others milled around. I thought my incredible access was because I was the only foreigner at this otherwise well-stocked gathering. But as it turned out, I was not even the only Londoner.

I quickly got chatting to Maulana Noor-e-Alom Hamidi, the genial, broad-faced prospective BNP MP for the Sreemangal constituency in the nearby Sylhet district. Hamidi presented me with his card and told me he was part of Hefazat UK, and that he ran a quasi-charity in the East London neighbourhood of Plaistow. The majority of British-Bangladeshis hail from the Sylhet region. As a result, Hamidi was working to raise money in London and Walsall in the UK for the Boruna Madrassa in Sreemangal. He was also politically active, with connections to Islamist groups in the UK such as Hizb-ut-Tahrir. This student-driven party is proscribed in Bangladesh but legal in the UK.

As I gazed at the sea of largely young men grouped in the crowd by their party affiliations, a Jamaat area waved placards on which Delwar Hossain Sayeedi's red beard shone out, and Hamidi ranted about 'Lady Hitler', as the opposition at that time were fond of labelling Sheikh Hasina. Hamidi would not go on to claim or even to contest the seat in Sreemangal. As it was, the Awami League, amid a hail of opposition protest, brickbats and shrugs of the shoulder, held its nerve and meandered towards an unprecedented second consecutive term in office.

Appeasement

A major obstacle in the Awami League's way that winter was another Hefazat march, planned for 24 December 2013. However, as the elections inched closer, the next 'siege' never materialised: at the last minute the protest was cancelled. In the subsequent months and years, it has become clear that this was because of a deal between the government or members of the Awami League and Hefazat. The madrassa movement was both appeased and bought off. One government bureaucrat, under condition of anonymity, described this as the government using 'divide and rule' tactics. By paying off Hefazat, the League lessened the chances of the madrassa group becoming the opposition's ally with narrowly political aims of toppling the government. But as Hefazat leader Mufti Fayezulla told me in the Old Dhaka madrassa that he runs, that did not mean that Hefazat's ideological battle was over. He trod a delicate line of argument: the group believed in the 'rule of law', he said, so superficially did not agree with the targeted killings of atheists. But the mufti was interrupted by a student who was more expressive in English—yes, they believed in law, but one that stated that blasphemy and unbelief should be met with capital punishment.

Since Hefazat's 2013 show of strength, the madrassa network has had a number of policy wins, some rather notional, others more substantial. This included the jailing of bloggers who were deemed to have offended Islam. One of these included committed atheist Asif Mohiuddin, who had been attacked in January 2013. His attacker's blade came within millimetres of killing him by decapitation. Asif would later meet his aggressors in jail, while he was still recovering from his wounds. Another metaphorical scalp the madrassa network claimed was that of Abdul Latif Siddiqui, a government minister. Siddiqui had not been the posts and telecommunications minister for long when he travelled to New York in September 2014 on an official junket. The minister took time off to address a gathering of Bangladeshi-Americans in the Jackson Heights neighbourhood of the city. While cameras rolled, he quipped that the Hajj pilgrimage to Mecca was a waste of money and added that the prime minister's son Sajeeb Wazed Joy was a 'nobody'.[11] His comments crossed two of Bangladesh's giant red lines, despite their banality or veracity. Yet again, Hefazat took to the streets, and once more the government caved. They first sacked and then jailed the minister, who had risked his life as a young man fighting not just for the country's independence but also for freedom of belief and secularism. However tactless or foolish Siddiqui's comments might have been, this pandering to Hefazat's sensitivity to criticism would not be applied to other belief groups. In other words, the Defenders of Islam were further enabling exceptionalism for the majority faith in Bangladesh and the breakdown of objective law and of the very notion of secularism—that the state not involve itself in matters of religion or favour a particular religious group. These were the sacrifices that Bangladesh's largest 'secular' party made in order to proceed with their unopposed election.

Hefazat-e-Islam: A Closer Look

The Hefazat movement is a loose agglomeration of what are known as Qawmi madrassas. These are the least regulated Islamic seminaries, and over the years they have steadily gained acceptance, status and power. Qawmi madrassas do not have to register with government agencies or local administration, and receive no financial aid from the government.[12] By 2005, an umbrella organisation estimated that around 1.85 million students attended these institutions and that the number was growing rapidly. These schools belong to different sub-strands, with Hefazat representing a cluster of madrassas in Chittagong in the south of the country. The movement's leader, Shah Ahmad Shafi, runs the Hathazari Madrassa, an institution in the Hathazari suburb of Chittagong, a few miles to the north of the port city.

Shafi was already in his nineties when the Hefazat movement started battling the government, and would fly to address rallies in a helicopter. He is suspected of profiting handsomely from his accommodations with the government who needed him to stand down in 2013–14. Months after police had killed dozens of his supporters, Shafi claimed that he never had a problem with the government.[13] He is said to have received a valuable plot of land formerly owned by the national rail ministry, purportedly as a bribe to abandon his organisation's relationship with the opposition.

While the groups in the Hefazat network have been in existence for decades, Shafi has turned the coalition into one of the most powerful Islamist forces in Bangladesh, if not the most powerful, since the repression of Jamaat-e-Islami. With millions of cadre in its charge, the organisation has huge potential for mobilisation. Generally in Bangladesh, being able to mobilise people nationwide means political power, and with that comes vulnerability to being targeted by rivals. But since its members are wrought from educational institutions, Hefazat has a degree of impunity in the face of attack from other political parties or movements. The fact that the network is comprised of religious institutions, moreover, affords Hefazat another layer of protection from repression, which straightforward political organisations can only dream of possessing.

Shafi is notorious for having claimed that women are 'like tamarind', the intensely sour fruit that is said to make the consumer salivate. According to his sermon, this alleged similarity was a justification for keeping women at home, or at least concealed beneath a burka. Much like equivalents from other religions, these pious institutions are obsessed with women and their supposed corrupting potential, treating them purely as sexual objects. But like Awlaki and his penchant for prostitutes, or the infamous cases of Catholic priests' abuse of those in their charge, Hefazat madrassas are replete with patently warped and hypocritical positioning, from corruption and political plays to a case of alleged rape of a young male student in a madrassa in the network in Pabna.[14]

Another institution whose head was a key leader in Hefazat was the Lalkhan Bazar Madrassa, located more centrally in the city of Chittagong. This institution's head was a man named Mufti Izharul Islam Chowdhury. Chowdhury reputedly travelled to Afghanistan to fight the communists in the 1980s, and allegedly met key fighters there, including Taliban supreme commander Mullah Omar and Osama Bin Laden. He and fellow travellers came back to a Bangladesh that was being transformed by General Zia's conservative policies. 'Ossified institutions like madrassas acquired a new lease of life.

The sites of reproduction of social orthodoxy became the recruiting centres for ultraconservative confessional political forces,' notes Professor Ali Riaz.[15]

The institution that Chowdhury headed, Lalkhan Bazar Madrassa, has had persistent connections to violent extremism. One October morning in 2013, a large explosion ripped through one of the third-floor dormitories of the school. Three people, including two students, were killed in the explosion. While Chowdhury claimed that the blast had come from a 'laptop', authorities reported that they had found grenades and bomb-making equipment at the institution.[16] The police did not arrest Chowdhury on that occasion. They would have been hard pushed to; according to press reports they did not arrive at the site of the deadly blast until 6.30 p.m., more than seven hours after it had occurred.

On returning from Afghanistan, Chowdhury and his friends decided to keep alive the jihadist spirit they had found there, and, under the leadership of Maulana Abdus Salam, formed an organisation called Harkat-ul-Jihad al-Islami Bangladesh, or HUJI-B. This was an offshoot of an eponymous Pakistani organisation that had fought jihad in the 1980s with the help of Pakistan's Inter-Services Intelligence agency (ISI). It first emerged in public in Bangladesh at a press conference on 30 April 1992, when it presented itself as a group of former Mujahideen celebrating the demise of the Soviet occupation of Afghanistan. The organisation would not be banned until October 2005. This was despite several assassination attempts on the Awami League leader, Sheikh Hasina, first in 2000 and again in 2004. In 2004, there was also a bomb attempt on the British high commissioner's life. Even after HUJI-B was outlawed, it was not until the BNP government left office after a military coup in early 2007 that the organisation's leaders were arrested. Some were detained even later in 2009, and then only because of their earlier mission to kill the newly appointed Prime Minister Sheikh Hasina. The HUJI-B chief and founder Abdus Salam was finally detained in November 2009, the year that the Awami League took office. Earlier that year he had been jailed over a bomb attack but was swiftly released on bail, apparently because the victims in that case were 'only' a leftist party. Arguably, HUJI-B had its remarkable political and intelligence connections to thank for this degree of impunity.

Removing Political Obstacles

On 21 August 2004, Sheikh Hasina, then leader of the opposition, addressed a rally of some 20,000 supporters at a gathering on the country's worsening terrorism situation. Only a few months before, British High Commissioner Anwar Chowdhury had been injured in a bombing while visiting a Muslim shrine in the northeastern town of Sylhet. Hasina was standing on the back of a lorry addressing the crowds when, just before 5.30 p.m., men from surrounding buildings started hurling down Arges grenades on the crowds. These are designed to 'inflict massive damage against soft targets' and spray 'shrapnel out to a distance of 30 metres.' While the grenades were originally designed in Austria, the Pakistan Ordinance Factory also produces them.[17]

Hasina was only slightly injured and credited her supporters with saving her life. However, twenty-four people were killed in the attack, and hundreds more were wounded. It rapidly became clear that HUJI-B were behind the incident. This had strong precedents; as a leaked US embassy cable related, HUJI-B 'has been linked to assassination attempts on intellectuals, journalists, and politicians, including two thwarted attempts on the life of Prime Minister Sheikh Hasina during public addresses.'[18]

However, the full nature of the 2004 attack would not become clear until the BNP government had left office. The words of alleged perpetrator and HUJI-B commander Mufti Hannan are incredible for their commentary on the nexus between politics and extremism, though it must be noted that his testimony might have been given under duress. Hannan claimed that days before the bombing he had met with then Prime Minister Khaleda Zia's son, Tarique Rahman, whom the US embassy described as running a 'parallel administration' from his 'notorious' office known as 'Hawa Bhaban'.[19] As well as the BNP heir apparent, at the meeting were Jamaat leader Ali Ahsan Mojaheed, then Home Minister Lutfozzaman Babar, and others, including a deputy minister named Abdus Salam Pintu and his brother, Maulana Tajuddin. According to Hannan, the Jamaat leader, Mojaheed, had said at the meeting that Hasina was 'working against Islam'. Hannan reported being told by Mojaheed that she could either be dealt with politically or be killed, thereby solving the 'problem' permanently. The violent route, again, did not work. As on a handful of other occasions, when shots were fired at her or bombs were planted in places where she was due to speak, she was fortunate to escape.[20] This was not to mention the occasion when her father was assassinated, which she had survived in 1975 by being away in Germany.

In any case, according to subsequent investigations, which had to wait four years, perhaps because of the fact that the BNP was in power, it was alleged that the Arges grenades used in the attack were brought to Mufti Hannan from the house of Maulana Tajuddin, the brother of BNP deputy minister Abdus Salam Pintu, a few days before the attack.[21] The grenades were apparently imported from Pakistan with the help of the ISI and Pakistani militant groups such as Lashkar-e-Taiba (LeT), and in particular an associate or friend of Hannan's from LeT named Maulana Obaidullah.[22] Over the course of two meetings between the political leaders and the HUJI-B men, the latter were allegedly assured that they would receive 'all administrative assistance'— in other words, impunity before the law.[23] In the event, out of those prominent individuals whom Hannan suggested were involved in the plot, only Tarique Rahman, heir apparent to the BNP, and Maulana Tajuddin would receive the said 'administrative assistance', in that they gained safe passage to leave the country when the change of administration occurred: Rahman to the UK, and Tajuddin, with the help of the Directorate General of Forces Intelligence (DGFI), to South Africa. The DGFI is Bangladesh's military intelligence agency, the equivalent of Pakistan's ISI or India's Research and Analysis Wing (RAW), and like those agencies, it is extremely powerful—and feared. Mufti Hannan was finally executed in April 2017.

Intel Connections

While Mufti Hannan's testimony hints at HUJI-B's political connections during the years when the BNP were in power, HUJI-B continued to wield relationships with power brokers like the DGFI after the BNP were forced from office. During a sort of military interregnum between 2007 and 2008 in which party politics was banned, the military government attempted to wipe the slate clean, before recommencing with competitive party politics. Among many others, both major party leaders, Sheikh Hasina and Khaleda Zia, were jailed by the authorities for corruption and election-related violence. Hasina was accused of bombing or ordering the bombing of transport infrastructure, including buses, which resulted in dozens of civilian casualties, as the Awami League tried to bring the country to a standstill in 2006.[24] This was the exact course of action that the BNP would take against the Awami League, which the latter, rightly, complained so bitterly about when they themselves were in government. The military's detention of the two leaders was known as the 'minus two solution'. Minus the two ladies, so the theory went, the country would be able to usher in a new, more open period of government. This was supported by a number of elites, foreign and domestic.

However, as the military looked to hand over power to civilian hands, there was also a scramble to put in place new parties and contestants for the polls. The DGFI, for its part, tried to promote a party called the Islamic Democratic Party (IDP), which was launched in May 2008. It was very evident that the party was little more than a front for HUJI-B, however. The outfit was launched around the time that the US State Department added HUJI-B to their Foreign Terrorist Organizations list. Members of Bangladesh's government at the time tried to explain to American diplomats that by creating and supporting the IDP, 'the Bangladeshi intelligence and security services could monitor and co-opt IDP leaders and arrest those HUJI-B members that remained outside of the political process.'[25] DGFI officials claimed that the move to support and create the IDP had been led by a brigadier general named A. T. M. Amin, who was then head of the agency's counter-terror division. The year before, in 2007, Amin had told the American embassy that DGFI had infiltrated HUJI-B and thus did not 'see them attacking western interests.'[26] This was clearly an attempt to mimic their Pakistani counterparts in the ISI, for whom co-option of jihadist outfits is systemic and promulgated as a means of using non-state actors to pursue policy goals.

As the history of such interactions shows, and from what we have seen from the likes of Hefazat, it is clear that religion is a powerful commodity. Therefore, for any political play, having a pliable religious party or entity to wield can be extremely powerful. In Bangladeshi politics, this manifests itself in two distinct ways.

First, Islamist parties don't tend to poll very well at elections, but the few seats they do win, and the automatic constituency they have, can make all the difference. In 2008, Jamaat-e-Islami, the largest Islamist party at the time, gained only 4.6 per cent of the vote, winning only two parliamentary seats of 300. Nonetheless, Jamaat and other Islamist parties are often seen as kingmakers. While the Awami League obliterated opponents in the 2008 polls, the previous 2001 elections were a much closer contest. The Awami League gained just over 40 per cent of the vote while the BNP won 41.4 per cent. It was here that Jamaat's 4.2 per cent of the popular vote came in. The alliance between the BNP and Jamaat had only formally been in place since 1999. In the mid-1990s, Jamaat had joined the Awami League in protesting the then incumbent BNP's handling of the elections, an almost mirror image of the situation that prevailed in 2013–14, except that on the latter occasion, the incumbent party or the Awami League managed to see off the alliance protesting against it.

Second, having a claim to the blessings of the pious is seen as a vital tool for proving the legitimacy of a party, ever since the country's first military dictator, General Ziaur Rahman, used this crutch to prop up his regime. The Awami League has also looked at strategic electoral alliances with Islamists in order to appear serious about 'promoting' Islam. For instance, on 23 December 2006, the League signed a memorandum of understanding (MOU) with the hard-line Islamist outfit Bangladesh Khelafat Majlish (BKM), even though it 'was well-known for its radical views and the involvement of its leaders with militant groups such as the Jamaat-ul-Mujahideen Bangladesh (JMB).'[27] The 2006 election never happened, perhaps luckily for the Awami League. For their agreement with the BKM was basically a shortened version of the list that Hefazat had insisted on, leading to deadly protests in 2013. It stipulated that if the Awami League and its allies came to power:

> the government would allow certified ulama [Islamic scholars] the right to issues fatwas [an Islamic legal ruling], impose a ban on enacting any law that goes against Quranic values, initiate steps for proper implementation of the initiative for government recognition of the degrees awarded by Qawmi madrasahs [unregulated seminaries], and ban criticism of the Prophet Muhammad, or in other words introduce a blasphemy law.[28]

Thus, Bangladesh's two largest parties, while having a stranglehold over the infrastructure of power, tend to rely on and therefore try to seduce and appease Islamists. As we have seen with Shahbag and Hefazat, the charge of being 'against Islam' is a powerful one. Indeed, Shahbag's precursor, a movement named the Ghatak-Dalal Nirmul Committee led by the now deceased Jahanara Imam, was mobilised to call for the trials of the alleged war criminals of 1971 after Jamaat leader Ghulam Azam was elected emir of the party in 1991. These secular protesters led by Imam were again labelled atheists or accused of apostasy—a crime that under many interpretations of Islamic law carries a punishment of death.

Religious Mobilisation in Times Gone by

Mobilisation of this sort is by no means new. As historian Richard M. Eaton notes, the mosque's special significance as a unit of social organisation and mobilisation in rural Bengal dates back to a time:

> when a religious gentry of '*ulamā* and *pīrs*—and in the institutionalised form, mosques and shrines—first emerged as nodes of authority around which new peasant communities originally coalesced …. Such people were attracted to the religious gentry not only as devotees of a religious leader but as groups of client peasants who had formerly been fishermen and shifting cultivators beyond the pale of Hindu society.[29]

Eaton describes how the eastern delta came to be populated by a large Muslim agrarian population, which came as a great surprise to the British colonialists in the nineteenth century when they conducted their first census. It was the carving out of the densely forested countryside that saw charismatic religious leaders being given land and encouraged to cultivate it by political leaders under both the Bengal Sultanate and the later Mughal dynasty. These efforts created settled communities in many of the regions that are now Bangladesh.

The political authorities that distributed land grants overwhelmingly favoured Muslims over members of other religions, leading to a giant agrarian Muslim population. The early pioneers were often Sufis and their heterodox interpretations of Islamic scripture enabled followers to mix Hinduism and animism with the new faith. Hinduism 'progressively diminished as one moved from west to east across the delta, rendering the preliterate masses of the east without an authority structure sufficient to withstand that of Islam.'[30] In essence, unlike other dominions of the Mughals or their Muslim precursors, the eastern delta had not been fully accepted into the sway of previous Hindu kingdoms and empires. This was in large part down to the hostile geography of the region, with its vast rivers and dense jungle. As such, these regions were like a clean slate on which pliant communities could be created for the benefit of the royal tax collector. The new settlements usually had at their centre the institution of faith of whoever had been granted the land. Without nucleated villages, 'homesteads are strung out along the banks of past or existing creeks. Or more often they are stippled throughout the rural countryside, dispersed in amorphous clusters.'[31] This pattern of organisation was again partly a response to the geography of the region, which necessitated building on higher ground to avoid flooding. It contributed to the organisation of society around religious institutions, as other local centres of authority did not exist.

However, 'Islam creatively evolved into an ideology of "world construction"—an ideology of forest-clearing and agrarian expansion, serving not only to legitimize but to structure the very socioeconomic changes taking place on the frontier.'[32] This fluid interpretation of Islam, which held on to its core egalitarian principles while adapting itself to suit local imperatives, gained Sufism a strong following. Indeed, these localised practices are still evolving and being created to this day.

As the country's many rivers shift, they create new land, often referred to as *chars*. Just across the river to the southwest of Dhaka is one such neighbourhood, Ati Bazar. Here, throngs of people come to the site of a shrine to listen to songs and musically venerate the late Sufi musician and poet Matal Razzak. His name means 'drunken poet', and he was famed for his irreverent sayings and poetry. To this day people gather to hear performances of his music late into the night at regular celebrations. From descriptions, Matal Razzak and the role he occupied seem akin to the charismatic holy men of old; he was almost shamanistic. The gatherings at his shrine are very far from the orthodoxy and stereotypical vision of piety that Islam usually projects.

It is hard to estimate how widespread adherence to such practices is. This may well be because such systems of religious ritual do not have binary notions of membership. Ever since Islam arrived in this part of the world, religious practices have often been fluid and combined elements of multiple belief systems. Practitioners today may, for instance, attend musical performances at the shrine of someone like Matal Razzak as well as attending a conventional mosque, for a variety of social or spiritual reasons. As noted earlier, however, conventional or orthodox mosques and madrassas are very much in the ascendant in Bangladesh, as the era of mass communication further pushes traditional, localised religious practices to the side and advances more austere interpretations, popular in places like the wealthy Gulf states and Saudi Arabia. Sometimes madrassas are effective merely through force of persuasion, or by offering the children of the poor free or very cheap education. Donors either in Bangladesh or abroad, in the UK or the Middle East, for example, often sponsor these institutions. However, at other times, recruitment of people to more orthodox belief systems is achieved through violence.

The Silent War on Sufism

Khizir Khan was a former chairman of the Bangladesh Power Development Board. In the nondescript building in north Dhaka in which he lived with his family, he ran a *khankar sharif*, a Sufi prayer hall or shrine. His son, Ashraful Islam, explained to me that Khan had inherited this position as a *pir*, a spiritual guide or master, from his father. It was an oasis of quiet on the morning that Ashraful showed me around. The walls of the main prayer room had a pulpit on one side and were lined with bookshelves on another. The upstairs study in the flat was similarly adorned with tomes on Islam and other faiths.

On 5 October 2015, Khan had some visitors. A group of young men 'came and rang the doorbell,' explained his son, and Khan 'told them to go downstairs' to the *khankar sharif*. The visitors had phoned ahead and enquired about renting out a room in the basement of the property. The *khankar sharif* had two small adjoining rooms. One was a sort of guest room where Khan sat and talked to the young men, the other a washroom where worshippers perform ritual ablution before prayer. It was here that Khan's wife discovered her husband, his throat slit. When the men had conned Khan into taking them downstairs, another gang broke into the flat a few flights of stairs above and tied his family up. Ashraful, who is a medical student, was at a loss to explain the motives of his father's killers: 'We are doing exactly as our Prophet said to us. We are not against our *sharia*.' Though Khan lived in the capital, his demise fits into an eerie pattern playing out in rural areas, and in particular in Bangladesh's northwest. Here, in many ways, the ancient, intractable rivals of Bangladeshi Islam are engaged in a quiet civil war.

Much like HUJI-B, a shadowy group formed by returning Mujahideen from the Afghan-Soviet conflict has been at the forefront of this bloodthirsty conflict over the last three decades. When I asked Ashraful about his father's killers, he explained that while the police's enquiry was still 'ongoing', it was evident from those who had been detained that they were followers of Jamaat-ul-Mujahideen Bangladesh (JMB). 'They explained to the police that they had a duty to kill all the *pirs*,' he said. Indeed, JMB has been a fixture in Bangladesh since the late 1990s, terrorising anyone who does not profess orthodox Sunni beliefs.

Jamaat-ul-Mujahideen Bangladesh

JMB was allegedly formed by Shaikh Abdur Rahman, a man whose life, travels and work speak volumes about this civil war over Islam in Bangladesh and some of its contradictions. Born in Jamalpur in the north of the country in 1959, Abdur Rahman grew up in the world of hard-line Qawmi madrassas, and in particular in the Ahle Hadith movement, in which his father was a prominent teacher. In 1980, Abdur Rahman was awarded a scholarship to the holy city of Medina in Saudi Arabia, the second most important city after Mecca in Islamic history, being the safe haven that the Prophet Muhammad fled to in order to escape persecution. By most accounts, Abdur Rahman's time in the city would prove pivotal to his career trajectory. There he became acquainted with the Muslim Brotherhood and joined its South Asian analogue, Jamaat-e-Islami, through the local chapter of the Jamaat student wing, Islami Chhatra Shibir. During his time studying in Medina he also allegedly had a spell fighting the Soviets in Afghanistan, although these claims are not properly verified.

In the mid-1980s Abdur Rahman returned to Dhaka, where he took up work at the Saudi embassy. It was during this period that he is said to have grown frustrated with Jamaat's attempts to achieve a caliphate or Islamic state through the democratic system, and so he decided to seek more aggressive actors with more direct routes towards this goal. He joined HUJI-B in 1995. However, Abdur Rahman soon began to fall out with the HUJI-B leadership and started to fish around for help in starting up his own organisation. His brother Waliur Rahman was still in Medina and had contacts with the Pakistani terrorist group Lashkar-e-Taiba (LeT).[33] Waliur Rahman put his brother in touch with Dhaka-based LeT operative and bomb specialist Abdul Karim Tunda. Through Tunda, Abdur Rahman was able to establish links with Al-Qaeda and Pakistani militant groups, and eventually travelled to Pakistan in 1998. 'There he met several LeT leaders, including its leader, Hafeez Saeed, and received training in arms, explosives, strategy and intelligence in Muzaffarabad along with guidance on how to build a jihadi organisation.'[34]

Lashkar-e-Taiba and Hanbali versus Hanafi

Like the Ahle Hadith movement Abdur Rahman had grown up with, Lashkar-e-Taiba differs from other major Islamist groups in Pakistan and Afghanistan in that it adheres to the Hanbali school of Islamic jurisprudence. The Hanbali school is considered to be the most absolutist of the four orthodox Sunni branches of jurisprudence, and crucially does not accept deferral to local custom when an answer to a dilemma cannot be found in scripture. This school of thought emanated from Saudi Arabia and is predominant—and the basis of law—in the oil-rich, influential state of Qatar (which at the time of writing is the country with the highest GDP per capita in the world). By contrast, HUJI-B and many other hard-line Islamist movements in South Asia, as well as most Hefazat madrassas, follow the Deobandi movement, which is indigenous to South Asia having originated in modern-day India. Deobandis generally adhere to the Hanafi school of Islamic jurisprudence.

The great empires that flowed from Central Asia and the Anatolian peninsula spread the Hanafi branch of jurisprudence across South Asia.

While parts of modern-day Pakistan had been conquered by one of the earliest Islamic caliphates in the seventh century AD, the indigenisation of Islam and the creation of a genuinely north Indian Islamic tradition was brought about by later Turkic empires and peoples, most famously the Mughals. Unlike the Hanbalis, Hanafis will, as a last resort, fall back on local custom to determine legal or moral conundrums.

The dichotomy between respective strains of jurisprudence points in part to earlier sources of validation and legitimacy that defined early Islamic rule in the region. In a sense this history provides a template for political positions taken to this day. Muslim rule in Bengal was often based in Delhi, under what was known as the Delhi Sultanate and later the better-known Mughals. While Islamic rule in Bengal started with the invasion of Muhammad Bakhtiyar Khilji in 1204, an independent sultanate took root by 1352, with the rise of Shamsuddin Ilyas Shah. As Eaton writes, 'The political and cultural referents of these kings lay, not in Delhi or Central Asia, but much further to the west—in Mecca, Medina, Shiraz and ancient Ctesiphon.'[35] In a sense, here we can see the birth of an independent Bengali Muslim state and identity, due in no small part to its definition of itself as different from the major Muslim power base to the west: Delhi. Referents in the Middle East were thus a vital tool for asserting a different identity and legitimacy—a distinctively Muslim one.

This still informs nationalism on the political right in Bangladesh to this day. While Hanbali Islam is seen as more absolutist in a jurisprudential sense, groups adhering to the Hanbali school as part of the Ahle Hadith tradition in Pakistan, such as Lashkar-e-Taiba, came to be seen as more politically convenient and less sectarian. In a sense, they were seen as being less interested in addressing domestic 'deviant' interpretations, and more concerned with a unifying Muslim identity.

The Rise of JMB

By 2002 Abdur Rahman had cemented his organisation and had quickly developed a following. JMB looked to institutions that already existed and that Abdur Rahman knew well: the Ahle Hadith madrassa and mosque network, and the Jamaat student wing, Shibir. The organisation turned to sympathetic teachers and imams who might be able to bring in and nurture young recruits.

These networks soon took hold in Bangladesh's northwest, and in particular in Rajshahi division. While Rajshahi is famed for its mangos, the entire northwest of Bangladesh is a quadrant that was isolated by rivers from the rest of the country and long haunted by abject poverty. To the south, the Padma (as the Ganges is known at this juncture) streams in from the west. Cutting off the region to the east is the Brahmaputra, which flows in from Assam and the Himalayas, creating thousands of shifting, silt islands, as it heads to the Bay of Bengal. These topographic challenges remain. It was not until 1998 that the Jamuna Bridge was opened, spanning the Brahmaputra, creating road access to the northwest from the rest of the country. For decades the region had only ferries to Dhaka, and informal, often-illicit access over the border to neighbouring India. As a consequence, the region has a distinct and more impoverished economy than the rest of Bangladesh. While chronic hunger, generally speaking, is today a thing of the past in Bangladesh, this part of the country continued to suffer seasonal famines prior to the opening of the bridge.

Much like in neighbouring West Bengal, since the 1970s poverty was at least partly responsible for leftist insurrections. In India, the most famous of these is known as the Naxalite movement. The village of Naxalbari, which gives its name to the movement, is situated in West Bengal not far from the Bangladeshi border. India continues to be troubled by the Maoist-inspired Naxalite insurrection, with a third of Indian states falling sway to this movement in some form or another. In then East Pakistan, the same forces and discontents over servitude and hunger were felt by poor villagers and peasant farmers, and leftist groups like the Purba Banglar Sarbahara Party emerged in the late 1960s. While they would join in the struggle against Pakistani rule in 1971, they would also wrack the new state with instability, as the proliferation of arms bedevilled the countryside, particularly in border regions. These leftist insurrections persisted into the new millennium.

It was in these perennially informal backwaters that JMB put down roots, through the networks and family connections that had endured throughout Abdur Rahman's life. The ideals of an Arabian Hanbali dream were disseminated via village mosques and imams, as the JMB sought to carve out a small slice of a caliphate in Bangladesh. The organisation did not begin particularly covertly or at a great distance from the authorities that its members hoped one day to overthrow.

In 2001 the BNP came to power with the help of its coalition ally, Jamaat. For the first time in Bangladesh, members of an Islamist party with the intention of dismantling the secular state took high office. And yet they had done so with a woman at the helm as prime minister. In a classic dynastic move, Begum Khaleda Zia, the widow of General Ziaur Rahman, had taken over the mantle of party leader in the 1990s. She followed in the footsteps of her nemesis Sheikh Hasina, Indira Gandhi in India, and Benazir Bhutto in Pakistan. Dynastic rulers are popular and effective in South Asia, and ones with liberation pedigree gain extra points.

However, this points ranking didn't tally up for the Islamists, for whom the issue of a woman leading the political alliance was a sticking point. But for the opportunistic, including former Jamaat member Abdur Rahman, the presence of Jamaat in government was correctly judged to be a huge opportunity. Unease with the female leadership had indeed been a push factor for members of Jamaat and its student wing to join JMB in the first place. At its peak, the organisation's top leadership board or Majlish-e-Shura was comprised solely of former Jamaat members. This included one Siddiqul Islam, whom the American embassy would later call a 'politically-connected mystery man'.[36] Islam would become better known by the moniker Bangla Bhai, translated literally as 'Bengali brother'. In 2004, echoing a common frustration with hypocrisy, Bangla Bhai told the press that 'as a college student, I joined Islami Chhatra Shibir. When I finished my study in 1995, I quit Shibir because Jamaat accepted female leadership although it said it considered female leadership sacrilege.'[37] Bangla Bhai would go on to become a notorious vigilante-cum-terrorist within the JMB fold, whose persona was transferred into adaptations of the popular video game Grand Theft Auto in cheap arcades in Dhaka until at least 2014.[38]

When the BNP–Jamaat government came to power in 2001 the alliance dominated the northwestern region, which included Rajshahi and Natore. These areas had members of parliament who were influential both at the national level within the BNP government and at the local level. The Rajshahi-1 constituency was the seat of the government's telecommunications minister, Barrister Aminul Haque, while Natore-2 was the constituency of Ruhul Quddus Talukdar Dulu, the deputy land minister. These positions gave ministers huge rent-seeking capacity. For Haque, the advent of mobile phones and the necessity of awarding contracts to install the infrastructure for the then budding technology presented a unique opportunity. In February 2004 this induced the nephew of MP Dulu, Sabbir Ahmed Gamma, to come up against one of the aforementioned leftist organisations, the Purba Bangladesh Communist Party, who shot the MP's nephew and an aide named Wahidul Haq Pakhi. They also murdered a number of other officials.[39] Gamma was an alleged local criminal with eighteen cases pending against him.[40] The MPs decided they needed to respond and so decided the way to hit back at the leftists was through counter-insurgents: right-wing Islamists. JMB fit perfectly. JMB formed a group called Jagrata Muslim Janata Bangladesh (JMJB) with Bangla Bhai as its leader. Indicative of how closely linked the group was to local MP Dulu were the names of two brigades JMJB formed: the Gamma Bahini and the Pakhi Bahini, named after the MP's deceased nephew and his right-hand man. The increasing patronage that the group was able to engender from this operation gave them licence to start performing their role as enforcers of their miniature caliphate, a triangle of land between Rajshahi to the southwest, Natore to the southeast and Naogaon to the north.

The Mini Caliphate

And so began a reign of terror in the region. Murders were often public affairs, with public hangings and public displays of victims hung from trees. JMB conducted many of its operations with police help:

> Noor Mohammad, Divisional Inspector General of Police in Rajshahi, told newsmen that Bangla Bhai and his operatives were assisting the law enforcers in tracking down left-wing outlaws. According to him, 'we've asked police stations to support them whenever they go to catch outlaws.' Reportedly, he justified such an action by indicating that 'You know Sarbahara [left-wing extremists] men have been quite active in the region for many years and it is not possible for the undermanned and under-equipped police to hunt them down.'[41]

The direct relationships between senior police in the area and Bangla Bhai continued until February 2006, when Rajshahi Superintendent of Police Masud Miah was forced from his job because of these connections. It is estimated that between 2001 and 2005 around 500 JMB arrestees were released in this manner. Among them was Bangla Bhai, who was caught by locals after attacking and attempting to murder a local Awami League leader and his children in August 2002. He was released a few months later.[42]

While the group had engaged in deadly bombings previously, largely of judges for attempting to levy secular laws, they were now emboldened to take on a variety of targets both at a local level in their mini-caliphate and more widely. These extended from secular writers like Humayun Azad to atheist ones like Taslima Nasreen, from judges and leftists to Nobel Laureate Muhammad Yunus, founder of the microfinance institution Grameen Bank. In 2006 the American embassy was concerned that the group would target an English-language training programme run by Peace Corps volunteers in the satellite town of Gazipur, northwest of the capital. A detained JMB operative claimed to have spent days staking out the volunteers, watching them as they played volleyball and walked around in T-shirts, revealing their shoulders.[43]

Stemming Secularism

One of JMB's principal projects was preventing all secular progress, or anything that offered an attractive alternative to the organisation's own medieval vision of how the world should be. The practices, provisions and ideals of NGOs that proliferate in rural Bangladesh were a particular target. NGOs like Yunus' Grameen Bank are both extremely successful and well known, but in many ways are so for one of the reasons that madrassas are: the gaping hole where the state should be but isn't, in so much of Bangladeshi life. Bangladesh has one of the smallest tax-to-GDP ratios on the planet, at around 10 per cent at the time of writing. As a result, organisations like Grameen and international development behemoth BRAC, supposedly the largest NGO in the world, run a variety of essential services in rural areas.

These include schools, which are often in direct competition with the madrassas. While NGO schools adhere to government standards and therefore use their curricula, they do so while having as a particular focus the need for a relatively gender-positive ethos. A core belief of many in the development sector in Bangladesh is that the increasing inclusion of women in the economy and their subsequent relative empowerment was one reason for the country's laudable development achievements. As such, the World Bank funded free primary school education for all girls in Bangladesh. These issues vex Islamists who see gender-positive judicial or legal moves as a threat. These range from implementation of equal inheritance laws to laws preventing rampant child marriage (of which Bangladesh has one of the highest rates in the world).[44]

While groups like JMB would attack and rob NGOs, Hefazat took to the streets soon after the Awami League came to power in 2010 to block their pledged progressive laws. Conservative voices often prevail on these issues; at the time of writing in 2018 it is legal to marry a minor in Bangladesh if the union has parental and court consent. In 2017, Sheikh Hasina met the head of Hefazat, Shah Ahmad Shafi, at a public gathering. Despite Hefazat's calls for men and women not to mingle in public, the two appeared to get along well on a very public stage. Hasina doled out concessions to the elderly preacher who had once compared women to tamarind. She stated that she too disliked a statue of Themis, the Greek goddess of justice, that had been erected outside a Dhaka court, which the Islamists had waged a campaign against. She further promised that Qawmi madrassas would maintain their unregulated status, but despite this their degrees would be recognised as equal to postgraduate degrees in the formal higher education sector. It was the equivalent of allowing a Sunday school preacher to offer certificates to students with no oversight and have those certificates recognised as equivalent to a university master's degree.

The denials of an 'alliance' from Awami League General Secretary Obaidul Qader suggest that Hasina at least had an eye on the elections scheduled for winter 2018.[45] Indeed, at the gathering Shafi was heralded as the 'spiritual head of the state'.[46] In acquiescing to Hefazat, she could at least hope to deny her opponents the support of a tested religious-political machine, if not create an ally of the sort she had hankered for in 2006 when she had formed an alliance with the far smaller Bangladesh Khelafat Majlish party.

JMB's Explosive Moment of Truth

By 2005 JMB and its offshoot JMJB were firmly ensconced in their Rajshahi fiefdom. The group was enjoying an astonishing level of impunity; police would occasionally pick them up, but soon let them go, often mysteriously losing or destroying evidence. This had enabled the group to spread its web across the country. As so often happens with such groups, aspirations swelled as well.

On the morning of 17 August 2005, at around 10.30 a.m., the network issued a show of force. Within an hour around 500 small bombs were exploded in sixty-three of Bangladesh's sixty-four districts. In Dhaka they were set off at sites of symbolic importance, such as the airport, the secretariat building and courthouses. The bombings injured around 100 people but killed only two, including a 10-year-old boy in Savar, just outside Dhaka. The attacks were arranged to coincide with the distribution of 30,000 leaflets. These were distributed by email and activists were told to print them locally.

The leaflets and the ineffectiveness of the bombs were probably important indicators as to the intent of the operation: to shift from having friendly government ministers and connivance, to a political situation where people lost faith in the government and supported a shift to Islamic rule. 'We urge the government of Bangladesh,' read JMB's pamphlet, 'introduce the rule of Allah in this country, and we will co-operate with you. We do not want power; we want Allah's law instead of the rule of the false god.'* It is telling that this episode, which had involved unprecedented co-ordination, had studiously avoided targeting politically powerful individuals. As is usually the case, the victims were the poor, or the poorly connected. The operation's main aims were, as ever, to create chaos so that the legitimacy of the government would be called into question, and to demonstrate a great flexing of muscles and inspire an outpouring of equivalent emotion. 'We carried out the bomb attacks to create a sense of disgust among people at the government, with the ultimate aim to unseat it' claimed Ataur Rahman Sunny, Abdur Rahman's youngest brother, in court in 2006. 'Our aim was to topple the

---

* JMB leaflet, quoted in Riaz, *Islamist Militancy in Bangladesh*, p. 131.

government through a mass upsurge, then capture the power and establish a rule of Islam.'[47]

In keeping with the times, the pamphlet focused attention on the government of George W. Bush and his 'war on terror'. 'Today the greatest terrorist of the world is George W. Bush. He launches attacks on innocent Muslims by resorting to terrorism and tries to make the Muslims non-believers by forcibly imposing a Kufri [non-believing/evil] constitution. He wants to bring the whole world under his control through a new world order.'* This theme is important for a number of reasons. When attempting to impose an austere Islam on the country, it helps inordinately to have conflicts that fit with scripture and the sense of being under attack, thereby requiring enforcement of strict interpretations of Islam in which the purveyors of piety become central. In the highly connected world that we live in, moreover, which was then just emerging in Bangladesh, the use of foreign conflicts or issues is regularly used to mobilise believers.

Palestine, for instance, is regularly referenced—all while Bangladesh has usurped land owned by non-Muslims in its Chittagong Hill Tracts. The similarities between Palestine and the Hill Tracts are unerring, but for most Bangladeshis the theft of land far away in the Middle East is far more egregious than in their own nation. Such conflation of narratives and conflicts is also helpful to maintain vigilance and mobilise people to a cause on the basis that they are under attack, and that they are one with their fellow Muslims. Through the internet, stories of Muslims being persecuted in the West, where a tiny proportion of the world's Muslims reside, fulfil a narrative that Muslims in general are under attack in a global conspiracy, threatened, as JMB and their alt-right Western counterparts would have it, by a 'new world order'. In this, the ideas of jihadists fuse with the average malcontent whose own insecurities meld with stories of genuine global injustices to generate the anger that fuels their actions.

Many in Bangladesh hold a view that secularism fosters corruption because in the messy years since independence, the country has called itself secular. Corruption is widely perceived to be what holds Bangladesh and other Muslim countries back. Thus the supposed

* Cited in Riaz, *Islamist Militancy in Bangladesh*, p. 133.

imposition of secularism, as opposed to theocratic rule, is held to be an intentional plot by other powers who would dominate the world at the cost of a broad, imagined Muslim community—or caliphate. It is the kind of proposition that is powerful in Bangladesh, as it is, say, in West Virginia, where similar arguments are made by Donald Trump, with secularism simply replaced by environmentalism or liberalism, which Trump supporters view as either a Chinese or a liberal conspiracy. In both spheres, the same angry young men are found moaning online.

Grudging Official Rebuke

The paradigm changed for JMB and Bangladesh after the bombings of 17 August 2005. While Abdur Rahman, Siddiqul Islam and co. still carried on trying to blow things up to achieve their Hanbali dream-state, the warm cradle that had enabled and emboldened their mission was rattled. The Bangladesh government and in particular Home Minister Lutfozzaman Babar had long denied the existence of Bangla Bhai and his clique, JMJB. Jamaat head Motiur Rahman Nizami had spuriously claimed it was a fiction created by the left-wing media.[48] Others, even more ridiculously, 'postulated that India and the [then] opposition Awami League were behind the JMB.'[49] As the US embassy noted with frustration:

> the [Bangladesh government] has failed to demonstrate it has the political will to recognize and combat Islamist extremism … it needs to hold coalition [government] figures accountable for their links to extremists. Virtually no one outside the [Bangladesh government] doubts that a BNP state minister, a BNP deputy minister, and a BNP MP set up and protected Bangla Bhai and Abdur Rahman as Islamic vigilantes to fight their local enemies. The lack of any censure, investigation, or even acknowledgment of these allegations projects an aura of impunity.[50]

Indeed, when the arrests did occur, that impunity presented itself in a very real sense. On 27 November 2005 the Rapid Action Battalion (RAB)—the country's principal counter-terrorism unit, notorious to this day for 'encounter killings', or extra-judicial murders—arrested Mahtab Khamaru. Khamaru was suspected of being Bangla Bhai's right-hand man, a kind of field lieutenant, albeit not important enough to be in JMB's governing Majlish-e-Shura. However, as soon as Khamaru was arrested, 'an agitated Home Minister of State Babar had complained that he had been forced to release him quickly after the intervention of Tarique Rahman, PM Zia's son and heir apparent, acting at the behest of State Minister for Land Dulu.'[51]

While Khamaru was alleged to have been involved in cases of murder, abduction, torture and extortion, he had a knack for getting out of detention. In spring 2016, he was even among a number of JMB cadres who ran for office in Union Parishad (local council) elections. Khamaru ran for the Jatiya Party, chaired by the former military dictator Ershad and nominally allied to the ruling Awami League, while other former JMB cadre ran for the League. Most prominent was Mohammad Abdus Salam, who was arrested in 2007 for his involvement with the JMB, but was soon released. In 2008, sensing which way the wind was blowing, Abdus Salam joined the Awami League, just in time for their thumping electoral triumph at the end of that year.[52] In September 2016 Khamaru was arrested for the fourth time.

In March 2006, Abdur Rahman and Bangla Bhai were finally arrested for the last time. Bangla Bhai's final battle saw him secure a sort of Pablo Escobar reputation. He was tracked to the northern town of Mymensingh, and in the dead of night the RAB closed in on a tin-roofed house where he was hiding out. After a long standoff, Siddiqul Islam emerged from the building in the morning and handed himself in. While Bangla Bhai and Abdur Rahman would be executed soon afterwards, they not only left behind the skeleton of their organisation, but had also firmly cemented a model for jihadist mobilisation.

4

THE URBAN JIHAD

Dhaka is reputedly the fastest growing city on the planet. Its physical urban landscape is changing at a mind-bending rate. The city grows faster as its infuriating traffic grows slower. Bangladesh's small state has been ineffectual, to say the least, at keeping up with the staggering explosion in urban growth. This has meant that the city has become the most densely populated in the world, with the smallest surface area proportionally given over to roads, or byways of any kind. Getting out of the city to another city is no mean feat, making the notion of commuting into Dhaka, or siting industry or business in other cities, impractical. Many of these factors give Dhaka a feeling that it is, in a sense, an apex of human activity: nowhere else have people strived, aspired and fought side by side for a future in such close proximity and with such mind-boggling connectivity amidst such deep poverty. With a population of about 14.5 million (and growing, fast) living on approximately 300 square kilometres of land, the city's density is around 44,500 people per square kilometre.[1] In other words, the city is roughly four times as dense as New York City, which has a population of about 8.5 million living across some 820 square kilometres. While this represents a host of planning nightmares for Dhaka, it has also led to a hugely swelling middle class: huddled aspirations, against many odds, being chased down. And as these odds are chased, so too are seams frayed and the human condition tested.

It is against this backdrop that urban middle-class youth are testing their frustrations and identities. In early 2016, Professor Ali Riaz noticed something many thought strange or surprising: in a study of those arrested for militancy in selected periods in 2014 and 2015, he found that while madrassa students made up a large cohort, 61 per cent 'have come from at least either middle-class or upper middle-class backgrounds.'[2] Although the Jamaat-ul-Mujahideen Bangladesh (JMB) had made moves to recruit from these demographics around a decade earlier, social forces and technological realities would prove to be far more powerful than their recruitment efforts seemingly were. While the JMB in rural Rajshahi had fed on isolated communities, which the authorities could not reach, a situation that engendered chronic insecurity, more connected urban youths would come to view the state and its failures in their world in a different way. Where the state was conspicuous by its absence in Bagmara, Rajshahi, in Badda, Dhaka it was conspicuous because of its apparent ineptitude and corruption.

The advent in 2009 of the Awami League government shed much light on and brought to justice a number of key militants who had previously existed with a degree of impunity. Some of these individuals were members of the Pakistani terrorist outfit Lashkar-e-Taiba (LeT).[3] The group is most famous for having conducted the Mumbai terrorist attacks of 2008, in which a handful of heavily armed militants stormed the luxury Taj Hotel, among other civilian 'targets'. The Awami League came in with a strong mandate from the people, and seemingly strong backing from India, issues which will be looked at more thoroughly in the next chapter. For Indian policymakers, Bangladesh's status as a safe haven for terrorists and a conduit for arms under the government of the Bangladesh Nationalist Party (BNP) and Jamaat-e-Islami had been extremely troubling. However, almost from the word go, the new administration faced challenges from Islamists. It is crucial to remember that their first, very legitimate parliament was wracked by at least two major attempts to unseat the government—both of which were murky episodes with probable Islamist connections. Yet it was during their second reign, with a more questionable mandate, that Islamist militancy took its most radical turn.

The murder of Ahmed Rajib Haider had occurred at the peak of the Shahbag protests, which called for the death penalty for convicted war criminals from 1971. After his murder, as counter-terror police chief Monirul Islam told me in an interview, pro-BNP/Jamaat newspapers slated all bloggers as atheists, which eventually brought the protests to a halt through the power of negative association. Thus, liberal expression was quashed as the country's realpolitik heavyweights did battle over the 2014 election period. The government manoeuvred to appease Islamist street counter-protests by jailing openly or supposedly atheist bloggers. It then violently removed Islamist Hefazat-e-Islam protesters from the streets of Dhaka in May 2013, but went on to bribe and appease the Hefazat leadership to prevent further agitation or Hefazat's alignment with the opposition parties. In all, the 2014 election was described as the most violent on record. The BNP 'again appealed to the Jamaat' to support its street agitation, leading to violence throughout the capital and elsewhere.[4] The government responded in kind, with a large number of 'encounter killings' or extrajudicial killings of people in custody, the killing of protesters, mass arrests and disappearances.

The Origins of the BNP–Jamaat Alliance

One reason often cited for the BNP's alliance with Jamaat is the inordinate strength of the latter's student wing, the Islami Chhatra Shibir. Shibir's cadres generally have more zeal than their BNP comrades, whose party, as previously noted, is not a political entity based on a singular ideological position, but is rather a patchwork coalition. The incorporation of factions from both the extreme right and the extreme left into one party was superimposed on the country to meet specific needs of its leaders, rather than as a bottom-up movement. When Ziaur Rahman came to power in 1975 in a military coup, he had to create a civilian party with a support base and even philosophy to justify his power out of the mess that was post-war Bangladesh. According to academic and NGO director Meghna Guhathakurta, these included 'policies of rural development [which] played into the system of developing this grassroots support from the top.' This meant that a lot of the BNP's 'clientele' or patronage relationships were created from the top down.

Simultaneously, to penetrate the grassroots both dictators, Ershad and Zia, by necessity pursued rural development policies that included both Western-funded NGOs and 'the religious parties, who had the structure at the grassroots'. Jamaat was allowed back into both grassroots development work and politics when Ziaur Rahman lifted a ban on religious politics towards the end of the 1970s, following the post-war period in which they were excluded and exiled, owing to their role in the genocide in 1971. Jamaat's activities in grassroots organising were helped by the fact that during the 1980s, many Bangladeshis were undereducated but pious, while madrassas were experiencing a new lease of life.

The BNP came into power as a civilian regime in 1991 after the fall of the Ershad military dictatorship. After a pro-democratic movement that briefly united various political groupings against military rule, three sets of alliances emerged: the Awami League and its fourteen-party alliance; the BNP with eleven parties; and Jamaat. In the words of Guhathakurta, Jamaat 'was very much legitimised in that whole process of democratisation, and it was only much later after the second election that they joined the BNP as a coalition.'

Modern Muscle

Thus on many occasions since their 1999 alliance, the BNP has by default had to fall back on Jamaat's student wing, Shibir, which has seemingly served almost as a finishing school for jihadists, such as the aforementioned JMB founder Abdur Rahman. In much the same way that Ziaur Rahman had in the early days provided patronage to grassroots actors, his wife Khaleda offered Jamaat patronage from the top in exchange for bodies on the ground or at the grassroots. The other option, which came to the fore during the efforts by the BNP in their campaign to unseat the Awami League in 2013–14, was the use of paid-for muscle, sometimes allegedly even in the form of street kids, who proved adept at hurling improvised incendiary devices at vehicles in exchange for a bag of glue for sniffing, or a tiny payment.[5]

By early 2014 some 500 people had been killed in election-related violence, a large cohort of whom had been burnt to death in horrific arson attacks on the public transport network of the country. Molotov cocktails would be hurled through the open windows of buses, with commuters trapped inside left to burn alive or suffer horrific burns.

Civilians would pay the price for the country's political failures in the form of scalded flesh and unimaginable pain. I met some of the more 'lucky' victims at the overwhelmed Dhaka Medical College Hospital burns unit that winter. One was a street-side vegetable vendor who could no longer see or hear with third-degree burns and blistered skin over much of his head and upper torso. The other large contingent of victims were opposition activists killed by the police and security forces in 'encounter killings' or confrontations on the street. Often, the thuggish Chhatra League, the student wing of the ruling Awami League, would assist the police in such confrontations. Buoyed by its party's ascendency, the Chhatra League has often come to be above the law.

These confrontations tend to wane with the coming of both hot weather in the spring months and rain in the summer ones—the seasons tend to push organised political violence to the dryer and cooler autumn–winter months. And so the following winter, in 2014–15, the political opposition jumped again to hold 'shut downs' and destabilising strikes on the anniversary of the elections, which they had boycotted the previous year. Yet more blockades and arson attacks proved gruesome and ineffective. Many of the orders, it appeared, came from Khaleda Zia's son, Tarique Rahman, in exile in London. It seemed that he wanted no compromise with the government, while senior members of the party on the ground tried to enact his desired stranglehold on the country. They were frequently thrown in jail by the government as a result.[6]

As the people suffered for the political conflicts of their leaders, February brought the annual month-long Ekushey book fair, which celebrates the Bangla language. One hot ticket from the previous year was at the festival. This was despite having written shortly before about finding himself:

> a target of militant Islamists and terrorists. A well-known extremist by the name of Farabi Shafiur Rahman openly issued death threats to me through his numerous Facebook statuses. In one widely circulated status, Rahman wrote, 'Avijit Roy lives in America and so, it is not possible to kill him right now. But he will be murdered when he comes back.'[7]

Avijit Roy

Writer, blogger and scientist Avijit Roy would not live to see the above words published. In his article, published in the secular humanist journal *Free Inquiry*, he went on, 'The phrase "religion of peace" gives me a belly laugh nowadays, and the association of Islam's followers with terrorism never surprises me.' He elaborated on the character of Farabi Shafiur Rahman, who had made death threats against him, saying, 'It has been revealed that Rahman is linked to the radical Islamist party, *Jamaat-e-Islami*, and a terrorist organization, *Hizbut Tahrir*. Last year, Rahman threatened to kill a Muslim cleric who officiated at the funeral of Ahmed Rajib Haider.' He rued that while Rahman had been arrested, he was granted bail only a few months afterwards, and since then had 'continued to threaten many progressives in Bangladesh'.[8]

Rahman was, as Roy noted, already well known to police for threatening an imam, and known to the public online for statements such as, 'To me atheists are nothing but insects, and it is best that insects should die.'[9] As well as disliking insects, Rahman had threatened an online bookseller who was selling Roy's work. The authorities had reacted with typical indifference to such threats.

Roy and his wife, Rafida Bonya Ahmed, arrived in Dhaka on 16 February 2015 from America, where Roy was a naturalised citizen. Roy was an IT worker by day, but was also a voracious reader and writer on science, rationalism and criticism of Islamic fundamentalism. His father Ajay Roy, a science professor at Dhaka University, had warned him against returning to the country because of the threats against him.

Avijit and Rafida took their time at the festival when they attended on 26 February. They had been invited to a gathering of scientists at the home of Dr Farseem Mannan, a professor at the university where Avijit had studied, the Bangladesh University of Engineering and Technology, known by the acronym BUET. The gathering of scientists was supposed to start at 5 p.m. As the evening wore on, Mannan kept delaying the start of the event as he awaited the arrival of his guests. Finally, at around 8.40 p.m, Avijit and Rafida left the grounds of the book fair, which was taking place on the same field that forty-four years earlier Sheikh Mujibur Rahman, the independence leader, had made his famous 7 March address, which had served as a starting gun for the campaign for independence. The park sits just over the road from Dhaka University and its Teacher Student Centre—a hub of student life, where students and idlers fill the streets for most of the day and night. Avijit and Rafida walked along a congested pavement, the streets even more crowded than usual with the book fair going on. They walked towards a waiting vehicle, which was to take them to the gathering at Dr Mannan's house. Police were out in force. At 8.44 p.m., grainy CCTV footage shows them walking past stalls on the street. Avijit turns round, and in the corner of the shot a man is seen following, periodically looking down at his phone. Within minutes, two assailants ran at the couple with machetes. Avijit sustained blows to his head that punctured his skull and killed him. Rafida tried to save him and lost a thumb, also suffering further severe wounds to her hands and to her head.

'We were stabbed again and again by machetes on the side of the road,' she recalled later when I interviewed her in 2016. Pictures show Rafida staggering on the pavement with blood pouring down from her head, reaching out to crowds on the dark pavement. 'Most of the media just mentioned that I lost a thumb, but I can't use four fingers on my hand, and I received four stab wounds to the head,' she told me. 'There are pictures of police standing in that crowd surrounding us; they said there were police 10 yards away and they just decided not to come. Why wouldn't the police come?' Rafida cannot recall the exact details of the attack. 'There was this photographer, the young photographer who came forward, who was the only one to actually help us. He took us on a three-wheeler and took us to the hospital,' she said.

'When [Mannan] heard we got attacked he still went on and had his dinner, his biryani, so that's what gets people very annoyed, how can someone in their right mind do that? Later on he got really nervous about it, and he went into hiding, he never came to the hospital.' Mannan, claims Rafida, was known to be an Islamist and a member of the Islamist group or party Hizb-ut-Tahrir, which is proscribed in Bangladesh, but not in other countries, including the UK and Australia.

Rafida was taken to the nearby Square Hospital and the next day many of her and Avijit's friends tried to come and see her. Raihan Abir, who co-authored the book *Philosophy of Disbelief* with Avijit, remembers that a young blogger named Ananta Bijoy Das was in the hospital waiting room, beside himself with grief. Inundated with tears, the blogger from the northeastern town of Sylhet was inconsolable, asking how and why Avijit could have been killed in such a way.

While the American FBI would later become involved in the investigation, the Bangladesh government, at the time of writing, has delayed publication of a 'probe report' on the murder and investigation over twenty times. According to senior Bangladeshi intelligence figures interviewed for this book, officers refused to work on the investigation because the victim was an atheist, or had 'insulted Islam'. The FBI allegedly was never sent DNA samples promised by the Bangladesh Detective Branch, according to individuals intimately involved with the case. Without the support of Bangladeshi authorities, the FBI was unable to proceed with any investigation. Why the Bangladeshi authorities refused to help or provide the DNA leaves uneasy questions. Rights groups, including Front Line Defenders, an organisation dedicated to the protection of human rights defenders, would go on to term the treatment that murdered bloggers and others receive from the government as 'victim blaming', in a report published in November 2016.[10]

A group called Ansarullah Bangla Team (ABT) claimed responsibility. This group, inspired by the teachings of Muhammad Jasimuddin Rahmani, was also responsible for the murder of Rajib Haider in 2013 and would come to be a major new strand of terrorism in the country. Its brand of attack was nothing new—atheist or secular writers had been targeted before. Machetes are, of course, hardly modern weapons, and had even been conferred some warped religious importance by Rahmani, who had written a book entitled *Open Sword* and had said, 'that is how they killed infidels during the prophet's time.'[11] The group's messaging, too, was copied from well-worn and distinctly foreign playbooks online. However, ABT would firstly come to represent a new demographic of attackers, and secondly would internationalise and disseminate its message in strikingly modern ways and with a searingly contemporary sense of vigour, in the same vein as famed Yemeni-American militant preacher Anwar al-Awlaki.

A Detested Minority

ABT's tactics work on the correct assumption that atheists are widely reviled in Bangladesh. While it is hard to accurately say how many of the population share this view, a Pew Research Center survey showed that 82 per cent of respondents believed in making *sharia* the official law of the land and 44 per cent were in favour of that as well as imposing the death penalty for apostasy, or renouncement of Islam.[12] In light of these findings, the murders of alleged or real atheists probably have great popular support. When interviewed, senior members of intelligence agencies, both of the civilian National Security Intelligence and the military Directorate General of Forces Intelligence, took time to blame the deceased for 'insulting religion' while also noting the dearth of those willing to investigate the killing, simply because of Avijit's criticism of Islam. The level to which atheism and apostasy in particular are despised manifests itself in institutionalised discrimination shared by many Muslim-majority countries.

Avijit had started his blog, called Mukto-Mona or 'Free Mind', in 2001. In other words, he had been a critic of religion and Islamists for a long time. His wife Rafida claims that despite this, he first received a death threat in 2014. There could have been several reasons for this. For one thing, Roy, along with other secular and atheist bloggers, had been involved in encouraging and mobilising the Shahbag protests. It is important to note that the man who sent that first death threat in 2014, Farabi Shafiur Rahman, had also threatened to kill the Muslim cleric who had conducted Rajib Haider's funeral. Even well-read blogs such as Avijit's did not resonate quite like Shahbag had, with its cacophonous political expression and round-the-clock news coverage. The brazen attack on powerful politicians through popular mobilisation seems to have been what elicited such a great pushback. As suggested previously, many, if not most, large-scale protests in Bangladesh are not spontaneous, bottom-up affairs. Rather, they tend to be staged processions brought out by vested interests with varying degrees of power behind them. The populism and mobilisation capacity of Shahbag were therefore seen by both the Jamaat party leaders on trial and their rank-and-file followers as a genuine threat. To opponents of the protests, those with the most non-conformist views could easily be vilified and sacrificed in order to destroy this free expression.

Indeed, in 2005 when Jamaat was in power with its coalition partner, the BNP, now deceased war criminal Motiur Rahman Nizami, who was then industry minister and leader of Jamaat, went on record to claim that 'speaking against Jamaat-e-Islami is tantamount to speaking against Islam and conspiracy against Islam means working against humanity,' before implying that since the fall of the Soviet Union, Islam was the only force standing between the United States and world domination. Any criticism of the party or Islamist orthodoxy, he claimed, was a 'worldwide propaganda campaign against Islam, a Zionist-directed strategy to destroy the religion.'[13] While Shahbag was principally a protest calling for stiffer sentences, it was soon regarded as effectively 'speaking against Jamaat.'

Another possible reason that Avijit received the brutal attention he did—and that he received it when he did—could have been the publication in 2014 of his book, *The Virus of Faith*, which had been a success. But this does not account for the huge body of work that he had previously produced. Undoubtedly the heightened political situation at that time, as previously discussed, had played some role in eliciting engagement, anxiety and anger. For Nisha Biswal, who served as the secretary of state for South Asia in the Obama administration, Islamists who had previously engaged in locally focused political violence in Bangladesh 'became kind of a rich fodder for exploitation by global networks there, because it is such a highly polarised society where institutions often lack credibility.' Indeed, in many ways 2014 was a watershed year. While the winter of 2014–15 represented the last time that the BNP and Jamaat attempted to unseat the government through street protests and agitation, the most persistent barrage of terrorist attacks began in 2015, as this overt campaign waned. 2014 also witnessed a renewed internationalisation of Islamist struggle in Bangladesh.

Al-Qaeda in the Indian Subcontinent

In September 2014, Ayman al-Zawahiri, leader of Al-Qaeda, launched Al-Qaeda in the Indian Subcontinent, or AQIS. In January of that year, perhaps more significantly, only ten days after Bangladesh's boycotted election, the Egyptian jihadist released a 30-minute video called 'Massacre behind a wall of silence'. The video's message is fairly incisive and localised and, coincidentally, chimes with the views of Jahidur, the Jamaat activist I had met at the Hefazat march in April the previous year, and with other fairly standard Islamist political narratives and positions. It posits the line that Muslims are an oppressed minority, who need to claim their rightful place by dominating the majority population (that is, Hindus) of the subcontinent. This vision is seen as representing a righteous return to the 800 or so years in which Muslim rulers dominated the subcontinent. Today, however, 90 per cent of Bangladesh's population is Sunni Muslim, with a declining proportion of embattled minorities.

As Zawahiri claimed in the message:

> The events in Bangladesh enjoy the blessings of both India and America, since their interests in fighting Islam overlap, and this is why their bilateral relations are becoming stronger day by day. ... My dear Muslim brothers, thousands of people are being killed in the streets of Bangladesh without any guilt, except that they have come out to protest against the collusion of the anti-Islam secular government with a bunch of transgressing secularists who are heaping insults and vulgar abuses on Islam and the Prophet of Islam. ... It is then that we get to understand that 'human rights' are the rights of their man, and not the rights of our man. The events in Bangladesh and Burma are not too distant from the oppression and killings of Muslims in Kashmir or the racial cleansing in Assam, Gujarat and Ahmadabad either.[14]

The inclusion of Bangladesh in a list of mainly non-Muslim-majority territories by Zawahiri is redolent of Pakistan's position in 1971—that Bengalis are not 'real Muslims.' The implication was that this peasant agrarian population on the fringes of northern India, who had to a large extent practised Sufism, were not 'authentic Muslims', unlike their fairer, taller and supposedly more orthodox co-religionists in other parts of the subcontinent, and that they needed to somehow be cajoled into being 'proper' Muslims.

This gives a glimpse into the schism of nationalist identity-politics in Bangladesh. The position of those on the right or the Islamist end of the spectrum is to look down upon indigenous Bengali culture, in favour of cultural tropes of the Middle East or Pakistan, as a way to exert a uniquely Bangladeshi-Muslim identity that is distinctive from the major regional power and supposed oppressors, India. This identity also actively engages with a broader worldwide Muslim community, and enables Muslims to empower themselves through unity derived from their religion. However, as a result of this condescension towards Bengali national culture, many secular Bangladeshis view the primacy of religion as part of a fetishisation of foreign beliefs and values, and thus view it as a self-hating ideology. In other words Zawahiri was tapping into something that was deeply divisive, a debate that at that moment was particularly explosive given that the elections had just concluded.

Zawahiri was additionally wrong about America and the West's attitude regarding the elections and India. In fact, US Ambassador Dan Mozena fell out with the Bangladesh government in private. Western diplomats spoke of being entirely frozen out by the Bangladesh government over their criticism of the boycotted polls. As one of Mozena's senior staff diplomatically put it to me some time later, 'We didn't see eye to eye with the Indians,' who supported the Awami League wholeheartedly for reasons of history and expedience that will be examined further in the next chapter.

The Local Affiliate

Ansarullah Bangla Team, or ABT, has gone by several names over its history and has possibly split. Initially Imam Rahmani formed the group in around 2007 under the name Jama'atul Muslemin, a venture that failed for lack of patronage and funding. Jama'atul Muslemin did seemingly have patrons who inhabited a world between middle-class educational institutions in Dhaka and the diaspora in the UK. The group re-emerged in 2012–13 and seemed to have a new lease of life on the campuses of the capital's private universities, in particular North South University in northwest Dhaka. Rahmani confessed that he was involved in the formation of an NGO and think tank named the Research Centre for Unity and Development (RCUD).[15] The RCUD was suspected to be a funding channel for ABT and Rahmani's aspirations, as well as an attempt to assert the intellectual case for their desired direction for the country.

Three members of the RCUD travelled to Yemen in late 2009, where they reportedly met with Anwar al-Awlaki. Among those who travelled to meet Awlaki was Tehzeeb Karim, the son-in-law of another Islami Bank founder, Abdur Rashid. Tehzeeb told Awlaki about his brother, Rajib Karim, an IT technician working in the UK for British Airways. Rajib was a supporter of the JMB, helping that group with IT and fundraising. Rajib had lived in the UK since 2006, initially relocating to seek treatment for a child. He said he originally wanted to travel to the Middle East, to join up with Awlaki and his brother Tehzeeb. But the Yemeni-American preacher saw huge potential in having an insider in British Airways. Awlaki was in direct contact with Rajib. He was 'exchanging emails with Anwar al-Awlaki that indicated he had made contact with "two brothers [i.e. Muslims], one who works in baggage handling at Heathrow and another who works in airport security. Both are good practicing brothers and sympathize."'[16] However, 'for Awlaki the priority was a strike at the United States … he pressed his new acolyte for support' and questioned whether it would be 'possible to get a package or a person with a package on board a flight to the US'.[17]

Rajib Karim was jailed for thirty years in the UK in 2010. He had no direct bomb-making experience, but represented that very middle-class jihadist trend: strong networking and web savvy and a lack of desire to actually get his hands dirty. Tehzeeb Karim was still missing at the time of writing. According to press reports, his family had not heard from him since 17 May 2016, when he allegedly arrived back in Bangladesh from Malaysia. Well-placed sources in Dhaka believe that Tehzeeb was detained by one of Bangladesh's intelligence agencies when he arrived back in Dhaka. However, he was allegedly radicalised after marrying banker Abdur Rashid's daughter, Seerat Rashid, in 2002. The pair both attended North South University, as had Rajib Haider's murderers.[18] Tehzeeb, like a good many other Bangladeshi jihadists and right-of-centre or Islamist ideologues, also spent time in Malaysia. According to his LinkedIn profile, he received a postgraduate degree in educational leadership from the University of Nottingham's Malaysian campus in 2015.[19] An indication of their affluence and of the circles in which Tehzeeb and Rajib Karim were involved, and a possible explanation for Tehzeeb's radicalisation, was the death of their older brother Atif Karim in an accident in London in 2001, which also claimed the life of the only daughter of Bangladesh's richest man, Salman F. Rahman. Those who knew him have suggested that Atif died in mysterious circumstances, which may have involved a romantic argument, and that of the three brothers he was the apple of the family's eye.

Developing Networks

The creation of supposedly altruistic institutions is not an abstract ruse. Supposedly innocuous institutions are often vital to forming networks, grooming recruits, and creating captive audiences and spaces in which outreach can flourish. In many ways, this is an end in itself. While from the outside investment in creating networks and indoctrination may seem superfluous without attack or violent confrontation, this is in many ways the real political project, which the attacks are but a temporary advertisement for. In spaces where formal structures do not exist, or even in ones where they do, these institutions form the political base for the germ of the protagonists' desired state to be created.

Rezaur Razzak, an alleged founder of ABT, is a private university teacher. According to some reports, Razzak was also involved with the Jama'atul Muslemin with Rahmani. At the time of writing he was the head of the Centre for Entrepreneurship Development at BRAC University, part of the sprawling NGO that had become a target of the JMB. Like Tehzeeb Karim he had spent time in Malaysia (as had one of Rajib Haider's murderers, Redwanul Azad Rana) between 2014 and 2017, when he was deported back to Bangladesh. These patterns and differences are distinctive and instructive. ABT reflects an almost alt-right culture, to appropriate a Western term. Its members are often characterised as urban, middle-class and educated. The group's modus operandi differs from the spectacular methods of the JMB and the Islamic State, or other famous jihadists. By targeting ideological opponents—the liberal proponents of diversity and secularism, for instance—ABT hopes to radically alter society from within.

The internet and the frustrations of the exploding middle class are ABT's greatest recruitment tools, and it has exploited both. Its supporters are frequently found to be university students—like Farabi Shafiur Rahman, who dropped out of Chittagong University and ended up taking to the internet to stalk and threaten atheists, or like the five North South University students who killed Rajib Haider. The students were drawn by Rahmani's sermons, which he had his followers film and upload to YouTube. Among those who attended his mosque was Qazi Mohammad Rezwanul Ahsan Nafis, the 22-year-old who went to the United States in 2012 on a student visa, where he planned to blow up the New York Federal Reserve.[20] Nafis had looked up blog posts on how to make a bomb at home, and found instructions that Rahmani had posted. He was caught in a sting operation by the FBI and sentenced to thirty years in jail in August 2013.[21] He wrote to the trial judge that, 'At my university in Bangladesh I did not have any real friends … So, when the radical students, who were influential and famous, were being nice to me I fell for them very easily.' The university in question was the very same North South University.[22]

Apart from students, one of the main demographics targeted for recruitment by groups like ABT and its ideological bedfellows Hizb-ut-Tahrir is members of the military. At the end of 2011, Major Zia-ul-Haq, an army major stationed in Dhaka who was allegedly a member of Hizb-ut-Tahrir, was implicated in a coup attempt; despite prominent allegations against him, he has never been found.[23] He was said to have been a gifted student from the Military Institute of Science and Technology. According to his father, Haq had been sucked into hard-line religiosity after the death of his wife.[24] In November 2017, progress was made in the case of Avijit's murder with the arrest of one of the attackers, Muhammad Abu Siddique Sohel. In his testimony Sohel suggested that Haq was known as 'boro bhai' or 'big brother', indicative of his leadership of the ten-member team that had killed Avijit. Sohel suggested that the former army major had been present and helped to coordinate the attack on the night that Avijit was murdered.[25] Similarly, other detained jihadists with links to the military have walked free with questionable ease.

This may explain why the investigation into Avijit Roy's murder has alternated between sluggish and incompetent and deadly. A key suspect in the case was a young man named Mukul Rana, alias Sharif, who, according to his family, was secretly detained by the Detective Branch on 23 February 2016. Researcher Tasneem Khalil has corroborated this suggestion.[26] Months later the Detective Branch first offered a bounty for information pertaining to his capture, and then shortly afterwards claimed that he had died in a shoot-out. Avijit's father, retired Professor Ajay Roy, claimed that 'through the killing [of Mukul Rana], the scope of getting more information on the killings has been closed,' adding that there were ghosts within the law enforcement agencies.[27] Could these 'ghosts' have not only killed one of the few people associated with the attack, but in doing so also intentionally destroyed evidence that would have helped solve other similar murder cases?

Blogger and secular campaigner Maruf Rosul agrees. 'The fact is that fundamentalism is in the brain of the administration, politics and law enforcing agencies,' he told me. In Maruf's view, 'Avijit Roy, along with our other comrades who are killed by the fundamentalists,' would always ultimately be regarded as atheists by the people at the top. 'The top persons' interviews published in media were really frustrating. They even accused the bloggers for their own death. They instructed bloggers, writers, about "How to Write".' He sighed, 'So you can understand their mentality.'

The Military's Silent Hand

Ever since the Awami League came to power in 2009, it has faced the threat of military dissatisfaction. The military in Bangladesh is, as in many countries, inclined towards conservatism and traditionalism. On 25 February 2009, a branch of the military then known as the Bangladesh Rifles, but which changed its name after the event to the Border Guards Bangladesh, mutinied in their central Dhaka cantonment. The mutineers killed some fifty-seven officers before the standoff ended. Instead of sending in the army straight away, Sheikh Hasina had tried to negotiate with the hostage-takers, thereby enraging some members of the military.

The mutiny, which some suggested had Islamist links, posed questions about the Awami League's ability to keep the military on side. Hasina 'clearly remains fearful about her ability to maintain her government', noted the American embassy after meeting with her in March 2009, weeks after the mutiny.[28] In November 2013, the government sentenced 152 of the mutineers to death in a single special trial hearing conducted in a converted schoolyard in Old Dhaka.[29] The convicts were sentenced while shackled in tightly packed cages in what was little more than a very well-guarded shed. Two years after the mutiny, an attempted coup by the previously mentioned Major Zia-ul-Haq and a still absconding businessman named Ishraq Ahmed would again challenge the stability of the civilian government. Ishraq Ahmed is most likely now based in Hong Kong.

Ever since this coup attempt, it has appeared that the military has been appeased, gaining major contracts and other financial rewards. This has included a license to form a bank for the Border Guards. For the regular army, appeasement has included new 'toys' and massive spending increases, as well as rank inflation, whereby dozens of extra senior posts were created to give lower ranking members higher status.[30] When the World Bank pulled out of its largest ever grant, which had been allocated to the construction of the giant Padma Bridge spanning the eponymous river, the military and Chinese companies stepped in, highlighting the ascendant power brokers in Bangladesh. In an informal economy where so little is paid in tax, and where civilian leadership is so routinely doubted and enfeebled, the power incrementally bestowed on alternative institutions, be they religious or military, perhaps shows how democracy dies.

A Deadly Trend

Avijit Roy's murder would set a trend in motion. Almost exactly a month after his death, 27-year-old Washikur Rahman left home for the last time in the Tejgaon neighbourhood of Dhaka. On the morning of 30 March, he left for work at the Far East Travels travel agency. Barely a few minutes out of the door, Washikur was attacked by three young men with machetes. The attackers hacked at his face and neck, in similar fashion to previous attacks, until Washikur collapsed on the ground. They continued to stab at his body before running away. Once again, nearby police could not catch the assailants, as Washikur's unrecognisable body lay in a pool of blood on the early morning tarmac. A local resident however, was more vigilant. Labannya Hijra, a 21-year-old hijra or transgender woman, saw the three young men running away from the site of the attack. She ran out as they passed and grabbed two of them by their T-shirts. As she did so, a bloodstained machete tumbled out of one of their backpacks. The two men fought her grasp, but to no avail. The third attacker managed to escape.

Washikur had often taken satirical swipes at orthodox religion, often on Facebook. He had been deeply affected by Avijit's killing, and had changed his Facebook cover photo to an image with the hashtag #IamAvijit, followed by 'words cannot be killed'. He had blogged under the name Kutshit Hasher Chhana, Bangla for 'ugly duckling'. He once compared the Islamists' behaviour 'to the way babies get upset and break a lot of things.'[31] His Facebook commentary had seemingly garnered him many death threats.

The two captured murderers were both in their early twenties. Zikrullah was twenty-two and had been a student at the madrassa run by Hefazat leader Shah Ahmad Shafi in Hathazari, just north of Chittagong. Ariful, the other attacker, had studied at a madrassa in the capital's Mirpur neighbourhood. Zikrullah had allegedly met attack planner Masum on a train as he was headed back to Chittagong. Neither Zikrullah nor Ariful apparently knew what a blog was, let alone read anything that Washikur had written. They claimed Masum had simply told them that he had written 'against Islam'. They had spent a short period in a flat in South Dhaka, where they had trained and planned the attack, and had even reportedly been picked up by police while practising walking with machetes concealed on their person.

To date, these remain some of the very few attackers to be caught literally red-handed. Labannya's bravery became symbolic given that the hijra community, like transgender people in many parts of the world, remain a stigmatised, excluded minority according to the conventions of orthodoxy. Labannya told press that she had left home aged nine. As in other parts of South Asia, hijras live together, rejected as they are by mainstream society and their families.[32] Theirs is a ritual exclusion, which forces them to get by from begging, with many people giving them money just to make them leave, in the belief that they bring curses upon others. Much like Washikur's comparison of Islamists to babies wanting to break things, the exclusion of hijras is not dissimilar to children believing that members of the opposite sex will give them 'cooties'. This belief is so strong that in nearby Bihar in

India, the authorities have been known to use hijras as tax collectors, so determined are locals to avoid being cursed that they will pay their taxes to make them go away.

The fact that the supposedly middle-class urban jihadist outfit ABT was now effectively exploiting madrassa students from the other end of the social hierarchy points to something very redolent of typical class dynamics. It is similar, perhaps, to the position of British Airways worker Rajib Karim, who wanted to use the computer with his hero, Awlaki, but was not prepared to engage in the actual act itself on the streets of his country.

Come May that year, yet another blogger would pay the ultimate price. 33-year-old Ananta Bijoy Das had helped moderate Avijit Roy's Mukto-Mona blog and had formed a 'Science and Rational Council'. Ananta lived in the northeastern city of Sylhet where he worked in a bank, but had come to Dhaka as soon as he heard of Avijit's death. He was known for his acerbic social commentary and support for Shahbag and other secular causes. With friends, he had published a magazine called *Jukti* and written a number of books, which took aim at dogma. This extended well beyond Islam and included, for instance, a February 2012 book entitled *Science and Revolution in the Soviet Union*, which tore into the politicisation of science under Stalin.[33]

Ananta also knew that his life was in danger and was already living a clandestine existence. He had applied for a Swedish visa to attend World Press Freedom Day events in Stockholm on 3 May at the invitation of Swedish PEN, the association of writers set up to promote literature and fight for freedom of expression. The Swedish embassy in Dhaka, however, had on 22 April refused his application, claiming among other reasons that 'there is always a risk involved when granting a visa that you will not leave (the) Schengen area after the visit.'[34] Ananta's friends claim that in the visa application process he had been interviewed harshly and at great length by two local embassy staff whom they suspect of being Islamist sympathisers. Ananta claimed that in the interview he had mistakenly admitted that he felt his life was under threat. At the end of the day the embassy was right, for he had very good reason to try to remain in Sweden. For a person who needs asylum, help or shelter, even from a country supposedly as generous as Sweden, the last thing to do is to admit that you are in danger until you have stepped foot on its soil.

And so, as Ananta went to work on the morning of 12 May 2015, at around 8.30 a.m. four masked men attacked him with machetes. Ananta initially ran for his life, but after a brief chase was caught by his assailants. Like those before him, he was ruthlessly hacked to death on the streets.

On 15 May, another blogger was on his way home in Dhaka from a protest to decry the killing of his friend and fellow writer Ananta Bijoy Das. Like Ananta and Avijit, 40-year-old Niloy Chatterjee, who blogged under the name Niloy Neel, was from a Hindu family background and an atheist. He was a member of the same rationalist society as Ananta had been, and had also blogged on Avijit's Mukto-Mona blog. Niloy was a graduate of philosophy from Dhaka University.

He recounted on Facebook:

I was on my way back from attending the rally organized to protest the murder of Ananta Bijoy Das. First, when I reached a certain place via public bus, they came with me to the same spot. Then, when I got on to a Laguna to reach my destination, one of them climbed aboard the Laguna with me. On the Laguna I realized this was the same guy who was on the bus with me, but there were two of them then. I thought to myself, well, it's possible; perhaps one of them was going somewhere else so he took a different route. Until then it seemed as usual. But on the Laguna, the young man was continually texting from his cellphone which made me suspicious. When I exited the Laguna before I reached my actual destination, he got off with me. I was quite scared, and hurried into [an] unfamiliar alley. Later when I looked back, I noticed that another young man, who had also been on the bus, had joined this young man, and they had not followed me into the alley; they were waiting at the alley entrance. Then I was quite certain that I was being followed. Because even if their destination was the same, they reached their [sic] through separate routes, following me. I went farther into the alley, and took a rickshaw keeping the hood up, and traveled to my destination. I reached in apparent safety with the help of a friend nearby.

When I tried to lodge a General Diary [with the police] about this incident, I faced an even more bizarre situation. A police officer had told me in confidence that the police do not want to accept General Diaries like this because the officer who accepted such a General Diary, related to the personal safety of an individual, remains accountable to ensure the personal safety of said individual. If the said individual faces any difficulty, then the relevant police officer may even lose his job for negligence in duty. This is what I saw when I visited the thanas [police station] to file a General Diary. When the surveillance on me had occurred, I had had to pass by several thanas, and so today when I visited one that had been in the vicinity, they refused to accept my General Diary. They told me this isn't under our jurisdiction, go to this other thana, it's their jurisdiction, and also, leave the country as soon as possible.[35]

In the summer of 2015 there had been a brief lull in killings. The country fasted over the month of Ramadan and endured the extremes of the seasonal weather. However, the respite for bloggers and non-believers would not last long. Niloy was at home on the computer on 7 August 2015 when there was a knock at the door of the apartment that he lived in with his wife, Asa Moni. It was about 1 p.m. when she answered the door to a man, perhaps in his early twenties, wearing jeans and a T-shirt. He claimed that the landlord had sent him up to have a look at the room. He immediately barged into the apartment and began typing furiously on his phone. Moments later, three more young men appeared and charged into the flat, carrying meat cleavers and a pistol. Niloy, dressed only in pyjama bottoms, had come to the door of the room he had been in. The intruders went straight for him. With their first swings they severed his hand and with the following blows almost beheaded him. He died within moments. Gruesome images show his semi-naked corpse in a pool of splattered blood, which had also sprayed over the books that he collected on the shelves. These included the Quran, the Bible and assorted other volumes on philosophy.

Reorganised Qaeda

Earlier that month, on 3 May 2015, a video with a speech from the purported leader of Al-Qaeda in the Indian Subcontinent (AQIS), Asim Umar, was posted to jihadist websites, claiming responsibility for the murders of Avijit Roy and Ahmed Rajib Haider. Initially Avijit's murder had been claimed by a Twitter account called Ansar Bangla Team-7. However, the ABT movement seemed to be formalising its practices under the name 'Ansar al-Islam', dropping the 'Bangla Team' tag. It was also in this month that the authorities banned Ansarullah Bangla Team.

Umar was seemingly appointed by Al-Qaeda leader Zawahiri to lead the AQIS outfit in 2014. Born some time in the mid-1970s, Umar is said to be of north Indian origin, and his real name according to Indian press is Sanaul Haq.[36] He reportedly grew up in the Deobandi madrassa system. Presumably attracted by the war against the Soviets, he is said to have moved to the Afghanistan–Pakistan border in the late 1980s and to have a long history with groups that developed around the fight against the Soviets in Afghanistan. In Pakistan, he allegedly helped facilitate Osama Bin Laden's stay in the garrison town of Abbottabad, where the Al-Qaeda leader had lived under the noses of the Pakistani military establishment in a large, conspicuous compound until he was eventually killed in 2011 by United States special operations forces.[37]

Umar is believed to have had connections with the Harkat-ul-Jihad al-Islami (HUJI) movement, with its long history in Bangladesh, as well as with the Pakistani Taliban and with Pakistan-based militant group Harkat-ul-Mujahideen (HuM). These links are said to have helped Umar in his promotion to the regional leadership position in AQIS. His numerous books are widely circulated and available in Pakistan, where he has long operated 'freely', according to Professor Christine Fair of Georgetown University.[38] There are suggestions, most notably made in a 2017 article in *Newsweek*, that Zawahiri himself has been given safe haven in Karachi by Pakistan's military intelligence agency, the ISI.[39] Fair claims that these suggestions are 'very credible', as 'we are continuing to learn more about the ties between the [Pakistani] state and [Al-Qaeda].' However others cast doubt on these suppositions, seeing them as efforts by the more hawkish Trump administration to put further pressure on their Pakistani counterparts to rein in their activities with non-state actors. It would of course be extremely troubling for Bangladesh if the Pakistani state had any sort of relations with AQIS, but these would not, of course, be unprecedented. The murky Karachi underworld is believed to be home to notorious, internationally wanted criminals, including Dawood Ibrahim and members of other well-armed groups. The ISI is famous for maintaining relations with groups like Jaish-e-Mohammed and for inventing and utilising others, such as Lashkar-e-Taiba and HuM.[40]

When the video of Asim Umar claiming responsibility for the killings of the two bloggers appeared online in May 2015, it represented a further sign that AQIS and Ansar al-Islam had reorganised. While blogger Washikur Rahman's name was not mentioned, his picture was included in the video, which was entitled 'From France to Bangladesh the dust will never settle down'. Umar also retroactively claimed the killing of University of Rajshahi academic Shafiul Islam, a sociology professor with secular values and an appreciation for Bengali culture whom Umar described as an 'accursed atheist'.[41] The video's title harks to an article by Awlaki from the first issue of his *Inspire* magazine in 2011, in which the Yemeni-American preacher called on Western Muslims to commit violent acts at home in retaliation against 'threats' to the religion that came from 'blasphemous' cartoons.[42]

In June 2015, the fluid, if somewhat chaotic, Ansar al-Islam group tried to clarify a few things. In another statement, they claimed that Ansarullah Bangla Team was merely a media outlet. The group also announced that:

> 'the Global Islamic Media Front (GIMF) will be the only official outlet for "Ansarullah Bengali" statements, hence, any statements, media releases, articles attributed to Ansarullah Bangla that are not published through GIMF are not authentic and are considered fake.'[43] GIMF is a propaganda organisation recognised as a communications arm of Al-Qaeda, and has been in operation since the early 2000s under various guises. Its principal role is to package, translate and disseminate material from regional Al-Qaeda franchises or sympathisers around the world.

The presence of a handgun at the scene of Niloy Chatterjee's murder, even if not used, and the alignment of Ansar al-Islam with AQIS in its claiming of the crime seemed to indicate that the group had officially been accepted as part of the Al-Qaeda network. Having grown from the blog or online presence that Rahmani and comrades had started, ABT had now become an official mouthpiece of AQIS and a subsidiary of GIMF. In other words, the group seemed to be trying to formalise and consolidate its messaging while its hardware also seemed to have taken a leap out of the mythology-laden machete era and moved on to handguns.

In the following months, members of religious minorities would be murdered by the remnants of the JMB in isolated corners of the country, part of the slow bleeding of Bangladesh of its diverse indigenous identities. In February of the previous year, one of the group's major bomb specialists, Zahidul Islam, alias Boma Mizan, was freed while being transported to a court in the northern town of Mymensingh while he was serving a thirty-six-year jail sentence. The renewed operations of the JMB would soon come to represent a different, major stream of resurgent militancy in the country.

Hacking the Messengers

In October 2015 two publishing houses came under attack almost simultaneously in central Dhaka. Both had published books by Avijit Roy, including *Philosophy of Disbelief*, which he co-authored with Raihan Abir. [44] Faisal Arefin Dipan ran Jagriti Prokashoni publishing house, which published the works of the cutting-edge, secular Bangladeshi literati. He fit the profile of many other victims, as a bright, bookish man from an intellectual family background. On 31 October, he was found dead and alone in his office.

Earlier that same day, Ahmedur Rasheed Chowdhury, also known as Tutul, was in the office of his Shuddhashar publishing house with two writers. Tutul had been receiving death threats on Facebook since February that year, cursing him for publishing books by atheists and threatening to bomb his offices. The month that the threats started, Tutul had met and been photographed with Avijit and Rafida at the Ekushey book fair, where his publishing company had a stall, on the very night that Avijit was killed. [45]

When two young men rushed into his office in October, Tutul was lucky. As he told me in an interview:

> I can only remember one thing, that, a boy of twenty to twenty-five said '*Allahu akbar!*' [God is great!] and hit me with a small sword. I fainted and fell down between the chair and table. Later I heard that they also tried to shoot me. But Ranadipam Basu [one of the two writers who was present] kicked a chair towards them—that's why the bullet didn't hit me.

The attacks were again claimed by AQIS and its local subsidiary, Ansar al-Islam.

A few days after Niloy Neel's murder in August 2015, another blogger and activist of the Shahbag movement in Sylhet thought he was being followed by four or five youths. Nazimuddin Samad, twenty-eight, was a master's student in the city and was so concerned that he stopped posting online. He looked to move and headed to the capital to continue his studies there. Nazim had responded to a friend's concern by stating, 'I am also scared, sir, scared of getting killed. But what else can I do? It's better to die rather than living by keeping my head down.'[46]

Nazim enrolled in Dhaka's Jagannath University and arrived in February 2016. He continued studying law. On the evening of 6 April, he was heading home from university and was stopped at a busy intersection. It was around 8 p.m. Nazim suddenly found himself surrounded by a group of four young men, who pulled out machetes and started hacking at his body on that busy Dhaka street, with all around them paused by the red light. To make sure their victim had no chance of survival they shot him with a pistol as his body lay bloodied and unrecognisable on the road, before making off along the bustling streets. The attack was quickly claimed by AQIS. The Awami League home minister, Asaduzzaman Khan, responded in similar haste to Nazim's killing. 'The bloggers, they should control their writing,' he said. 'Our country is a secular state. … I want to say that people should be careful not to hurt anyone by writing anything—hurt any religion, any people's beliefs, any religious leaders.'[47]

Striking Sexual 'Deviants'

As has been established earlier in the book, sensitivity of belief and thought are extremely relative. In April 2016 Bangladesh attempted to celebrate the beginning of the Bengali New Year of 1423, a festival known as Pohela Boishakh. The celebration most probably dates to the reign of Mughal emperor Akbar in the sixteenth century and was created on the basis of harvest time, when taxes were also collected. Its origin presents many telling examples of how an ostensibly liberal Muslim ruler ruled and taxed an agrarian, religiously diverse population who were wedded to their fertile deltaic rice paddy. Pohela Boishakh may also have tagged on to more ancient Hindu or Buddhist festivals, which occur at this time of year in the region. It is an important and distinctively Bengali festival, which has been cherished by both Muslims and non-Muslims for around 500 years.

In 2016, 460 years after Akbar's official adoption of the proto-Hindu-Islamic calendar that formally began this tradition, members of the LGBTQ+ community wished to participate in the usually colourful Pohela Boishakh festivities with a Rainbow Rally to celebrate LGBTQ+ culture and rights. While such events had already been held for the past two years, this year the organisers had advertised the rally on Facebook and the police warned that they could not guarantee its security and advised people not to take part. The Facebook event page was inundated with threats. 'Make your parade, do what you want, but we have a list with your names and we will hunt you very soon,' read one.[48] When a handful did try and hold the rally, the police arrested them. An activist named Xulhaz Mannan, forty years old, who in 2014 had set up *Roopbaan*, the country's only magazine for the LGBTQ+ community, and who worked for the United States Agency for International Development (USAID), came down to try to help. However, as recalled by a friend and LGBTQ+ activist, who did not wish to be named, 'four were detained for trying to hold the rally— Xulhaz went down with a few friends and spent the whole day trying to get them out' of the police lock-up. It was around that time that Xulhaz started to receive a large number of death threats. Rainbow Rallies aside, Pohela Boishakh festivities are a target for some Islamists who see it as 'un-Islamic', and as a result celebrations have been attacked. Most notably, in April 2001 ten people were killed in Ramna Park near Dhaka University in an explosion perpetrated by HUJI-B.

On 25 April, about ten days after the Rainbow Rally arrests, Xulhaz Mannan and his friend Mahbub Rabbi Tonoy were at Xulhaz's flat in the Dhanmondi neighbourhood of Dhaka. At around 5 p.m., six young men arrived at the building and told a security guard named Parvez that they were couriers. The men proceeded up to the first-floor apartment and forced their way in through the front door. There, in what had once been a centre of convivial activity and hope, the interlopers chanted '*Nara-e-takbeer, Allahu akbar*'—Arabic for 'God is great'—as they hacked at the two young men with meat cleavers. They then shot their defenceless victims, covering what had once been a place of sanctity for a small part of an embattled community with blood. There to witness the bloodshed in the apartment that day were Xulhaz's mother and a household helper. Parvez, the security guard, heard the screams and gunfire coming from above and made his way up the stairs to investigate. He was met by the fleeing assailants, who stabbed him in the face.[49] Xulhaz's mother was apparently so traumatised by the horror of witnessing her son being torn apart that she suffered amnesia, and has lived ever since in the belief that her son Xulhaz is abroad.[50] Ansar al-Islam, under its AQIS banner, swiftly claimed responsibility for the double murder and a week later released a deeply political screed condemning Xulhaz for 'spreading the filth of homosexuality' in Bangladesh as a 'paid and chosen servant' of America and India:

> We are astonished by the shamelessness of these Americans. They are the ones who are continually committing crimes against fundamental human ethics, morality, civilizational values and humanity. They are the ones who are working relentlessly to spread their own depravity, obscenity, perversion, wickedness & debauchery throughout the world. They are the ones who want to drag the whole world into the abyss of sin, perversion and debauchery with them. And these are the shameless ones who dare to teach the Muslims of Bangladesh humanity & morality?[51]

The AQIS statement takes time to discuss American actions in Iraq, Vietnam, and elsewhere. It reads much like the frustrated essay of a nihilistic student justifying acts of horror with whataboutism. Its attribution of homosexuality to the West and more specifically to America is a common trope. The irony, of course, is that the criminalisation of homosexuality in the subcontinent is a legacy of British colonialism. In the Victorian era the British government shared Ansar al-Islam's fears about an imaginary 'abyss of sin, perversion and debauchery', so it passed a law about it in 1860, three years after locally hired Indian soldiers, or sepoys, as they were known, had rebelled across northern India. The empire decided to consolidate its rule with a new penal code. Under Section 377, which deals with 'unnatural offences', the law (which Bangladesh has never re-written or struck down) states that:

> Whoever voluntarily has carnal intercourse against the order of nature with any man, woman or animal, shall be punished with [imprisonment] for life, or with imprisonment of either description for a term which may extend to ten years, and shall also be liable to fine. Explanation:

Penetration is sufficient to constitute the carnal intercourse necessary to the offence described in this section.[52]

Despite the very clear, Victorian wording that only the specific sexual act constitutes an offence, as opposed to promoting or living a particular sexual identity, the day after AQIS's essay was released, Home Minister Asaduzzaman Khan claimed that, 'Our society does not allow any movement that promotes unnatural sex. Writing in favour of it is tantamount to criminal offence as per our law.'[53]

Xulhaz's death had caused shock among his colleagues at USAID, as well as from Nisha Biswal, then the US assistant secretary of state for South Asia. After Xulhaz's murder, Biswal had expressed concerns to Home Minister Khan about the safety of American citizens living in Bangladesh. As Khan put it, 'I told her that we have been investigating every murder giving highest priority. We have arrested many criminals. Capability of police has also been enhanced. Security of every foreign national living in this country has been ensured.' Before long, this statement would be exposed as ringing deeply hollow. Still, the home minister added that he had shown Biswal:

> some contents of bloggers written on different blogs, and told her that no religion of the world approves such remarks. None has the right to hurt the religious sentiments of people belonging to different religions. Action will be taken if anyone is found written such remarks criticising religions. ... We hate the bloggers' writings criticising the religion.[54]

Corruptions

All the murders by AQIS's local outfit, Ansar al-Islam, were described as targeted killings. In effect, they represented a sort of vigilantism by people who viewed society as deeply corrupt and in need of cleansing through the elimination of supposed transgressors of their interpretation of a supernatural moral code. As the statements from the government suggest, the killings were also based on deep societal concerns and anxieties, and served as warnings to members of targeted demographics. This made them deeply political. The government was forced to coalesce and cede ground, adopting a warped interpretation of the law and spirituality to appease the killers and their supporters.

But part of this movement was not simply scriptural. As anthropologist Arild Engelsen Ruud told me after conducting fieldwork and interviews with Jamaat supporters, 'The main reason cited for supporting Jamaat is not about Islam and the Muslim identity of the country. It is rather about governance and corruption.' Those anxieties about corruption within society, seen through an Islamist lens as stemming from secularism and godlessness, are the driving force behind young men's support for Jamaat, which might shed light on Islamist opinion in general and perhaps on the motives of those behind the AQIS attacks.

In many ways this leads to a crisis of nationalism, which is not just a Bangladeshi phenomenon or even solely a Muslim one, but rather an anxiety that the way of our politicians and political orders is not working. As we have seen, there are some who believe that this can be easily remedied by looking for answers from those who are seen to command discipline, and who have always complained most loudly about corruption, real or imagined. Many of the most powerful have majoritarian religious backing.

5

A DYSFUNCTIONAL NEIGHBOURHOOD

In the early hours of 2 April 2004, two shipping trawlers, the *Kazadan* and the *Amanat*, sidled up to the government-owned Chittagong Urea Fertiliser Company Limited's dock on the Karnaphuli River in Chittagong, southern Bangladesh. The trawlers had trans-shipped and carried their cargo from a larger vessel, which was moored at sea near St Martin's Island, Bangladesh's southernmost point. The larger vessel was purportedly owned by a local Bangladesh Nationalist Party MP and businessman named Salauddin Quader Chowdhury.[1] Probably acting on a tip-off from Indian intelligence, police arrived at the jetty at around 4 a.m. and were astonished by what they found. According to *Jane's Intelligence Review*, the police stumbled on arms being loaded from the two boats onto ten trucks. The haul was 'worth an estimated US$4.5m–$7m' and 'included around 2,000 automatic and semi-automatic weapons, among them 1,290 Type 56-1/Type 56-2 Kalashnikov-type assault rifles; 150 T-69 rocket propelled grenade (RPG) launchers; quantities of 40mm RPG ammunition; 25,000 hand-grenades; and 1.8m rounds of small-arms ammunition.'[2]

It was only in January 2014, weeks after the Awami League swept back into power and almost ten years after the haul was discovered, that any of those involved in the case were sentenced. Among them were BNP former minister of state for home affairs Lutfozzaman Babar; former industries minister Motiur Rahman Nizami, who had been the

111

head of Jamaat-e-Islami; a former director general of the National Security Intelligence (NSI) agency, Brigadier General Abdur Rahim; and a one-time head of the Directorate General of Forces Intelligence (DGFI), Major General Rezzakul Haider Chowdhury.

In all, the court sentenced fourteen individuals to death after an investigation that produced details described by the Indian National Security Review of 2009 as 'astounding'.[3] Their crime had been involvement in and planning one of the largest arms hauls in South Asia's history. 'There was no question' that the arms were destined for Indian separatist outfits, the United Liberation Front of Assam (ULFA) and the Isak-Muivah faction of the National Socialist Council of Nagaland (NSCN-IM).[4] Assam and Nagaland are two of the seven states in Northeast India collectively known as the Seven Sisters, which are home to a large number of distinct ethnic groups. Many of these groups did not agree to join the new nation when India declared independence from Great Britain in 1947. This region, moreover, is almost cut off from the rest of the giant country by Bangladesh. It is wedged between Myanmar to the east, China to the north and Bangladesh to the south. These 'seven sisters' are topographically like the stalls of an amphitheatre ascending into the Himalayas around deltaic Bengal.

In September 2013, I spoke to barrister Fakhrul Islam, who was defending BNP politician and shipping magnate Salauddin Quader Chowdhury at the International Crimes Tribunal (ICT). Fakhrul told me that his client had been implicated in the dreadful killings of 1971 because of a 'successful Indian plot' against him. This kind of rhetoric usually sets off a well-known alarm bell: 'communal conspiracy theory incoming'. Fakhrul's line that day was that his client was accused and in detention because India was trying to control and subjugate Bangladesh, using its proxy, the Awami League party, as a tool to quash his client. Without such subjugation Bangladesh would be so successful, the barrister claimed, that other Indian states would want to secede from the union. This struck me as fanciful, until I considered Salauddin's alleged involvement in the arms haul to Indian separatists, and his part in the persistent proxy conflict that the region's two hegemons wage. The conflict fosters a deep distrust of India that serves to fuel Bangladesh's Islamic identity, and also directly impacts Islamist agitation in Bangladesh.

Almost like clockwork, Bangladesh becomes an accommodating place for Northeast India's separatist rebels every time the BNP comes to power. In the mid-1990s, before the Awami League were elected in 1996, journalists could meet the ULFA leadership in safe houses provided by Bangladesh's intelligence agencies.[5] These were ideal locations for the separatists, close to their conflict-riddled homelands, with convenient transport connections and, most importantly, an administration that, as the 2004 arms hauls proved, was essentially hostile to the Indian state.

As Deb Mukharji, former Indian high commissioner to Bangladesh, told me:

> When I went to Bangladesh as high commissioner in 1995, I could see that elements of the government were collaborating fully with the ISI [Inter-Services Intelligence, the Pakistani intelligence agency] and helping these insurgent groups from India—it was very evident to me. I had information to that effect—hard information. This was certainly going on.

As Salauddin's lawyer hinted, Pakistan actively wanted to help dismember India, in much the same way that India had assisted in dividing Pakistan in 1971: by supporting insurgencies and by stimulating proxy conflicts. Salauddin was never tried for his involvement in the arms shipment. There was, according the American embassy, however, 'widespread speculation that he was involved with the Chittagong arms haul shipment. After the latter incident, Kamal Siddiqui and then Foreign Secretary/now Ambassador to U.S. Shamsher Chowdhury predicted his exit from the PMO [Prime Minister's Office].'[6]

A Family Affair

Salauddin Quader Chowdhury had essentially inherited a fiefdom in the bustling port city of Chittagong. His father Fazlul Quader Chowdhury was a native of the city and had been one of the few political leaders based in East Pakistan to prosper in the then unified country. As an important member of the Muslim League Party, he had been the speaker of the National Assembly and periodically stood in as president of Pakistan when Ayub Khan left the country. He ruthlessly fought for the union of the two wings of the country. Fazlul died in jail in 1973, shortly after the country gained independence. He was one of very few people to be jailed for crimes committed during the struggle in its immediate aftermath. His son, however, would carry on the mantle as his scion in the city. The wealth of Salauddin and his family is based on two, or perhaps three, lucrative, symbiotic industries: politics, shipping and smuggling.

Fazlul's Muslim League was banned in Bangladesh by Sheikh Mujibur Rahman in the aftermath of the 1971 war, along with Jamaat and political parties that were deemed only to serve the interests of one religious community. The country's military rulers, however, rehabilitated leaders of these parties in the years after Mujib's assassination in 1975. It was only after General Ziaur Rahman came to power that Salauddin returned from exile in London. The next dictator, Muhammad Ershad, gave Salauddin his first break in national politics, but it was Zia's widow, BNP leader and two-times prime minister Khaleda Zia who took Salauddin's career to new heights by giving him a position in her inner circle when she took power in 2001.

Salauddin isn't the only family member in politics. His cousin A. B. M. Fazle Karim Chowdhury is also in the shipping business and an MP for Chittagong—but with the Awami League, for whom he represents the Chittagong-6 constituency. Fazle narrowly defeated his cousin, Salauddin's younger brother Giasuddin Quader Chowdhury, in the 2008 elections. Their relations and dealings are not always a picture of family unity, nor of strict party loyalty. Before the 2008 elections, it was suggested that Salauddin was favouring cousin Fazle over his younger brother because, owing to his recent fall from grace, Salauddin 'needed' Fazle with the ascendency of the League.[7]

On the morning of 1 October 2013, Salauddin did not seem worried. As he sat in the dock of the ICT, his family a few metres away, he joked and laughed with journalists with garrulous bravado. He was the personification of untouchable confidence, a strange mix of charm and intimidation—traits that are often a magnetic projection of the kind of impunity that comes from underworld power. At around 12.30 that afternoon, with utter contumacy, he stared down the judges as they read out their sentences for his purported crimes, committed in co-ordination with his father some forty-two years before. Salauddin's defence rested on the claim that he was not in Chittagong at the time of the crimes, which he tried to prove with a university certificate and eyewitness testimonies of those he alleged he had met in Karachi in then West Pakistan in March 1971. In those terrible months in 1971, gangs had hunted down Hindus and other assorted perceived non-conformists and had tortured and killed them. The prosecution fell back on contemporary news reports that suggested that Salauddin was injured in a grenade attack by the freedom fighters, the Mukti Bahini, in Chittagong that year. Hospital records suggested he was admitted for treatment in the city for related injuries.

Prosecution witnesses complained of intimidation and of receiving death threats. One Wahidul Alam Junu died shortly after testifying against Salauddin on 12 February 2013. Junu had recounted that on the evening of 5 July 1971, he had been abducted at around 7 p.m. He claimed to have been taken by Salauddin to the family's Goods Hill residence, where he was abused and tortured in the presence of Salauddin's father. In the mortuary of the dilapidated Chittagong Medical College Hospital, where Junu's body was found ten days after he testified in court, the doctors who examined his body later told me that Junu had 'died of nothing.' The police in the city further said that Salauddin's wife had been contacted about the case, but they told me that she had not wanted to come to the police station, so they did not take the matter any further. The case of Junu was one to which few paid attention, and one of many that might forever be left unexplained, despite bizarre inconsistencies in official narratives.

Bangladesh does not have a witness protection programme as such. The ICT has seen witnesses being killed in more definitive cases. Mustafa Howlader, who testified against the crimson-bearded preacher Delwar Hossain Sayeedi, was attacked in his home in the early hours of 9 December 2013. Howlader had confirmed to the court that Sayeedi had been a member of a pro-Pakistan militia, known as a 'Peace Committee', which had looted Hindu homes and shops.[8] The authorities had assigned him some police protection, but Howlader could not afford to feed the officers meant to guard him, so they paid scant attention to his safety and left.[9] His attackers burrowed into his modest home in Pirojpur, Sayeedi's home district, and hacked him with machetes to within an inch of his life. Howlader died in hospital, and his wife who witnessed the attack sustained injuries. Another prosecution witness, Sukharanjan Bali, was seemingly turned by threat, inducement or his own conviction. When he tried to testify on behalf of Sayeedi's defence he was abducted by police. After several weeks of secret detention in Bangladesh, Bali would later show up in India.[10]

Geo-politicised Trials?

Out of all of Bangladesh's ICT verdicts, what was produced in court on paper or given in testimony regarding the 1971 war probably mattered the least in the case of Salauddin Quader Chowdhury. Salauddin used his stellar connections to try to beat the charges till the end. These allegedly extended high into the government of Prime Minister Sheikh Hasina and her incredibly wealthy private sector adviser Salman F. Rahman, who offered to act as a witness in Salauddin's trial. Such is Rahman's stature that when I met him in 2015, he freely admitted that he had been able to 'borrow' and still owed $800 million from state-owned banks. However, in the end, perhaps outweighing these connections in importance were Salauddin's long-standing connections with Pakistan. It was likely these connections, many of which he had inherited from his father, that sealed his fate.

In July 2015, Salauddin lost his appeal at Dhaka's Supreme Court over his death sentence. The authorities beefed up security as the cogs of the ICT turned towards an eventual end for the 66-year-old. It was in these months that, coincidentally or not, terror would ratchet up in Bangladesh and a bold new menace would emerge. Despite a further unorthodox appeal to allow more witnesses to testify in the case, Salauddin Quader Chowdhury was hanged at 12.55 a.m. on 22 November 2015.

Few in Dhaka doubt Salauddin's close ties to Pakistan, but his relationship with that country's powerful intelligence agency, the ISI, is hard to measure because of the very nature of the organisation. Still, respected investigative journalist David Bergman has claimed that according to 'multiple well-placed sources', 'at some point after 1975 … he became a key agent' for the ISI.[11] As Bangladeshi intelligence officials told me, 'Salauddin Quader Chowdhury had a very good relationship with the ISI [partly] because he had a shipping line.' Having worked his way into Khaleda Zia's inner circle during her last years in power, when he served as her parliamentary affairs adviser, and was also an MP in Chittagong (a post he held in six separate parliaments from 1979 onwards), he strenuously fought to impede Indian investment in Bangladesh.[12] This included blocking a potential $3 billion investment by the Indian industrial giant Tata. And so it was rumoured in Dhaka that autumn that if Prime Minister Hasina did not hang Salauddin, India would hang her.

The details of the arms haul case would only become evident once the BNP government fell at the beginning of 2007. As well as implicating members of that government, those giving evidence suggested that the funding for the arms had come from Pakistan's ISI. According to Brigadier General Abdur Rahim, he had travelled for 'several meetings with a Dubai-based gold company in connection with bringing in the arms that were seized in Chittagong.' In court the then Home Minister Lutfozzaman Babar claimed that 'ULFA and the embassy of a South Asian country bribed "higher-ups" in the former Khaleda Zia government to ensure safe passage of the consignment.'[13]

Suggestions of involvement of a foreign intelligence agency in the arms haul, however, were hinted at by *Jane's Intelligence Review* as early as August 2004, when it noted that, 'According to JIR sources, the purchases were financed by a foreign intelligence service seeking to destabilise India's northeast, and payment for the original shipment was made by the NSCN-IM to an agent in Hong Kong.'[14] ULFA, for their part, 'made no secret of the fact that Pakistan supported ULFA and encouraged him [Barua] and his comrades to step up their activities in Assam,' according to veteran journalist and writer Bertil Lintner, who met ULFA leader Paresh Barua several times, both at a safe house in Dhaka and in Bangkok, Thailand.[15]

The Struggle over Kashmir

Pakistan has something of a myopic focus on the Kashmir region that lies on the border it shares with India. The country, as one former senior Pakistani official described it, does not have a foreign policy; it simply has a policy towards India. The restive northwestern Indian state of Jammu and Kashmir is majority Muslim by some margin and borders the Pakistani territories of Azad Kashmir and Gilgit-Baltistan.

After India's independence, the Hindu maharaja of the princely state of Jammu and Kashmir, Hari Singh, stalled in his decision over which of the two new nations the state should join. Most probably, he wanted to maintain the state's independence. In the First Kashmir War, citizens of the Poonch district rebelled to pressure the maharaja to accede to Muslim Pakistan, and tribesmen from the North-West Frontier Province and elsewhere in Pakistan poured into the province in autumn 1947 with a small contingent of uniformed troops. Singh summoned help from New Delhi, which was delivered on the condition that the maharaja join India. India initially seemed prepared to offer the people of Jammu and Kashmir a plebiscite on their future when order had been restored, if Pakistan withdrew its forces and non-state actors, including tribesmen or *lashkars*, from the region. As soon as Singh had agreed and signed the Instrument of Accession, Indian troops arrived in the capital of the state, Srinagar, and fought the Pakistanis out of most of the province. A sliver of territory to the west, known as Azad Kashmir or 'Free Kashmir', and one to the north, Gilgit-Baltistan, stayed in Pakistani hands, where they have remained till today.

Kashmir never had the plebiscite it was promised to decide its constitutional future. The issue of a vote was pushed down the agenda when the idea of a third option, of Kashmiri independence, gained traction. This naturally dampened Pakistani enthusiasm. To this day, Jammu and Kashmir is ruled in a draconian militarised fashion by India. Of particular note is India's controversial Armed Forces (Special Powers) Act, which ensures impunity for India's military personnel in 'disturbed areas' of the country despite a plethora of accusations of brutality. While Kashmir is a hotly contested issue, militarily and emotionally, it is not alone.

Pakistan and China have, since the 1950s, supported ethnic separatist groups in India's northeast region, the Seven Sisters, which sits adjacent to Bangladesh. Often this has simply been in order to split India's military by inducing greater deployments in the east that would otherwise be facing off against Pakistan in the west and checking militant infiltration into Kashmir. But this tactic also works on a deeper and longer-term level. It is an attempt to prove the fallibility of the idea of unified India, just as Bangladesh's war of independence and the country's rejection of its singularly Islamic identity asked such existential questions of Pakistan in 1971. India, meanwhile, has in turn been accused of stimulating secessionist movements in Balochistan in Pakistan, where certain groups are prone, like Bengalis were in the mid-twentieth century, to see their ethnic or cultural identity as more important than their religious one.

Pakistan as a state has always struggled with civilian rule. Instead, it has been an 'army with a country', to borrow a phrase used to describe the militaristic Prussian state of old in Europe.[16] With an army that owns a country, the idea of that country is reduced to a simplistic adversarial one. Pakistan imagines itself above all as an Islamic entity, which could and should dominate the subcontinent, as the Mughals and Delhi Sultanate had for some 800 years. The country that Pakistan's army dragged along with it did not fare well against its non-believing neighbours, however. Between 1947 and 1972, India and Pakistan fought three wars, all of which saw India prevail on the conventional battlefield. India was only restrained by Pakistan's patron states, principally China and, to an extent, the United States. Just as Pakistan's conventional military ventures against India most often failed, so too India's prominence and success in the world, economically and more broadly, started to outpace Pakistan's. From at least the 1970s, this led Pakistan's military to develop an obsession with trying to hold India back. This fixation is fed by the idea that the problems confronting Pakistan, and by extension the Muslims of South Asia, are all due to the non-believing Hindu or secular rulers of India. Thus the Pakistani state can be seen to be held together under this ethos by the military, which needs to protect its citizens or co-religionists from divisive forces.

Pakistan developed tactics of using non-state actors as far back as 1947, particularly from lessons learnt in Kashmir. However, in the 1980s, the country's planners came up with an insurance policy. They saw the need to prevent adversaries from retaliating against attacks by Pakistan's non-state actors through waging conventional war, which Pakistan would probably lose. This had been the case in 1965, when India responded to the infiltration into Kashmir by some 30,000 men under Pakistani military command, which Pakistan had hoped would induce a popular rebellion. This foray, known as Operation Gibraltar, had some early success but led India to launch a full-scale attack and occupation of sovereign Pakistani territory, which forced a settlement in 1966. The insurance mechanism against a repeat of this scenario was, of course, nuclear weapons. This allowed Pakistan the freedom to prosecute 'jihad under a nuclear umbrella', as Professor Christine Fair of Georgetown describes it.[17] Pakistan was now able to weaken its opponents through attrition-heavy insurgencies, chipping away at the enemy with minimal costs to the state and a degree of plausible deniability that the actions were theirs or conducted under official state policy.

While the Pakistani state initially supported the Jammu and Kashmir Liberation Front (JKLF), a notionally secular group whose primary goal is an independent Kashmir, in the 1980s the ISI 'requested the group stop calling for sovereignty and instead focus on self-determination.'[18] The JKLF leader rejected the request, leading the ISI to cut off funding to the movement and to adopt two new approaches to shape the insurgency: encouraging JKLF members 'to break away and form pro-Pakistani militant groups'; and building up the Kashmiri separatist terror group Hizb-ul-Mujahideen.[19] In 1989 Hizb-ul-Mujahideen was adopted as the 'military wing' of the Kashmiri wing of Jamaat-e-Islami Pakistan, which shares some of its ideology and origins with the Bangladeshi party that bears the same name. The hardening of communal identities and conflicts along religious lines in the conflict over Kashmir helped push what was often a secular movement for an independent, sovereign Kashmir towards hard-line pro-Islamist movements. This was demonstrably in the interests of the Pakistan military, given its role as the protector of what it views as a singular Muslim polity in the subcontinent. This sectarian ideology is not remarkably different in direction from that of Islamists in Bangladesh.

Entwined in this is the notion of '*Ghazwa-e-Hind*', a prophecy found in the *hadith*, a body of Islamic texts based on the sayings of the Prophet Muhammad and written down about a century after his death in 632 AD. This prophecy foretells a war between good and evil over Hind—or South Asia. It has helped foster enthusiasm for the Pakistan military's strategic objectives against India, fed by the army's own desire to maintain power and unified control over Pakistan. This ideological position is shared by groups like Lashkar-e-Taiba (LeT), for whom 'external jihad also serves the state's supreme interest: its integrity.'[20] When Ayman al-Zawahiri launched AQIS in September 2014, he made a reference to this very prophecy.

LeT provides the most glaring example of Pakistan's use of non-state actors to pursue specific foreign policy objectives, which it wraps up in this prophecy in order to curry favour in Kashmir and beyond. 'Throughout the 1990s, Pakistani official media also encouraged discussion of the Ghazwa-e-Hind Hadith to motivate jihadists. In fact, every major Pakistan-based jihadi group that launched terrorist attacks across the border claimed that their operations were part of the Battle for India promised by the Prophet,' writes Hussain Haqqani, former Pakistani ambassador to America.[21] 'For these Pakistani groups, supported by Pakistan's Inter-Services Intelligence agency, the target of jihad should be the modern state of India and its "occupation" of Kashmir.'[22]

As Christine Fair contends, 'Pakistan's interest in proxy wars may have been piqued by the training in counterinsurgency it received from the United States during the 1950s, when the two countries were formally allied against the communist threat,' well before the Soviet invasion of neighbouring Afghanistan.[23] Not unlike the insurgency in Kashmir, the Soviet–Afghan War, as we have already seen, was a major networking opportunity for jihadists from across the world, including Bangladesh. When the Soviets pulled out of Afghanistan in 1992, the ISI attempted to redirect many of these foreign fighters towards Kashmir, where, at the time, the Indians were having some success in waging a counterinsurgency and convincing the local populace of the benefits of Indian rule.[24]

America–Pakistan–China

Pakistan has been a long-term, if difficult, ally of the United States. At times this has been a relationship of utmost importance, particularly with regards to Afghanistan in the late 1980s, and then again in the early 2000s. The 11 September 2001 attacks in America forced the Pakistani state to take difficult positions towards some militant groups whom they had previously supported. Under the pressure of military retribution, Pervez Musharraf, Pakistan's then military dictator, joined the war against Al-Qaeda and the Taliban. This induced some militant groups to turn against the state and fight their jihad within Pakistan. The groups that did so were largely Deobandi movements, and did not include the Ahle Hadith-affiliated Lashkar-e-Taiba.[25] LeT has been largely uninterested in sectarian attacks against minorities within Pakistan, meaning that it has greater utility to the state as its actions are directed outwards, principally towards India. Not only does LeT prosecute Pakistan's external policies, it also undermines the militant Deobandi groups that advocate attacking within Pakistan, thereby working 'to preserve and protect not just the state but also the state's ideology.'[26] Thus, while the Deobandi groups have been tied up with interpretative issues and the religious practices of the population, LeT has been much more prepared to enforce a bigger-picture, pan-Islamist vision, more in keeping with the foundational ideology of Pakistan. Pakistan and the United States initially entered an alliance specifically to work against the Soviet threat. As was discussed earlier, this also led to a convenient tie-up for Pakistan that is only growing in importance: its enduring relationship with China. This three-way relationship grew out of a strategic alliance in the 1970s, when the Nixon administration sought to isolate the Soviet Union. However, it also stems from Pakistan's long-term antipathy towards India, which is shared by Beijing.

In the restive Seven Sisters in India's northeast, China holds a claim over much of what is today the Indian state of Arunachal Pradesh. China's stake is based on its annexation of Tibet in 1950, and the fact that Arunachal Pradesh had once been part of Tibet but had been claimed by the British as part of India with the drawing of the McMahon Line in March 1914. In 1962, a unified China under Chairman Mao, having put down a rebellion in Tibet in 1959, looked to territories that had been claimed by India. In the west this included a slice of Kashmir, and in the east, the remote mountainous region of Arunachal Pradesh.

The Chinese routed the ill-prepared Indian forces in a swift war in 1962. After making quick territorial gains in both the western and eastern theatres, the Chinese announced a ceasefire and withdrew, having pushed the Indians back to what is referred to as the 'Line of Actual Control', a few miles behind the border. However, more importantly, they had severely bruised Indian egos and asserted themselves as the dominant regional force. While the Kennedy administration was heavily distracted by their stand-off with the Soviet Union over the Cuban Missile Crisis during those weeks of October 1962, the US was broadly supportive of India in the conflict. This support, however, had limitations; the Kennedy administration turned down Indian requests for manned combat aircraft, which would have been decisive for India. India did not know that the Chinese could not wield aerial capabilities, so in fear did not deploy its own, which could have halted the Chinese army's advance through the difficult, mountainous Himalayan terrain.

In any case, the humiliation of this brief spat with China pushed India closer to the Soviet Union for military hardware and support. This relationship was sealed three years later in 1965, when war with Pakistan saw the United States cut off military aid to both rival nations. This meant that India looked to Moscow for arms, and Pakistan to Beijing. Nixon and Kissinger, meanwhile, would usher in an almost complete repudiation of usually democratic India, in line with their desire to make allies in Beijing in the 1970s.[27] Essential to this were Pakistan's generals, who became the secret bridge between Beijing and Washington. This was one of the principal reasons for the callous attitude taken by the US towards the savagery of the Bangladeshi war of independence. During this period the Nixon administration went as far as to illegally sell weapons to the Pakistanis, by routing fighter jets through Jordan for resale to Pakistan for subsequent use in the conflict with India in 1971.[28]

Regional Rivalries, Local Clients

Since the nation's birth, there has been a partisan division in Bangladeshi foreign policy orientation and allegiances, which has been maintained ever since. Bangladesh's military dictators, who ruled after the assassination of Sheikh Mujib till 1991, overwhelmingly looked to the United States and Pakistan. This coincided with the uptick of madrassa education and the spread of Saudi-inspired Wahhabism. As Saudi Arabia's heir apparent and Crown Prince Mohammad Bin Salman has claimed, 'investments in mosques and madrassas overseas were rooted in the Cold War, when allies asked Saudi Arabia to use its resources to prevent inroads in Muslim countries by the Soviet Union.'[29]

Indeed, the initial independent government, which had been created with Indian help, had looked to the Soviets and to New Delhi because of staunch opposition from Beijing and Washington over what they saw as Indian expansionism. The advent of democracy in

1991 meant that both of Bangladesh's civilian political parties would seek, and receive, patronage from either Delhi or Islamabad. This began immediately and a sum, believed to have been in the region of 50 million Pakistani rupees, of ISI money helped Khaleda Zia to win the 1991 elections.[30] Similarly, India provided financial support; in the words of *The Economist*, 'bags of Indian cash and advice' helped the Awami League prevail in the 2008 elections.[31]

The events of 2004 and earlier—including another smaller arms haul in 2003 in the town of Bogra, when an unattended truck full of explosives and bullets was discovered by accident—drove Indian imperatives to new heights. Not only was the BNP–Jamaat government an ideological enemy, but it was seen as a direct threat to India's national security and the fragile integrity of its northeastern states. According to Deb Mukharji, who served as the Indian high commissioner to Bangladesh between 1995 and 2000 (under both BNP and Awami League governments):

> From my judgement, she [Khaleda Zia] is very, very deeply anti-Indian, and I think this comes from a deeply communal mind-set. I think she is anti-Hindu. She considers India to be Hindu and therefore dislikes India. I'm afraid that is my conclusion; her approach to India is not that of a rational leader.

While Delhi tends barely to notice Bangladesh, when it does so, it often views Bangladesh, rather condescendingly, as a weak, impoverished backwater and source of instability. But the reality appears very different nowadays. Bangladesh often sees itself as the plucky smaller neighbour, which has to show guile and at times belligerence to survive subjugation by India. As Salauddin Quader Chowdhury's lawyer Fakhrul Islam had it, the success of the country allegedly shows up a supposed fallacy or weakness of a unified India.

This is not an altogether far-fetched theory. For many on the political right in Bangladesh, sovereignty and success run counter to India's dominance of the region. Not only has Bangladesh leapfrogged India in many, if not most, human development indicators, the country has also prospered by inviting India's rivals into its backyard.[32] While China is a traditional ally of Pakistan, and thus by extension, in theory and historically, of BNP governments in Dhaka, Beijing has increasingly looked to do business with whoever is in power in Dhaka. With China's growing prominence, its $900 billion Belt and Road Initiative (BRI), and Sheikh Hasina's longer-than-usual tenure in office, there has been an extraordinary strengthening of bilateral ties between the Awami League-led government and Beijing.

China's President Xi Jinping visited Dhaka in October 2016 and brought with him an unbeatable $24.5 billion worth of 'bilateral assistance' to be spent on some two dozen projects and programmes in Bangladesh as part of the BRI. Some Western diplomats have since bemoaned that simply no one can compete. Hasina's government, for its part, has taken to mimicking the rhetoric of its Pakistani adversaries in describing China as an 'all-weather friend of Bangladesh.'[33] This wilfully purges the memory of China's position towards Hasina's father Sheikh Mujib, and what official Chinese state press called his 'puppet countenance'.[34] Today these opinions could not be expressed in Bangladesh under the country's Digital Security Act 2016, which proscribes '"carrying out propaganda" against or spreading false information about the War of Independence or Sheikh Mujibur Rahman. This could be punished by life imprisonment, a fine of up to 10 million taka (US$127,000), or both.'[35] A precursor of this law was used to harass critics of religion and atheist bloggers, most prominently in 2013, when four bloggers were imprisoned after several lists of purported blasphemers were submitted to the government by Islamist groups. Amongst them was Asif Mohiuddin, who was almost killed by assassins' machetes shortly before his detention.

Bangladesh expects its nominal GDP to overtake Pakistan's by 2020. As it has with India, Bangladesh has also surpassed its erstwhile overlords in most development indices and has witnessed far more robust and stable GDP growth rates over the last two decades.[36] Thus, an attitude of condescension from India and its attempts to dominate the region have been driving forces for a spiky Bangladeshi nationalism, tinged with communalism and the need to assert sovereignty.

China's new-found fondness for Bangladesh under the Awami League has not been transmitted to Pakistan. Just as India saw the dominance of the Awami League as an absolute priority in Dhaka, to ward off a government prepared to smuggle trucks full of arms to secessionist rebels, noises out of Islamabad have been overwhelmingly negative towards the League.

Almost immediately after Salauddin Quader Chowdhury was hanged in November 2015, Pakistan's Foreign Office released a statement reacting to the execution with 'anguish'.[37] Salauddin's son Hummam Chowdhury said at the funeral that his father was a 'tiger' who would not bow down to anyone and that the people would not accept the execution, which he decried as a 'murder'.[38] The funeral was well attended and was presided over by a prominent local cleric, Hefazat-e-Islam's secretary general, Junaid Babunagari. Babunagari had once threatened to cut one of the Shahbag organisers 'with a sword into a hundred pieces' if the protesters came to Chittagong.[39]

Babunagari's threat not only chimed with at least one student from a Hefazat madrassa, who attacked the blogger Washikur Rahman, but also reflects politics in a city the American embassy described as comprising 'some of the most violent areas in the country'.[40] In keeping with this tradition of political violence, it is here that we have seen some of the most tangible connections between violent Islamist militancy and politics.

Numerous BNP members were found to have been funding a little-known militant group called the Shaheed Hamza Brigade, which was formed in 2013. Among them was a businessman and local BNP politician Manzur-e-Elahi. Bangladesh's elite anti-terrorism police unit, Rapid Action Battalion (RAB), alleged that Manzur had transferred about half a million taka to the group and its leader, former Jamaat student wing member Moniruzzaman Masud, alias Don. Also arrested in connection with the Shaheed Hamza Brigade was a barrister named Shakila Farzana, the daughter of another BNP leader from Chittagong named Syed Wahidul Alam. An old comrade of Salauddin Quader Chowdhury's, Alam was alleged to have taken part in the murder and torture of Hindus in the city back in 1971, as part of the Al-Shams Brigade, a pro-Pakistan militia that emanated from the Muslim League Party, in which Salauddin's father had been a prominent member. Alam had been a parliamentary whip for the BNP in the 2001–6 parliament and served as the MP for Chittagong-5, which covers Hathazari, the neighbourhood just north of the city where Ahmad Shafi's Hefazat madrassa is located. Farzana is a UK-trained lawyer and part of a pro-BNP group of lawyers in the city. In April 2015, the RAB made a series of raids in the city connected with the Shaheed Hamza Brigade, in which they uncovered arms and ammunition purportedly belonging to the group. These included AK-22 semi-automatic weapons, cheap knock-offs of the more famous (and powerful) AK-47. They believed the weapons had entered the country from India. Farzana and another lawyer were alleged to have deposited around 10 million taka in a bank account associated with the group, and were arrested in August of the same year.[41] Twelve of the suspected members of the Brigade were detained from a madrassa in Hathazari.

The Shaheed Hamza Brigade episode is a rare case in which we gain a possible picture of the organisation of a conspiracy, and how money and patronage flow down from the associates and comrades of an internationally connected 'godfather', as Salauddin was known, to extremist, foot-soldier cadres. Crucially, it demonstrates the impact and transmission of regional geo-politics. At the top are people like Salauddin, who had supposed links to the ISI and who along with his associates sought to enforce policy via extremist auxiliary groups. These people are able to operate with a greater degree of plausible deniability in their constituencies but enjoy tight relations with religious institutions and those with a firm grip on politics and financial muscle.

Prosecuting Regional Cold War

However, 2015 would produce more tantalising evidence of direct, sensational Pakistani collusion in Bangladesh's extremist landscape. In February that year, Bangladesh managed to 'out' an alleged ISI agent at Pakistan's High Commission in Dhaka. Mohammad Mazhar Khan, officially a visa clerk, was withdrawn and sent home. It was alleged that Khan had been involved in forging currency and funnelling funds to Ansarullah Bangla Team, Hizb-ut-Tahrir and Jamaat.[42]

India has alleged that Pakistan's ISI runs a counterfeiting operation, where it produces fake Indian rupees in the Middle East and Pakistan and pumps them into India via Bangladesh.[43] Fake Indian notes were seized at the port in Chittagong as well as from passengers arriving in Dhaka and Chittagong by plane. On 20 September 2015, customs officials discovered almost 30 million fake Indian rupees in 500-rupee notes, hidden in Chittagong port in concealed sections of a shipping container that had been sent from the United Arab Emirates by a Bangladeshi expatriate, originally from the Hathazari area of Chittagong. Of those arrested was Asad Ullah, the son of another war crimes convict, Mobarak Hossain.[44] Two days later, yet more fake Indian rupees were discovered at Dhaka's international airport on a passenger arriving from Dubai.[45]

The ISI's use of counterfeiting as both a means of funding terrorist activity and of waging economic warfare against India was confirmed by David Headley, who was convicted for involvement in the 2008 Mumbai terror attack, committed by Lashkar-e-Taiba. In fact, Headley is not the only LeT cadre to have been discovered with fake notes. Syed Abdul Karim, alias Tunda, the Indian-origin LeT leader who was arrested in 2013, allegedly used a network of Bangladeshi migrants to smuggle counterfeit rupees printed by the ISI into India.[46] India's abrupt decision in November 2016 to decommission large-denomination bank notes, namely 500- and 1000-rupee notes, was seen, at least in part, as a way of fighting back against this scourge.[47] The Nazis had used a similar tactic, counterfeiting fake pounds and dollars during the Second World War to undermine Allied economies.

By the end of 2015, the Pakistan High Commission in Dhaka was making more headlines. When police arrested four suspected Jamaat-ul-Mujahideen Bangladesh members, they found that at least one of them, Idris Sheikh, a dual citizen of Bangladesh and Pakistan, had had dealings with a second secretary at the Pakistan High Commission. Sheikh claimed that in 2012 he had been given a special phone with which to communicate with a handler. In a confession in December 2015, he named the handler as an official at the Pakistan High Commission, Fareena Arshad. The second secretary had allegedly given Sheikh money when they met.[48] Sheikh had returned to Bangladesh from Pakistan in 2007, lived there for several years and had a family. Bangladeshi authorities alleged that prior to his arrest, he had made regular visits to Pakistan.

Thus, in the words of senior Bangladeshi intelligence officials I interviewed in early 2017, 'It is obvious they [Pakistan] are trying to bring down the [Awami League] government—they'd be very happy if that happened. They always try to have a friendly government here.'

6

THE ROHINGYA

In November 2016, across golden paddy fields, dispossessed citizens of neighbouring Myanmar poured into Bangladesh. Bangladesh's border guards were reportedly under orders to 'seal' the border, but no border guards were evident as I stood watching desperate Rohingya Muslims run through the first fields of Bangladesh, before melting into the countryside near the Leda refugee camp, not far from the town of Teknaf. Refugees in the fishing village of Shamlapur later described how their home villages in northern Rakhine State in western Myanmar had been attacked by military helicopters, as well as by ground forces from Myanmar's military, known as the Tatmadaw. The soldiers had been assisted by civilian auxiliaries from the local Buddhist community—amidst the harrowing tales that the refugees shared, it seemed a particularly pernicious note to the tales of utter dread. Many of these attacks were assisted, or indeed carried out, by people who had only days before been friends, neighbours or colleagues. The Buddhist population in Myanmar has periodically turned against the Muslim minority with whom they have shared this strip of coastal land for hundreds of years, but since 2012, things have turned particularly vicious.

That year on 1 April, in the rural constituency of Kawhmu, Myanmar's Nobel Peace Prize Laureate democracy campaigner won a seat in the country's parliament in a by-election. Naive hope had rippled out that spring from Aung San Suu Kyi's dusty delta constituency as her victory neared. Thousands, including journalists such as myself, lined the usually quiet rural road into the town. This had encouraged a Western halo to be placed around the country and its emerging economy. Western capital and its cheerleaders rushed in. The country's once struggling hotels were packed. Mobile phones emerged on the market for a population long starved of information technology. Foreign brands set up shop to sell the impoverished population branded dreams and shiny new products.

Less than six weeks after Suu Kyi's electoral victory, a young Rakhine Buddhist seamstress was returning home after work when she was raped and killed. Local authorities alleged that the perpetrators were Muslim Rohingya. This incident led to vicious pogroms, killings and sexual assaults. It was as if a dark cloud had very swiftly descended to tarnish the hope that a veneer of democracy had produced. At the time, an activist from the Chin ethnic group wearily (and prophetically, as it turned out) lamented to me that it looked like, 'we might go back to the dark age before we have even stepped into the path of light.'[1]

Soon, Rohingya populations in the state capital Sittwe and elsewhere were burned out of house and home and corralled into ghettos.[2] An apartheid-like situation dawned, as access to formal services such as schooling had a religious and ethnic wedge inserted into them. The issue of the Rohingya population's citizenship and belonging suddenly became a pressing issue. For mainstream opinion in Myanmar, the minority were seen as interlopers—illegal immigrants who had entered from Bangladesh, either with the British colonisers or subsequently. It was not just traditionally chauvinistic nationalists who were suddenly up in arms about the Muslim minority on the fringes of the country. U Win Tin, an ally of Suu Kyi's, had campaigned for democracy and human rights and spent almost two decades behind bars in horrible conditions. Indicative of Myanmar's paradigm, he told me in our last conversation before he passed away that the Rohingya minority should not, as many had suggested, be pushed out to sea—yet he called for their DNA to be tested to clarify their 'true belonging.'

The Demonisation of the Rohingya

It was after the horrific events of 2012 that a Rohingya insurgent group supposedly started mustering among Rohingya in exile and in northern Rakhine State. The group was initially known as Harakah al-Yaqin, Arabic for 'Faith Movement'. Its existence, activities and nature have been clouded by opacity. This draws attention to a number of salient points about the Rohingya, a group often associated with Islamist insurrection in Bangladesh even if it is virtually impossible not only to find any acts of terror they have committed in the country per se, but also to ascertain whether Rohingya groups have had any connections to transnational jihadist groups.

However, since George W. Bush's declaration of a so-called 'War on Terror' after the 9/11 attacks on New York and Washington D.C., the Myanmar regime seemed determined to try to convey apparent connections between Rohingya groups and the transnational jihadist groups that were suddenly in the headlines and in the sights of Western military planners. With perhaps no coincidence, the day before Congress in Washington, D.C. voted to grant the president the power to attack Iraq to remove Saddam Hussein from power and eradicate his imaginary 'weapons of mass destruction', Myanmar shared rare 'intelligence' with the American embassy in Yangon, which in most probability had the same providence as Western intelligence on Iraqi weapons. This was strange, because at the time Myanmar's regime, and specifically its ruling military, was under strict sanctions from the Americans. There was little to no official communication between the two on matters such as these. However, the Burmese intelligence agencies, then under the wily Khin Nyunt, a mercurial politician-cum-general, told their jittery American adversaries about how an organisation called the Arakan Rohingya National Organisation (ARNO) had met and trained with Osama Bin Laden, then the most wanted man in the world. The Myanmar intelligence claimed that, 'Ninety members of ARNO were selected to attend a guerrilla warfare course, a variety of explosives courses and heavy-weapons courses held in Libya and Afghanistan in August 2001. Thirteen out of these selected members participated in the explosives and heavy-weapons training.'[3] It further added that around the time of the

9/11 attacks, members of the Taliban had visited Rohingya groups in southern Bangladesh.

The ARNO at this point was likely a rag-tag group of aspirant organisations, some of which had perhaps a limited stock of arms. According to the Burmese intelligence report, under pressure in Bangladesh, they wanted to emulate the handful of ethnic armed groups who tended to take shelter on the Thai–Myanmar border. These other ethnic groups, some of whom ARNO met, according to the cable, waged secessionist struggles against Myanmar's military, and engaged in smuggling and generally advocating for greater self-determination for the non-Bamar (Myanmar's majority ethnic group) peoples who inhabit Myanmar's hinterlands. The ARNO were in Bangladesh and lacked the connections that helped many of those other groups tick. The Myanmar intelligence alleged that an ARNO leader had travelled to Thailand in August 2002. The Americans suspected that this intelligence was provided not only to draw questions about the Rohingya groups, but also of the groups ARNO members had supposedly met in Thailand.

Soon after the Americans received the intelligence, some ARNO members named in the cable were rounded up by the Bangladeshis. I tracked down one of those named, Salim Ullah, in 2011, after he had been released from a Bangladeshi jail and was living in exile in Chittagong. To all intents and purposes, he was leading an unarmed and largely limited campaign for rights for the Rohingya. It was ineffective in that even by 2011, the UN Refugee Agency (UNHCR) were describing the conditions of Rohingya refugees in Bangladesh as a 'protracted emergency'. At that point, there were 200,000 Rohingya in Bangladesh, and around a million living peacefully as second-class, stateless residents of the impoverished backwaters of northern Rakhine State, in a condition that the American embassy in Yangon described in 2006 as a 'vast internment camp', where the population had an infant mortality rate four times Myanmar's national average.[4]

Things would deteriorate rapidly from that grim state, as Myanmar supposedly democratised over the next decade. As far as I could tell, the demonisation of the Rohingya and associating them with violent extremism became a greater priority for Myanmar's military intelligence as this process took root. While the deliberate characterisation of Rohingya groups as extremists and radicalised fifth-columnists worked, at least in othering the population in the eyes of the Myanmar public, in many ways it also serves as a drastic example of how extremism and religious tension are used in and around Bangladesh's hinterlands. In many ways, just as Pakistan and Bangladeshi politicians seemed to be using and supplying ethnic armed groups in northeast India to commit foreign policy goals, so too has Myanmar characterised and painted the Rohingya as Islamist extremists to maintain control in an era of flux. A major question, however, was the possibility that such a characterisation would end up being a self-fulfilling prophecy. Would the abject treatment received by the Rohingya on the basis of their assumed otherness and fifth column predilections actually elicit real radical extremism?

From 2012 to 2017, Rohingya civilians were treated abominably, facing worsening isolation and repression. The state became effectively apartheid-like: Rohingya were separated in schools and prevented from travelling to receive medical treatment, conduct business or visit relatives. They were restricted from marrying and worshipping. They were harassed to register as Bengalis in a national verification process, which included option to 'verify' as a Rohingya, the identity that the group chooses for itself. While the international community looked on at the dreadful manner in which the Rohingya were treated prior to 2012, the situation became drastically worse in 2012 and thereafter. By 2014, international NGOs such as the UN, MSF and the Red Cross who provided basic services to the Rohingya pulled out after they were attacked, threatened, harassed and criticised for giving aid and voicing concern about how the group was being treated.[5]

ARSA

During this period, according to the International Crisis Group the Harakah al-Yaqin group was running around committing very low-level insurgency activities.[6] Between their probable formation in 2012–13 and August 2017, Harakah al-Yaqin's attacks killed fewer than fifty members of Myanmar's security forces altogether. Meanwhile, in the first half of 2016 alone, a non-state armed group from the very same state, the 'Arakan Army, an insurgency fighting for ethnic Rakhine rights, killed at least 300 soldiers' from the Myanmar military.[7] In 2017, Harakah al-Yaqin became the more secular-sounding Arakan Rohingya Salvation Army (ARSA) and carried out its most prominent series of attacks at the end of August that year. The attack on thirty police outposts killed twelve policemen and an immigration official, and would result in vicious pogroms against civilian populations and see the exodus of the majority of the Rohingya from Myanmar.

If evidence were needed that the Rohingya were being treated with exceptional harshness and brutality, 2017 would provide it in abundance. Myanmar soldiers and paramilitary auxiliaries openly disclosed to journalists how they had partaken in massacres in September 2017, digging mass graves in Rakhine State villages such as Inn Dinn, resulting in the complete clearance and exodus of Rohingya from the area.[8] In many of these incidents, Buddhist Rakhines had taken part in the atrocities, but more significantly the population of Myanmar as a whole had seemingly stood behind the Myanmar military. Not only had they supported the Tatmadaw's actions against the supposed Rohingya terrorists, they had also joined the military in rebuking international condemnation of the massacres. For while Myanmar had seemingly 'transitioned to democracy', as was repeated ad nauseum for some years, the military had retained crucial ministries and its grip on power. In some ways, it had increased in influence after the 2015 elections, which saw Suu Kyi and her National League for Democracy (NLD) party take power.

For a start, the Tatmadaw was in control of the defence ministry, the home ministry and the border ministry by virtue of the 2008 constitution, which was passed into law by Myanmar's military in an extremely farcical referendum. This document also guaranteed that 25 per cent of parliamentary seats went to the military. To change the constitution, more than 75 per cent of parliamentary votes were needed. From 2010 to 2015, after the end of military dictatorship, the country had been led by a military proxy party named the Union Solidarity and Development Party (USDP)—which had promulgated an economic liberalisation that saw military cronies and companies gifted productive state assets in phoney privatisation drives—meaning that the Tatmadaw, at least at that stage, trusted the newly civilian government. Once the supposedly liberal NLD took over, the military doubled down and re-established control over institutions such as the police and other crucial levers of power. In other words, the more formal the civilian administration appeared on the surface, the more the military fought back for control. As ever, the Tatmadaw proved adept at fomenting ethnic tensions to assure its own supremacy.

Whereas the Myanmar public had always seemed to unanimously resist the Tatmadaw's authoritarianism and brutality throughout the long years of junta rule, with hatred of the Tatmadaw uniting otherwise disparate segments of the population, the Rohingya issue was cunningly used by the Tatmadaw as a classic divide-and-rule tactic in order to redirect resentment toward the spectre of a perceived common enemy. Starting in 2012, the Tatmadaw-backed USDP party would need to fight in elections against the overwhelmingly popular NLD. Therefore, demonisation of the Rohingya became an easy way for the Tatmadaw to increase public support for ethnic nationalism and the military's essential place in governance, and to convince the electorate of the need to support militarism against the perceived threat of Islamic terrorism.

The NLD were backed into a corner, unable to denounce the violence or stand on a platform of human rights for the Rohingya with public opinion mobilised against them. Yet, it turned out that the NLD had few Rohingya sympathies to hide from the public in the first place. International observers who had long admired the resolve of Myanmar's people in the face of the dictatorship were shocked to see supposed human rights and democracy activists stand united with chauvinistic ethnic nationalists in support of the 'clearance operations' against the Rohingya.

Years before the emergence of ARSA or Harakah al-Yaqin, scholar Dr Kyaw Yin Hlaing recounted in an American legal journal how:

> Before former intelligence chief General Khin Nyunt was dismissed and his intelligence agency disbanded, the junta could almost always uncover opposition groups that were planning to organise protests. In 1997, for instance, the junta became aware of monks' plans to protest a regional commander's improper renovation of a famous Buddha statue in Mandalay. Before the monks could launch the protest, a rumour emerged that a Buddhist woman had been raped by a Muslim businessman. The government diverted their attention from the regional commander to the Muslim businessman, eventually causing an anti-Muslim riot.

He concluded that, 'intelligence agents have often instigated anti-Muslim riots in order to prevent angry monks from engaging in anti-government activities.'[9]

As far back as 2003, the American embassy corroborated this, noting that, 'We frequently hear stories of pro-SPDC "fake monks" allegedly inciting violence against Muslims to deflect anti-regime ire,' and similarly that they were training paramilitary militia in Rakhine to put down uprisings.[10] In other words, the military long used religious and ethnic tensions to maintain control across Myanmar, and in particular in Rakhine State. Moreover, it has a long track record of actively fabricating spark incidents to further its aims.

ARSA's Disappearance

By the spring of 2018, with the majority of Rohingya chased out of Rakhine, ARSA seemingly disappeared. The group's Twitter account went quiet and its once vocal and charismatic leader, Ata Ullah, had, at the time of writing, similarly vanished.

There are several possible reasons for this. It could well be that with virtually the entire Rohingya population removed from Rakhine State, the militants simply lacked the infrastructure in which they had previously operated: the Rohingya villages and their communities in the north of the state. It might also be that once the Rohingya had crossed the border and entered Bangladesh, the security forces there were able to instantly shut down this group, which had previously been able to muster hundreds of men and posed in videos with automatic weapons. Among the refugee populations, there is undoubtedly some support for any group campaigning on behalf of the Rohingya. At the same time, there are also many who resented ARSA, seeing its actions as exacerbating the Rohingya's suffering.

Meanwhile, it is important to note that this area of southern Bangladesh is relatively lawless. From the Myanmar side of the border, a vast tide of methamphetamine flows. If the growth of this industry is anything to go by, there is a flourishing underworld. In 2006, Bangladesh authorities seized 1,670 methamphetamine pills, known as *yaba*. By 2017, that number had risen to an astonishing 40 million pieces interdicted.[11] The Bangladesh authorities have taken a range of positions, from expressing frustration that the authorities on the Myanmar side of the border have shown indifference to the flow of narcotics, to openly suggesting that the Myanmar military has involvement in the smuggling.[12]

In a similar vein, senior members of Bangladesh's Directorate General of Forces Intelligence (DGFI) suggested that ARSA was somehow a creation of the Myanmar government. Awami League MP Abdur Rahman Bodi echoed this suggestion when I met him. Conversely, Zaw Htay, the spokesperson for Aung San Suu Kyi, claimed in May 2018 that 'Bangladesh is unwittingly allowing extremists to rear its [sic] ugly head in this part of the region. ARSA is already having a foothold in the camps, soon will become a stronghold of terrorism!'[13]

It could well be that ARSA finds it impossible to operate in Bangladesh without some sort of patronage. The Rakhine insurgent group, the Arakan Army, is almost certainly involved in the *yaba* trade and has links to groups in Bangladesh's Chittagong Hill Tracts, where it has a limited presence. It could well be that Bangladesh's security services were able to clamp down on ARSA in the camps, despite their vast size and chaotic nature. Crowded Bangladesh is not an easy place to hide out without patronage or support of local power brokers. Despite many attempts, ARSA's attacks seemed to lack equipment, training and coordination.

The human tragedy has been responded to by Al-Qaeda in the Indian Subcontinent (AQIS), who called for Muslims to join some sort of jihad against Myanmar. ARSA's leader, a man named Ata Ullah, grew up in Karachi, Pakistan and studied in Saudi Arabia, and is supposed to have met AQIS through the Harkat-ul-Mujahideen networks in Pakistan.[14] However, if these connections did exist, they have been remarkably ineffective. The ARSA attacks have been poorly equipped to say the least, though reports from groups such as the International Crisis Group have reproduced Myanmar government propaganda about Pakistani nationals in Rakhine State, and of Ata Ullah having been trained in 'modern guerrilla warfare.'[15] This seems to be clutching at straws provided by Myanmar intelligence. If foreign fighters or AQIS cadres were joining a fight in Myanmar, one would imagine that the insurgency would be more effective and/or that Myanmar would be able to provide evidence of this happening. They have not. This is probably not surprising. Jihadist groups gain much mileage from high-profile incidents of Muslims suffering, but have little to gain from supporting the futile struggle of a desperately poor population. Meanwhile, the huge influx of refugees prompted a greater security presence along the border with Myanmar.

The Rohingya Crisis' Impact on Bangladesh

The Awami League government in Dhaka had been jittery about Rohingya militancy in Myanmar in the years leading up to 2017's vast exodus. The government saw it as a potential nuisance, and seemed suspicious of those wanting to work with the group. Sheikh Hasina personally stated in 2012 that the Rohingya issue 'is not our responsibility.'[16] They were especially wary of international Islamic charities, and banned Muslim Aid and Islamic Relief among others, because they were believed to 'encourage radicalism and provide funds to militants, and we cannot let them do so with Rohingyas.'[17]

However, once the magnitude of the exodus became apparent, Muslims and non-Muslims both inside and outside Bangladesh were horrified by the human suffering, Islamist organisations not least among them. Meeting the very first waves of refugees in 2017 were members of the large Deobandi missionary organisation Tablighi Jamaat. Very quickly, they were followed by groups such as Hefazat-e-Islam, who rushed in to camps to provide services such as madrassas for the refugee population. It appeared that Bangladesh's central government was not only allowing these domestic Islamist non-state actors to provide services, with little oversight, to a population whose conditions—by the government's own admission—made them vulnerable to radicalisation, but it was also winning plaudits from groups like Hefazat. Mufti Fayez Ullah, a general secretary of the group, was full of praise for the Awami League when we met at his old Dhaka madrassa in May 2018. MP Bodi, from the Teknaf area on the border, corroborated this approving relationship when he told me in April 2018 that he had no concerns about Hefazat operating in the area—partly he said, beaming, because the madrassa network 'love me.' At the same time, while Hasina had baulked at allowing refugees into Bangladesh in 2012, in 2017 her party was actively hailing her as the 'mother of humanity' on posters near the camps.

The Chittagong littoral which protrudes like a leg in Bangladesh's southeast is, on the whole, not a natural bastion of the Awami League. It is socially conservative, and its vote was split in the 2008 elections, which the League won handsomely overall. Chittagong returned Jamaat-e-Islami's only two parliamentary seats in 2008. There was a belt of rural constituencies from Chittagong, down to that of MP Bodi, which is the furthest south in all Bangladesh, which went to the BNP. Bodi, meanwhile, is not an ideological natural fit for the League. He is a local operator, a man who appeals to pan-Islamic identity as he would to any other ideological driver. When he returned from a spell in jail in November 2016, I happened to be departing the airport shortly before his arrival back at Cox's Bazar. Awaiting him were celebratory crowds, mainly of men, dressed in their finest Arab-style costumes to receive the returning MP. His party machine had paid for triumphal arch after triumphal arch from the airport, right down to his constituency and fief in the Ukhia-Teknaf area, a crucial Wild West spit of land. It is wedged between the Naf river and Myanmar to the east and the Bay of Bengal to the west.

The League's stance on the Rohingya requires striking a delicate balance locally as well: the rural Cox's Bazar district has borne the brunt of the impact of the crisis, with local markets, forests and livelihoods significantly disrupted by the sudden influx of 700,000 new refugees. The League must be careful not to appear to be granting too many opportunities and allowing aid to the refugee population while the local electorate remains poor and disenfranchised. Controlling this area in many ways necessitates working with acquiescent Islamists or acquiescent smugglers, especially if they can control independently minded rebel groups like ARSA, or the disquiet of an impoverished population.

Hop over the Naf river into Myanmar and things do not look very different: the Buddhist Rakhine community is impoverished, conservative and vengeful towards centralised power. They have long clamoured for greater regional autonomy from the government over the Arakan Yoma mountain range, which made it easier to travel to Chittagong than to Yangon for centuries. Allowing access, succour and power in both provinces to religious chauvinists is therefore crucial. These are the identity ties that prosper on the frontiers of these national cultures. It is often only this religious identity that marginal groups such as the Rohingya have been able to hang on to.

In other words, just as in Myanmar, government policy in Bangladesh had coalesced around the pulpit. Not only this, but both countries were able to appropriate the Rohingya issue—one steeped in religion and identity politics—to project the ire of the religious right outwards towards their neighbour. Both countries found that inciting popular religious enmities served to deflect public anger outwards, and away from government.

7

THE BLACK FLAGS

Sometime in 2013 or 2014, a group calling itself Junud al-Tawheed wal-Khilafa emerged in Bangladesh. As Bangladeshi counter terror chief Monirul Islam told me, JTWK 'tried to bring all groups into a common platform to declare jihad against non-Muslims in Bangladesh, but that attempt failed to recruit members from other outfits, like Harkat-ul-Jihad Bangladesh or Ansarullah Bangla Team or Hizb-ut-Tahrir.' The group was seemingly short-lived, but in October 2014 it released an amateur video on the Internet. The video declared the group's 'allegiance to Shaykh Abu Bakr Al-Baghdadi (may Allah protect him). We pledge that we will listen and obey him in all matters unless we see clear kufr [disbelief] from him for which we have proof from Allah.'[1]

The message additionally saluted Al-Qaeda leader Ayman al-Zawahiri and his citing of the *Ghazwa-e-Hind* prophecy in September of that year. It also showed off the military training of around ten fighters. Some of this amounted to the protagonists hopping rather comically in a circle, bearing pistols (real or otherwise). Some were barefoot; all were masked and dressed in haphazard black outfits. They jumped in front of a black flag, which has become well known as the symbol of the so-called Islamic State (ISIS). Abu Bakr Al-Baghdadi, born Ibrahim Awad Ibrahim al-Badri, proclaimed his 'caliphate' in June 2014, with himself as Caliph Ibrahim, far away from Bangladesh in the chaos of war-torn Iraq and Syria. Baghdadi and his group of former Al-Qaeda militants had captured Mosul, Iraq's second largest city, earlier that month.

It was this JTWK group that apparently attracted a Canadian of Bangladeshi origin who arrived in the country in October 2013. Tamim Chowdhury would go on to become a supposed mastermind of some of the worst terrorist violence in the country. According to Monirul Islam, 'The first man he met, we think, was the founder of Junud al-Tawheed wal-Khilafa, and he joined the group. That guy was called Abdus Samad,' a man arrested by police in December 2017. 'We think first he [Tamim] met some boys of Ansar al-Islam in Dhaka, [who were] well educated and English-medium background [educated at English-language schools], and they introduced him to Abdus Samad.'

Tamim Chowdhury seems emblematic of a pattern of quietly disgruntled young men who are attracted to jihadist groups such as ISIS. They are part of an angry, reactionary sub-culture. A resident of Windsor, Ontario, Tamim was an athlete for the J.L. Forster School, which he attended in the town till 2004. He graduated from the University of Windsor in spring 2011 with an honour's degree in chemistry.[2] He seems to have been a bright, quiet student.[3] After graduation he travelled to Calgary, where he became friends with a group of young Muslims, some of whom travelled to, and died, in Syria.

Baghdadi had not declared the supposed ISIS 'caliphate' when Tamim entered Bangladesh, as Bangladesh counter-terror police are keen to point out. Its precursor organisation was, however, already in existence. Baghdadi had been a leader of Al-Qaeda in Iraq, which used the name Islamic State in Iraq. This group had spread across the border into war-torn Syria, where in April 2013 Baghdadi deliberately tried to merge with or take over the Syrian Al-Qaeda franchise, Al-Nusra Front.[4] He called this entity the Islamic State of Iraq and the al-Sham (the Levant), ISIS or ISIL. This bold move inevitably led to a power struggle, which Al-Qaeda central leader Ayman al-Zawahiri was called in to mediate. Zawahiri called for the two groups, Baghdadi's Iraqi branch and Syria's Al-Nusra, to remain separate, but the ambitious Baghdadi carried on regardless.

It is unclear how or why Tamim ended up back in Bangladesh, his country of birth. He seems to have arrived on a flight from Abu Dhabi on 5 October 2013, into the political tinderbox that Bangladesh then was, but it is uncertain whether he had first travelled to Syria or Iraq. In 2012, Damian Clairmont, an acquaintance of Tamim's from the small 'Calgary circle' of jihadists, had left to fight in Syria for the Al-Qaeda-affiliated Al-Nusra.[5] Several of Tamim's friends also left around that time.

A First Strike

The first attack that was claimed by ISIS in Bangladesh occurred on 28 September 2015, almost two years after Tamim arrived in Dhaka. In many ways, this was a pivotal moment, the details and timing of which provoke more questions than answers, but are nonetheless worth examining. Cesare Tavella, fifty years old, was an Italian aid worker who had been in Dhaka since May that year. He worked for a Dutch food security NGO. After work that September afternoon, he left the American International School Dhaka at around 6 p.m. Tavella reportedly exercised frequently and used the gym at the school, which was located in Dhaka's swanky diplomatic quarter, known as Baridhara. This enclave houses embassies as well as the homes of diplomats and the very wealthy. Tavella made his way by foot on the short journey back towards his apartment in the adjoining Gulshan-2 neighbourhood. At around 6.15, a motorbike with three men on board pulled up near him on the street. Tavella was shot three times with a pistol, before the vehicle made its swift getaway. Before long, ISIS had claimed the murder on Twitter.[6] Almost as quickly, Bangladesh's government denied the presence of the group in Bangladesh. This was despite having previously claimed to have arrested an ISIS recruiter in the country in 2014.[7]

There were several noteworthy things going on at the time of the murder. On Friday, 25 September, the Australian High Commission in Dhaka had released an unusual travel warning. It had 'reliable information of a possible militant attack against Australians.'[8] Its American and British counterparts followed suit on Monday, hours before Tavella was shot. One obvious target for the Australians was that their national cricket team was due to visit the country. Only that weekend, its official security team had arrived to assess the suitability of the tour. The team left the day after Tavella was murdered and the cricketers did not tour.[9] Also cancelled was an alcohol-fuelled Antipodean expat gathering, known as the Glitter Ball.

Denial

At the time, Prime Minister Sheikh Hasina was in New York, where she was due to address the United Nations General Assembly and to attend a number of high-profile events along with world leaders including American President Barack Obama. These were the kind of events that a 'small' nation like Bangladesh is keen to make the most of, and they provide a great deal of legitimacy and prestige domestically.

Over the weekend before Tavella's murder, American officials briefed members of Hasina's entourage in New York of the threat. The warning was almost certainly gleaned through monitoring the internet by an intelligence agency for one of the 'five-eyes' countries: the USA, UK, Australia, New Zealand and Canada, which have an intelligence-sharing arrangement regarding electronic surveillance or signals intelligence. Officials are reluctant to discuss exactly where this intelligence emanated from, but it seems likely that it was from sig-int, as opposed to a more traditional form of spy-craft.

Hasina dismissed the threat and warnings out of hand, and seemed to take them personally. She was due to extol the virtues and development successes of the country at the UN, and it was her birthday on the twenty-eighth.[10] However, when she did address the assembly two days after Tavella's murder, she took the time to discuss terrorism in her speech, claiming it to be one of the two 'greatest threat[s] to sustainability of the human civilisation', the other being climate change. She added that 'Terrorists do not have any religion', and emphasised that:

> I am myself a victim of terrorism and violent extremism. My father, the Father of the Nation Bangabandhu Sheikh Mujibur Rahman, my mother Begum Fazilatunnesa Mujib, three brothers and other close relatives were brutally assassinated on 15 August 1975. I was subject to terrorist attacks nineteen times. My government, therefore, maintains a 'zero-tolerance' policy to all forms of terrorism, violent extremism and radicalisation. We are steadfast in tackling the extremists and anti-liberation forces who

continue to remain active in destroying the democratic, progressive and secular ethos of our nation.[11]

Officials suggest it was unlikely that Hasina was briefed properly by her own security agencies before dismissing the Australian warnings of the imminent threat. Thus, the overwhelming impression given by the Bangladesh government was that whoever had shot Tavella had done so not only to spoil Hasina's UN General Assembly appearances—and the domestic photo opportunity of appearing with the then world-champion Australian cricketers on her return from New York—but also to destabilise her rule and her government.

To put this knee-jerk reaction into context, with horrible timing, hours before Tavella was shot, the Bangladesh Nationalist Party held a press conference to blame the government for Australia's cricket cancellation. They singled out the leftist information minister—whose Jatiya Samajtantrik Dal party and ideological bedfellows have long warned about the problems of religious extremism in the country—saying:

> We [the BNP] agree with their [the government's] statement—there is no militancy in Bangladesh. However, several other ministers, including Information Minister Hasanul Haque Inu, have been vociferous about the presence of militancy in the country for so long that a sense of insecurity about Bangladesh has already developed among the international community.[12]

The government's initial denial of ISIS involvement in the 'isolated incident' of Tavella's killing would colour official Bangladeshi responses to the later murders claimed by ISIS. It would also induce uncertainty and a lack of trust in the accountability of subsequent investigations.

Opportunism

On 3 October, the weekend after Tavella's murder, 66-year-old Japanese national Kunio Hoshi was riding in a cycle rickshaw at around 9 a.m. near the agriculture project he worked on in the remote northern Bangladeshi district of Rangpur. On an isolated lane, a red motorbike pulled up, blocking the path of the rickshaw, which was being driven by Abdul Monaf, who regularly drove for Hoshi. Monaf testified in court that the men on board the motorcycle opened fire at Hoshi from close range, killing him instantly before driving away. ISIS quickly tweeted that, 'There will continue to be a series of on-going security operations against nationals of crusader coalition countries, they will not have safety or a livelihood in Muslim lands.'[13] The bizarre implication was that Hoshi, who it was reported was a Muslim convert, came from a country involved in the Crusades of the Middle Ages, which Christian European nations had fought against the Levant in the Middle East.[14] Japan, of course had nothing to do with the Crusades. In fact, when it was finally known at all by people in the Middle East, Japan was most often lauded for its resistance to European power or militarism. The tweet gave the distinct impression that foreigners were being targeted at random and in an opportunistic fashion, and that those attacked had only been chosen because they were the easiest targets.

Hoshi was in one of the most sedate and remote parts of Bangladesh imaginable. He reportedly lived alone, and it seems he was engaged in and had affection for the local community. These were the kind of backwaters where formal law enforcement is generally absent, and where informal networks are strong. Hoshi was probably, as a result, well known, not only because of his enthusiastic engagement with the community, but also presumably as one of the few foreigners in the area. Pictures emerged shortly after his death of him smiling, posing for a photo in a mosque with other men. Like all the others, Hoshi is wearing a white *tupi* or Muslim skullcap. Rangpur is a northern district similar to those where the Jamaat-ul-Mujahideen Bangladesh (JMB) had been successful setting up a brief, thuggish semi-state in the mid-2000s.

Tavella was likely chosen because he walked out of an emblematically foreign establishment: the American embassy's school. It seems that he was just an unlucky victim, emerging from the school gates at the wrong time, but was not otherwise pre-selected or targeted. It must be noted that the American International School, at least in 2015, did not have armed guards at its gates. Indeed, there would have been armed police several hundred metres away, at the nearby British High Commission, or perhaps even nearer, but they would not have been able to prevent determined, armed individuals from entering the school premises. Even so, Tavella's attackers waited and followed him for a little over a kilometre. They struck on a relatively quiet, poorly lit street, just before it hits a major thoroughfare. They seem to have intentionally been avoiding a major confrontation or spectacle.

When one considers attacks that have been claimed by ISIS in other parts of the world, the spectacle is often the most important element of the act. Arguably, the spectacular element here was simply the fact that the victims were foreign, which undoubtedly garners greater headlines and panic in Bangladesh than the usual JMB murders of vaguely defined, vulnerable non-conformists in rural northwest Bangladesh.

A few weeks later, on 24 October, a Shia procession in Dhaka was attacked with improvised explosives. One teenaged boy was killed. Again, ISIS claimed the attack. Bangladesh has a very small Shia population and attacks on the community are rare, especially in comparison with those on more prominent minorities, such as Hindus or Ahmadiyyas. The Shia, however, are such a small community in Bangladesh that they are not seen as serious rivals to Sunni Islam, unlike elsewhere in the world, such as Pakistan and the Middle East.

The following month, on 18 November, yet another Italian, 64-year-old Piero Parolari, another lone foreigner in a less-trodden corner of northern Bangladesh, Dinajpur, was cycling to work at around 8 a.m. Three men on a motorbike shot him with a 'silenced pistol' because he was a 'crusader', according to the claim made by ISIS.[15] Parolari, a doctor and missionary, survived. A week later, on 26 November, more Shia came under attack. Again in the north, multiple gunmen killed one victim. Again, ISIS claimed the murders.

Panic Stations: Very Bangladeshi Attacks

The attacks had an alarming effect. Security was tightened and foreigners cancelled business trips, suddenly vanishing from the streets of the Dhaka neighbourhoods they had frequented. Fears emerged about the vital garments sector, which exports primarily to Western retailers. The regularity of attacks was more consistent, and the time between attacks smaller than the concurrent attacks on bloggers, which by autumn 2015 were being claimed by AQIS, as discussed in chapter 4.

But the attacks also had a Bangladeshi hue. Bangladesh is regularly beset by terrorist attacks. Between 2000 and 2015, there were 944 terrorist attacks in the country, according to the Global Terrorism Database. In 2014, the data and survey outfit Pew found a strikingly high support for suicide bombings against civilian targets that were carried out to 'defend Islam'. Of the small sample of respondents, 47 per cent claimed that suicide bombings were justified often or some of the time—a higher rate than in the Occupied Palestinian Territories as a whole, and only surpassed by the rate of agreement in the Gaza strip.[16]

Importantly, 'the victim yield[s] for these [944] attacks [catalogued by the Global Terrorist Database] are quite low with an average of one fatality and under 7 persons wounded per attack,' notes a statistical analysis by academics from Georgetown University. By way of comparison, the study points out, Lashkar-e-Taiba attacks in India killed six people on average per attack.[17] Thus, the first wave of ISIS attacks was very much in keeping with the previous national averages since 2000.

There are several things worth mentioning here. First, if we compare attacks in Bangladesh with, say, Pakistan, the sophistication of weaponry used in Bangladesh has been basic to say the least. Even the presence of 'silenced pistols', of which ISIS had boasted, was something of an aberration in Bangladesh. Bombings, meanwhile, are commonplace in Bangladesh and decidedly weak. Politics is often conducted with shutdowns, which are enforced by the hurling of what are locally called 'cocktails' and are basically a variant of the Molotov cocktail. The only bombing to have had a high casualty rate was the grenade attack on the Awami League gathering by the Harkat-ul-Jihad al-Islami Bangladesh (HUJI-B) in 2004, which was discussed in chapter 3. The most widespread bombing campaign by far was by the JMB, when hundreds of bombs went off almost simultaneously in 2005, killing two people.

Political Nexi?

The Awami League government's early, emphatic denials of ISIS's presence in the country in 2015 cast doubts on arrests that were made following investigations into the attacks. On 10 October, plain-clothed officers detained a young man named Rasel Chowdhury in the Badda neighbourhood of Dhaka.[18] Two others were picked up around this time, and a few weeks later, Abdul Matin, the brother of a BNP leader named M. A. Quayum, was arrested. The authorities claimed that Quayum had paid for the attack and that his brother, Matin, had co-ordinated it. Quayum, a Dhaka city convenor of the BNP, later denied both these allegations in an interview with The Daily Star, saying that they were politically motivated and that the government was seeking to scapegoat him. He had left the country on 28 April that year and since then had allegedly been in Malaysia (where a good number of Bangladeshi militants and members of the political opposition have taken up residence) and Dubai, as well as spending time in London.[19]

One of the supposedly for-hire hitmen, alias Rubel, whom police alleged had been the shooter, claimed that he had been tortured to induce a confession.

Confessions are often one of the few means by which law enforcers in Bangladesh gain 'solid proof' in a case—such is the limited capacity of law enforcement. This is a huge inducement for security forces to detain suspects for long periods and, of course, to use torture to gain confessional statements. Senior intelligence officials bemoan that if law enforcers follow the letter of the law, '50 per cent of suspects walk free after much hard work.' The press, meanwhile, found that the detained youths who supposedly carried out the killing had been local 'druggies' who were associated with BNP politics in the Badda neighbourhood.[20]

The case would come to be seen as a textbook example of how the opacity of the judicial and law enforcement systems, and the probable politicisation of vital institutions of state, would produce no clear justice or reckoning. This left the impression that party politics and inter-agency rivalry had likely perverted the legal process. This was most evident in two vital law enforcement agencies contradicting one another.

Bangladesh's new anti-terror priority produced fresh avenues for competition between the black-clad RAB and the conventional police's Counter Terrorism and Transnational Crime Unit, the latter of which had been in the ascendency. In 2016, the RAB claimed that Sarwar Jahan, a militant working with Canadian Tamim Chowdhury, had been behind the killing of Tavella. The CTTU, however, was sticking to claims that Quayum and his BNP associates in the area were behind the killings. The discrepancies between accounts of the events and confessions by the alleged BNP shooters suggest that the CTTU's story was indeed a red herring, an intentional and clumsy attempt to associate members of the opposition BNP with the killings. Sarwar was, according to the RAB, an old JMB stalwart who had spent nine months in jail in 2003, before being released on bail and then disappearing. The RAB claimed to have found documents suggesting that in July 2015, Sarwar had become the *ameer*, or leader, of the group the government termed the neo-JMB.[21] In all likelihood, this relationship between Tamim and Sarwar had formed the basis of the Bangladeshi franchise of ISIS. Tamim had brought an international credibility, instilling vigour and sophistication into the group, and Sarwar's network was one of several under the umbrella grassroots JMB network. This would breathe new life into sections of the movement that had been stamped out incrementally since 2005. The message of foreign piety, dislocation and anger would in many ways be vital in sparking this revival.

Arrests were also made in connection with the Hoshi murder. Four young locals, supposedly members of the JMB, were detained and two people, including an alleged mastermind of the attack named Saddam Hossain, were killed in encounter killings with the police.[22] This method of addressing terrorism in the country would increasingly come to cloud understanding of the threat, and the basic search for justice, as many alleged militants would simply never testify or see the inside of a court house.

A History of Islamic Revivalism

While Tamim brought an international aspect with him to Bangladesh, foreign-inspired Salafi or Wahhabi political agitation is far from new in the region. Eighteenth- and nineteenth-century Bengal was a hotbed of turbulent rule by the British East India Company. By the time the Company acquired vast swathes of territory in Bengal from 1757, it was comprised, by most accounts, of a strange mix of paranoid administrators and rapacious profiteers. Their practices of continually breaking treaties for petty reasons, aloofness and aggressive profiteering followed them as they turned into a political administration, which initially maintained an uneasy rule through attempts to use the systems inherited from their Mughal forebears. However, in the 1790s the Company sought a new system whereby landholders paid it fixed revenues, inspired by a belief amongst British parliamentarians of the virtues of property rights and their rigorous maintenance, and as a way of mitigating corruption amongst Company officials.

In 1781, Haji Shariatullah was born in Faridpur district, which lies just over the vast Padma river from Dhaka. Prior to colonial rule, areas such as Faridpur were wealthy from producing and exporting some of the finest cotton cloths—in particular, muslin. Shariatullah studied Islamic jurisprudence in both Mecca and Cairo, but returned to his native Bengal in the 1820s.[23] On his return, he started a campaign to 'eliminate various traditional practices (riwaj) that contradicted the teachings of the Quran.'[24] This religious revivalism 'converged with militant resistance to Hindu zamindars' [landowners'] tyranny on the part of predominantly Muslim tenant populations.'[25] Shariatullah instructed his fellow Muslims to stop paying 'unofficial taxes for the celebration of pujas and the worship of the Hindu gods and goddesses', practices he viewed as idolatrous.[26] His preaching sparked what became known as the Faraizi movement: a symbiosis of revivalist Islam and agrarian revolt, with a tinge of communalism owing to the demographics of mostly Muslim peasants confronting largely Hindu *zamindars*.

At a similar time, in what is now West Bengal, another Islamic revivalist revolt took place under the leadership of Titu Mir. Like Shariatullah, Titu Mir had visited Mecca, but only on pilgrimage in 1821. On his return, he similarly instructed peasant followers to abstain from *shirk* (idolatry) and from paying taxes to the *zamindars*, preaching revivalist Islam inspired by the Saudi religious leader Muhammad ibn Abdul Wahhab, who had then only recently died in 1792. Titu Mir would serve as an inspiration for jihadist and nationalist causes in the subcontinent for many years after. His rebellion was loud and violent, as compared with the subtler, more ambivalent revolt of the Faraizi movement. In contrast to Titu Mir, the Faraizis 'never launched armed resistance directly against the [British] Raj. Instead they concentrated on broadening their social base and finding ways to act against any threat to their agrarian domain.'[27]

Revivalist religious movements are a recurrent feature of Bengali politics, as relevant today as then. The question arises as to the centrality, in this snapshot of history, of economic turmoil and societal change as stimulating factors in the resurgence of Islamic revivalism or radicalisation. To what extent are these factors driving forces of Islamic revivalism and agitation in other times? Similarly, the external influence of ideas and actors from the Middle East can also be seen in the reimagining of Bengali identity today. It seems evident that the British East India Company's disturbance and destruction of political and economic structures in the eighteenth and nineteenth centuries drove the hardening of sectarian identities, communal divisions, a sense of Muslim humiliation, and the search for hard-line Middle Eastern answers. These are questions that pertain to analysing contemporary Bangladeshi society and the challenges of militancy it faces today.

It may seem incongruous to compare the chaos of British colonial-constructed economic deprivation to the economic circumstances of today, given Bangladesh's growing affluence and widely applauded improvements in human development indicators. However, some of the more prominent battlegrounds for Islamist-inspired agitation would suggest that, like the changes resulting from colonial rule, economic and social change brought about by globalisation prompt anxiety and other comparable emotions. The turbulence and rapid change in Bangladesh, at least in part induced by the globalised economy, are a cause of angst and anger. This was made manifest in the 1990s when groups like the JMB attacked the facilities of rural NGOs, such as the famous Grameen Bank.

NGOs in Bangladesh have long worked to try to empower women and this simple challenge to orthodoxy is another important avenue to look at. But as well as ruffling gender roles, the introduction of new money, jobs and class aspiration also hints at the role of globalisation in driving anxieties among traditionalists. The inclusion of women in the workforce is blamed by some for the failures of modern economics or political economy in remedying poverty and inequality in Bangladesh.

In fact, since the early 1990s Bangladesh's economy and human development fortunes have improved greatly, partly because of the ready-made garments industry. While it is most commonly known in the international press for the health and safety risks faced by its largely female labour force, the foreign capital the industry earns for the country, of which small portions trickle down to its workers, have been and are transformative. In a few decades, millions of young women have migrated from rural areas, where they were often relatively unconnected and dependent on traditional agrarian existence, to peri-urban sites of industry, where they are given their own earnings. Thus, a newly empowered demographic of women, who have been handed a small though potent sliver of agency through wage work—and, of course, a class of capitalists who through guile and patronage have accrued vast wealth—have changed Bangladesh. This has, in many ways, as in other countries, pulled the elite out of the domestic cultural sphere into a more cosmopolitan, international one, in line with globalisation. This symbolism is potent in the nature of targets chosen by jihadists and in eliciting emotions that serve as powerful recruiting tools.

JMB Reloaded

The silenced pistol attacks claimed by ISIS soon stopped. Parolari's attack occurred almost a month after Matin, the co-ordinator whom the police claimed was involved in Tavella's murder, was arrested. However, the regular killings of individuals from minority or unorthodox religious groups continued, usually with the more traditional method of slaying by machete. These attacks included the 22 February murder of a senior Hindu priest, Jogeshwar Roy, aged fifty. Roy was hacked to death early in the morning by five or six assailants on the veranda of the Deviganj temple in the far northern Panchagarh district. He was conducting morning prayers when he heard a commotion and explosions close by. The attackers had run into the temple compound, fired shots and thrown improvised explosives, causing Roy to go investigate. The men ran at the priest and hacked him to death. His assistant, Gopal Chandra Roy, tried to intervene and was shot in the leg as the attackers fled.

ISIS swiftly assumed credit, claiming that as part of a 'security operation facilitated by the almighty God, soldiers of the Caliphate liquidated the priest Jogeshwar Roy, the founder and the head of the Deviganj temple that belongs to the infidel Hindus.'[28] The attack strongly resembled the ongoing killings claimed by the JMB.

The spectre of the JMB was never far during this time. On 23 February 2014, a prison van carrying three JMB members, two of whom were on death row, was travelling between Dhaka's Kashimpur jail and the northern town of Mymensingh, where the men were due to testify in court. From the Dhaka satellite town of Gazipur, the police van was trailed. In the town of Trishal, about 120 kilometres north of the capital, a small lorry blocked the van's path. From the trailing vehicle and a bevy of motorbikes, around twenty men emerged, some of whom hurled small explosives at the van. In the ensuing gunfire one policeman was killed on the spot, and the convicts were released. One of the three, Rakib Hasan, was found the next day and killed in an 'encounter' with police. The other two convicts, Salauddin, alias Salehin, and Zahidul Islam, alias Boma Mizan, disappeared and made it across the border to India.[29]

On 2 October that year, a huge explosion ripped through an unassuming rented room in the small West Bengal town of Burdwan, killing one person. When police and fire-fighters arrived on the scene, two armed women prevented them from entering the property. Investigators in the country believed that this had been a JMB bomb-making den. Those operating it were said to have been acolytes of Boma Mizan. It seems likely that Boma Mizan and his associates had resuscitated what authorities began terming the 'old JMB', which had to a large extent shifted its focus to India after Mizan and others fled there. Mizan was finally apprehended by Indian authorities in August 2018. In January of that year, he had tried to assassinate the Dalai Lama with a small explosive at the holy Buddhist site of Bodhgaya in Bihar. Mizan was a JMB cadre who actively attacked NGOs in rural Bangladesh because of their secular agenda and goals for women's empowerment.

Tamim Chowdhury, meanwhile, had moved on from the failure of JTWK to what authorities described as 'neo-JMB', which would utilise some of the more eager remnants of JMB whom Sarwar Jahan and other former members had been able to mobilise. These old cadres seemed to have had a drive to strike the iron hardest and with most vigour, and to wage a spectacular, all-out jihad as opposed to a more targeted attrition campaign. Their lives and deaths are shrouded in a certain layer of mystery. This is partly because many witnesses and protagonists have died in 'encounter killings', and because police officers involved in raids or the Detective Branch unit investigating these cases have been unwilling to disclose much information about what has been revealed during interrogations.

On 5 June 2016, Bangladesh was shocked by the rare targeted killing of a woman by suspected jihadists in Chittagong. Mahmuda Khanam Mitu, a 32-year-old mother of two, was taking her six-year-old son to the school bus at around 7 a.m. when she was rushed at by three armed men, who first hacked her to the ground with machetes and then shot her.

Mahmuda's husband, superintendent Babul Akter, was seen as a leading light in the Chittagong police force's anti-terror division. The previous year, he had been involved in a supposed encounter killing. Babul and his colleagues had allegedly apprehended a suspected JMB member, Mohamed Javed, in early October 2015, and claimed they were taking him to a quiet area of the port city where, according to police, Javed had said he would show them the location of the group's weapons stash.[30] Babul and his fellow police officers then claimed they were ambushed by a group of JMB members and had come under fire. The detained suspect, it was claimed, was killed by a grenade or improvised explosive device thrown by the ambushers. Ever since the incident, Babul had been protected by armed police guards outside his house. It is likely that they had just left their posts when Mahmuda was escorting her son to the school bus. The subsequent investigation has seen many strange turns, including Babul's departure from the police force. Two suspects of Mahmuda's murder were killed in an encounter, and it was widely reported that one of Babul's undercover sources had hired two men to carry out the killing.[31] That month, there was a huge round-up of militant suspects, prompted at least in part by Mahmuda's murder.

While Mahmuda's death may have acted as a spur, the country had also been rocked by the double murder of two LGBTQ+ activists by AQIS' local subsidiary Ansar al-Islam the previous month, one of whom had worked for the American embassy. Days before, ISIS had also claimed the killing of a professor at Rajshahi University. Professor Rezaul Karim Siddique, sixty-one years old, was a practising Muslim who taught English at the university, where four professors had been murdered in recent years. Siddique had been involved in Bengali cultural societies, playing music, writing poetry and editing a cultural magazine. He had also set up a music school in the Bagmara area that had once been carved out by JMB founder Abdur Rahman and 'Bangla Bhai' as the site of their mini-caliphate. On 23 April 2016, he was on his way to work and waiting for a bus when at about 7.40 a.m. he was attacked from behind by a group of men who virtually decapitated him.[32]

The Bangladesh security forces began rounding up tens of thousands of supposed suspects and filling up the already heavily overcrowded prison and overloaded judicial systems. A senior official told me at the time that the situation was so dire that the authorities had little choice but to take drastic action. Many, it was alleged, were rounded up in order for local police to collect bribes from those arbitrarily detained. Others were simply alleged members of the political opposition, known to be part of the rough-and-tumble world of politics, but suspected of little else.

That June, as a relative quiet settled, I wondered whether the Bangladesh authorities had succeeded. Could detaining some 15,000 loosely selected suspects actually work? Of course, things were not that simple. During those weeks, a foreign diplomat told me that a lawyer connected to Jamaat had visited their mission, voicing concern that he was representing a few 'well-connected families' whose children had gone missing. Some of these families were allegedly British citizens, and the lawyer had purportedly taken his concerns to the British High Commission. Months later the High Commission denied knowledge of any such visit. The diplomat had told me they were not sure why the lawyer had visited them, but feared he might have been trying to mitigate association with some bad news that would soon emerge.

Missing Youth

One person who had not been caught in that June's round-up was a young man named Rohan Ibne Imtiaz, a student at BRAC University. Rohan was twenty years old and had not been seen at home since 30 December 2015. His parents had already been away in Kolkata, India, for medical treatment for a few days when Rohan left home for the last time, taking his passport with him in his college bag. He reportedly told the security guard at the family's house in Lalmatia, Dhaka that he was going to college. Not only was Rohan solidly middle class, attending a private university and having been educated at an English-medium private secondary school, but his father was also a leader in the ruling, supposedly secular Awami League. Imtiaz Khan Babul returned on 1 January and began desperately searching for his son:

> I asked all my relatives and his friends whom I knew, if they knew his whereabouts. He was nowhere. Then I filed a [general diary] with the police station. Then I met the honourable Home Minister, and talked to him. I talked to [the inspector general of police], Rab, every source I had, searched, provided his photo. But we didn't find any trace of him. There was no information about where he went to, no communication. We have tried a lot (to find him), searched a lot. He was my only son.[33]

Rohan was pious—his father said he prayed five times a day—but did not show signs of being particularly radical. He appreciated many of the ordinary obsessions of twenty-year-olds anywhere in the world and was a fan of English football club Manchester United.

On 3 February 2016 in the middle-class Uttara neighbourhood in Dhaka, Nibras Islam left home for the last time in a similar manner. Nibras was also educated at a private school, the Turkish Hope School, which is part of an international network of educational institutions formed by followers of Turkish cleric Fethullah Gülen. After finishing school, Nibras enrolled at the North South University. He did not last long at North South; after a single academic year at the institute he headed to Malaysia, where he enrolled in a course in computer science at the Australian Monash University's Malaysian campus. There he was described as a fun-loving, good-looking ladies' man. 'He used to maintain multiple girlfriends,' claimed counter-terror police chief Monirul Islam. Nibras was a fan of Bollywood and had once met Bollywood heroine Shraddha Kapoor, a video of whom he had excitedly shared on Facebook.

It was here in Malaysia, however, that at around the end of 2014, radical Islam became part of Nibras' life. He seems to have become involved through online interactions and perhaps also through people he met, quite possibly in the Bangladeshi diaspora in Malaysia, which by this point included a number of disgruntled opposition figures and more radical members of the religious right. By 2015, Nibras was showing signs of support for radical ideologues, including the UK's Anjem Choudary and his celebration of the attacks on the *Charlie Hebdo* newspaper offices in France. Nibras' father told the press: 'We are an ordinary Muslim family. We say our prayers but Nibras was never too interested in religion. We had to push him to attend Jumma prayers on Friday. But he started praying regularly after returning home from Malaysia, where he was studying at Monash University, in 2015.'[34]

Nibras returned to Bangladesh in October 2015, when the first attacks claimed by ISIS in Bangladesh had begun. On 3 February 2016, the day that Nibras left home for the last time, police allegedly apprehended three youths in central Dhaka who 'named Nibras as their associate'.[35] The police learned from Nibras' family members that he had disappeared and launched a search for him.

Three more young men would go missing at around that time, one of whom was from a similarly privileged background. Mir Saameh Mubasheer, eighteen years old, was taking his A-levels when he left home in the upmarket Banani DOHS area of Dhaka on 29 February. The family driver was taking him to a weekend private tutoring lesson when, because of heavy traffic, Mobasheer got out of the vehicle and told the chauffeur that he would make his own way. Mobasheer's mother was a teacher at the expensive private school Scholastica, which Rohan had attended. His father worked for the French-American multinational telecommunications company Alcatel-Lucent. Like others, Mir Hayat Kabir immediately started searching for his son when he disappeared.

The police investigated Mubasheer's disappearance and told his father that there had been four or five other disappearances in the area around that time. They searched Mubasheer's possessions and found his passport still at home. They examined his online footprint and found communications with Nibras and Rohan, the two other young men who had gone missing from affluent Dhaka neighbourhoods. Yet, they were unable to track him down. Journalist and writer Nuruzzaman Labu interviewed Mubasheer's father, who dismissed suggestions that his son had been radicalised, instead suggesting that someone might have 'trapped him'.[36]

Hayat was right in a way. Someone had trapped his son. The three young men had met online and been sucked into a world in which supposed answers were given not only to their insecurities and personal anxieties, but also to the broader apparent maladies of the world. Initially, the online efforts that were focused on Bangladesh had largely been part of a recruitment drive to the so-called *jihad* or holy war that was drawing disgruntled young Muslims to groups in Iraq or to fight the regime of Bashar al-Assad in Syria. These developments shared elements with the events that led to the formation of HUJI-B and the JMB after the Afghan-Soviet war—but in fast-forward.

Much of this clandestine recruitment took place through expatriate Bangladeshis or members of the Bangladeshi diaspora. Of note was a Facebook group called 'Ex-cadets Islamic Learning Forum'. This was moderated by a Bangladeshi expatriate in Japan named Saifullah Ozaki, who was himself part of that newly decisive demographic suddenly at the forefront of Bangladeshi Islamist extremism: middle- or upper-class students and members of the military and their children. Ozaki was also a convert to Islam, having been born a Hindu. He had won a scholarship to the University of Kyoto and gone on to teach business administration there. With comrades back in Bangladesh—in particular an individual named Aminul Islam Beg, who had studied in Malaysia—Ozaki would recruit young, relatively educated, capable yet disgruntled Bangladeshis, helping them to get Japanese visas, which would then enable them visa-free travel to Turkey.[37] From Turkey it was relatively straightforward to head, via Gaziantep, to the massacres, torture, bloodshed, barbarity and land of supposed religious sanctity—the caliphate.

Some people from the diaspora in the UK also looked towards the subcontinent to recruit for the then newly declared caliphate in the Middle East. In September 2014, Londoner Samiun Rahman, who worked for a minicab firm, was arrested in Bangladesh. Samiun was labelled an ISIS recruiter by the Bangladesh government. He had travelled to his ancestral home to recruit naïve young Bangladeshis to go and fight, and die, in Syria. The recruits included young men such as Asif Adnan, once a gifted student and rock musician, who was also the son of a judge.[38] Samiun had arrived in Bangladesh in February 2014, having previously visited Syria and Morocco.[39]

There were suggestions that some of these diaspora individuals, as well as seeing Bangladesh as an easy recruiting ground, were turning there in fear of returning to their home countries in the West, where they thought they would be picked up by the more capable security services. By this stage a degree of hysteria had developed about young Western Muslims travelling to fight in Syria. This included the so-called 'Britani Brigade Bangladeshi Bad Boys', alternatively known as the 'Pompey jihadis'. These were a group of British-Bangladeshis from Portsmouth in the south of England who had travelled to Syria to fight. Most died in Syria, but one, Mashudur Choudhury, returned home, where he was jailed for four years.[40] Mashudur and his friends from Portsmouth had been recruited by a British-Bangladeshi man named Ifthekar Jaman. One of the first Britons to join ISIS, Jaman had followed the group's successful copybook and used social media to recruit, sharing pictures portraying the attractive side of life in the caliphate, replete with kittens and comfortable accommodation.

In 2015, Bangladesh changed from a sender country to an area of attention in its own right. It is notable that just as militants were increasingly coming from the upper classes of Bangladeshi society, so too were these disgruntled youths found among affluent expatriate Bangladeshis—students and teachers, and young people aspiring to white-collar professions. The ISIS recruits were not the poor Bangladeshi construction workers in Qatar, but more comfortable individuals in Canada, Malaysia, Japan and the UK. These were disillusioned people who had been promised social equality but, for whatever reason, had found that to be a hollow promise.

While the more affluent areas of Dhaka were seeing cherished sons vanishing, the capital was not the only affected area. In Bogra, Rajshahi division, two young men from far more ordinary backgrounds had also vanished from their families in 2015. Shafiqul Islam Ujjal, twenty-six years old, came from the small village of Kaiyagari in the Bogra area. His father Badiuzzaman Badi was an agricultural labourer and a supporter of the Awami League. Ujjal had completed secondary school and gone to the local Azizul Haque government college. He did not last long there, and in 2014 left college and travelled to Ashulia, a sprawling satellite town just north of Dhaka where garment factories have sprung up in recent years. This area was once the site of the Tazreen Fashions factory, which made clothes for Disney and Walmart and burned down in 2012, killing over 100 workers who were trapped inside.[41] Ujjal's brother, Asadul Islam, worked at a garments factory in the area. Ujjal moved to Ashulia to join his brother and found a job there as a kindergarten teacher.

Another young man from Ujjal's area went missing in 2015. Khairul Islam Payel, aged twenty, was last seen at home in December 2015, when he had returned to his native village in rural Bogra on a motorbike with a friend named Abdul Hakim. The pair said they were off to Dhaka, where Payel claimed he was enrolling in Jagannath University. Payel had graduated from a local Qawmi madrassa (a seminary that runs without government oversight or regulation) only the previous year. His agricultural labourer family were devout and allegedly supporters of the Jamaat party. Payel had seen out his entire education in local madrassas. His family would later claim they were too scared to approach either the police or journalists to attempt to track down their son, another indication of the suffocating effect Bangladeshi politics can have on public institutions.

8

RAQQA, MEET DHAKA

Friday, 1 July 2016 marked the beginning of the last weekend of Ramadan, the holy month of fasting which gives way to the celebration of Eid al-Fitr, one of the most important Muslim holidays. That year, 2 July had been marked as Laylat al-Qadr, a significant date in the Islamic calendar, seen as the anniversary of the first revelation of verses of the Quran to Prophet Muhammad in 610 AD. For much of the country, the pious and the less-than-pious alike, this was the beginning of a serious holiday season. The weather that weekend was muggy but the worst of the heat had been ameliorated by the advent of rain and deltaic humidity.

Restaurants were doing a roaring trade in the swanky Gulshan neighbourhood in Dhaka. In one of the leafiest and most salubrious corners of the area, a converted late-twentieth-century two-storey house was perhaps the best place to be having dinner that weekend. The venue had originally started out as a bakery but was evolving into perhaps the only serious European restaurant in town. Its initial incarnation had been known as the Holey Bakery. The owners had brought in a French baker to teach the staff how to make croissants, puff pastry, and much else besides. The prices were eye-watering for Dhaka, and over the top even by international standards. But the restaurant had a niche for several reasons. The property had a lawn and handsome garden, which overlooked the languid green lake that divides the Gulshan-2 and Baridhara neighbourhoods. The garden was a rarity and would often cause casual bystanders walking along the public path by the lake to stop and gawp at what to most Dhakaites was another world within. This being the most densely populated city on the planet, and with scant planning legislation to boot, all corners of the city sprout multi-storey apartment buildings at an insatiable rate. The Holey Bakery garden was surrounded by high-end apartment blocks on two sides.

The restaurateur's in-laws owned this property and it had come to be the setting of the owners' culinary dreams. On one visit shortly after it opened, I chatted with a few of the owners, one of whom fondly described how he had courted his wife here, as he sat on the verdant lawn, pointing up at a balcony that overlooked the lake from the upper floor. He recounted with pride how the restaurant had grown up on a site where his life's dreams were made. It was a blossoming enterprise. From a bakery with impressive imported ovens emerged a cosmopolitan, full-service restaurant, which became known as O' Kitchen. A gelato counter soon followed, where scoops changed hands for four (American) dollars.

The bakery had had its setbacks. Initially, the owners had quietly sold sausage rolls with real pork, and a ham sandwich once appeared on the lunch menu before a patron had become so upset as to write to a local newspaper to complain. The ensuing uproar ensured that the forbidden swine had swiftly disappeared by September 2015. Pork is not illegal in Bangladesh; a few places run by Koreans or other foreigners sell pork in upmarket restaurants, and local Christians quietly go about selling and consuming the meat. The irksome issue seemed to be that here Muslim-born Bangladeshis were the purveyors, and thus straying from their Muslim identity.

To some, this represented the dynamic of a Bangladeshi elite who had fashioned successful businesses in the garment export sector, enabling them to drift away from their roots to entertain notions of themselves as less Bangladeshi and, more importantly, less Muslim. The garments industry is a sector built on the hard work of mostly poor women. The ostentatious swagger of that elite class, who represented 'moral failure'—as clerics were prone to interpret the bulging inequality of the economy—was in the bones of the Holey restaurant.

Not only did much of the wealth of its customers derive from the garments industry, but some of the owners were in the business as well. The garments industry also has deep political connections and as a result, the upper echelons of the sector—the businesses that export to Western brands—receive distinct favours. For instance, Bangladesh has a tiny domestic tax base, so it taxes imports heavily to try to balance the books. The garment export industry, however, comes under a special clause: so long as the entirety of a business' produce is exported, it receives tax-free imports of the vitals for its business. In contrast, successful local businesses producing garments or other goods for the domestic market pay taxes on imports. To get into exports in the tax-free, higher-end business requires connections, or capital, or both. This has created a two-speed economy, where one industry outperforms, to the detriment of others.[1]

The Holey restaurant was the kind of place where diplomats and their children might be seen on a weekend morning—perhaps enjoying the hip brunch classic shakshuka with friends in the echoing dining room, or simply moseying in to pick up a baguette to take home. That 1 July, staff had arrived at around 7 a.m., it being the weekend— the only days when the restaurant opened for breakfast or brunch. Come evening and the thirteen staff would be busy working under the direction of head chef Diego Rossini, one of two Argentine chefs who brought some authentic Latin expertise to the kitchen.

The work was steady; there were some twenty-five reservations and all was under control as guests started to arrive for dinner at around 7 p.m., recalls pasta maker Shishir Sarker. By eight o'clock a few guests had already left, but the restaurant was nonetheless relatively busy. A party of Japanese consultants was at one table; they had been in Bangladesh working for their country's aid organisation, JICA. Koyo Ogasawara, Nobuhiro Kurosaki, Tamaoki Watanabe and Makoto Okamura were all in the country to help with infrastructure and traffic management as consultants. Koyo was due home in a few days. Next to the Japanese was a large table of Italians, most of whom worked in the country's flourishing garments trade. Among them was Simona Monti, who was pregnant at the time. She was out with her friend Claudia d'Antona and Claudia's husband Gianni Boschetti. Gianni had stepped out of the dining room and was in the garden talking on the phone. Claudia was soon due to travel back to Turin from Dhaka and had reportedly delayed her return by a few days.

Three young students had just arrived and were having a reunion of sorts. Faraaz Hossain, American national Abinta Kabir, and Indian national Tarishi Jain had all only recently graduated from the American International School, which lay just over the lake from the restaurant and was where Italian aid worker Cesare Tavella had been followed the previous September. The three students, aged between nineteen and twenty, sat just inside the main door. All three had returned to Dhaka for the summer from universities in America. Tarishi was studying at the University of California, Berkeley, while Faraaz and Abinta were at Emory University in Atlanta. Near the students in the restaurant's dining room were Bangladeshi-born Hasnat Karim and his wife Sharmina Parveen, both British nationals, and their children.

The restaurant was dimly lit in the evenings, as affluent guests pored over pricey food, some sipping glasses of wine. At a table on the patio outside sat a Sri Lankan couple, Pepetha Shayama Wijesekera and Harikesha Wijesekera, Indian national Sat Prakash, and Ishrat Akhond from Bangladesh. Also outside, eating ice cream in a gazebo on the lawn, were Tahmid Hasib Khan, Fairooz Maliha and Tahana Tasmia, all young Bangladeshis. Near the main gate of the compound was a newly built pizza oven sheltered underneath a roof, manned by the pizza maestro, Saiful Islam Chowkidar. Saiful's wife, Sonia Akther (who was seven months pregnant at the time) awaited the regular call from her husband that night.[2] He was scheduled to visit his wife and two daughters in their home village over the coming Eid holidays.

It was just before 9 p.m. when the white gates to the restaurant were flung open and five young men, whose families had not seen or heard from them for months, walked into the premises. They all carried backpacks and were dressed in cosmopolitan attire—T-shirts and jeans. They would not have looked particularly out of place. Although they would not leave the premises alive, over the course of the evening they would transport the restaurant to the heart of international jihad and cause a vision of depravity to be visited upon this self-consciously aspirational corner of Dhaka. Within minutes, the five pulled out semi-automatic AK-22s—and machetes. They were soon shouting jihadist slogans and crying out 'Allahu Akbar'—'God is great'.

Panic

As the young men fired into the air, panic ensued from those outside on the patio. Some, including the Sri Lankan couple, Sat Prakash, and Gianni Boschetti, bolted and tried to hide in the garden. The assailants circled the restaurant and corralled most of those who had been outside into the restaurant.

In the meantime, 'everyone had been busy … cooking food, me as well,' recalls assistant chef Delwar Hossain. 'I was cooking food, and I needed shrimp so I went out [of the kitchen] to get the shrimp.' As he left, he heard a commotion and saw head chef Diego Rossini running. 'I saw that, so I put the shrimp back and I thought maybe there was fire, or accident. After I saw my boss running, I went back into the kitchen and went inside and everyone said that terrorists were coming.' Diego ran away without a word to his colleagues. He had reportedly been worried about terrorism since the killing of Cesare Tavella. He quickly made it to the roof, from which he jumped to an adjacent property, injuring himself, but making it out alive. Those still in the kitchen quickly closed the kitchen door and ran out to the back, locking themselves in the staff toilets. There were eight staff members in total in the small bathroom.

Inside the restaurant, pasta chef Shishir Sarker was 'making pasta and taking it to the chiller, which was to the right of the ovens.' The chiller was a room where fresh pasta was stored, and was next to the two large tables at which the Italians and Japanese were sitting. From the chiller room, Shishir remembers that he:

> heard a guest say something like 'help', screaming. And then I was thinking, what's happened outside? I looked outside [into the main room of the restaurant] and saw guests running, and I saw one guy [with a] big rifle and one big knife, a machete, and one rifle was firing, and all the Japanese people were sitting under the table.

Shishir retreated back into the chiller room. As he did so, a middle-aged Japanese man ran in and pleaded for help:

> so I took him and we went back into the chiller and locked it. The chiller was a little bit cold—not too much, normal cold. Then actually inside it's not well locked; you just pushed it and it opened, so if you

pulled it, it opened. So I took one bit of plastic and [secured] the door from the inside. Then I listened and heard firing—about three minutes after entering the chiller—firing and the *jongli* people [terrorists] were shouting '*Allahu Akbar*'.

Sat Prakash was waiting for a friend and was on the porch when the attackers burst through the gates. He ran towards an old pizza oven in the opposite corner of the compound from the main gate. He told police:

> I tried to hide myself behind a tomb. Within seconds, I saw a guy running with hands on his face. There was blood on his face. He looked like a person from Far East countries like Japan, China, Korea. I was thinking about leaving the place by any possible means. There was a Sri Lankan couple, whom I knew before, who came behind the tomb to hide … I saw through a window that one of the attackers was hitting a … person [lying down] with a sharp object. I turned my eyes immediately. Soon after the couple came, one of the attackers appeared and said, 'Don't hide, we are not going to harm you. You are not safe here, come out immediately.' We came out following the instruction. The same guy asked us not to use mobile phone.[3]

The wounded Far Eastern man was most probably Tamaoki Watanabe, the only person from the group of Japanese diners who survived. He ran out of the building and hid in the garden, nursing a bullet wound.[4]

While Shishir was hiding in the chiller room with one of the other Japanese diners, the young attackers, Nibras, Rohan, Mubasheer, Ujjal and Payel, had entered the building. Within minutes, the young men began shooting all those who appeared to be foreign and who had not made it out of the main room. Tarishi, Abinta and Faraaz had managed to dash into the customer's bathroom, which was close to their table. The attackers told the diners that they were there to kill non-Muslims and foreigners. Ishrat Akhond, forty-five years old, was a Muslim but was dressed in supposedly Western attire and was drinking wine. She reportedly responded belligerently to the young men, who began demanding that their hostages recite verses of the Quran to prove their faith. By most accounts, Ishrat refused to oblige, even though she most likely would have been able to. By this stage the attackers had gathered a few gas canisters, which had been used to power the kitchen's cookers. Coroners' reports suggest that Ishrat was beaten to death with one of these, or another blunt object, killed by several blows to the head for taking a brave stance. All those who were still alive and who had been rounded up were made to sit at the tables. At this stage, Nibras, the tall, good-looking attacker, appeared to take a leadership role and lectured the staff on Islamic virtues, standing next to the corpse of a pregnant Italian woman and a dozen other dead civilians. He expounded on the evils of alcohol as blood splattered over the white stone floor.

Shishir, the pasta chef, was still in the chiller room. He recalls:

> The Japanese person was so afraid, crying like that. 'How can I help him,' I was thinking, 'how can we be released from this moment?' Then we [thought that] if anybody called him and his mobile went off and it made a sound, people would know there was someone inside [the chiller room] … people would catch us. So that's why I turned my mobile off and told the Japanese person to turn his mobile off, so we are same, together we turned our mobiles off. Then we were saying, 'Please God, just help.' Then I asked him his name, but I have forgotten this name, and then he asked what work I did, and I said I am pasta maker. Then he said maybe we should call the police, but I said, 'No problem, the police are coming. This is a big problem, the police will be coming, don't worry, you just be silent.'

Before long, having received word of gunfire, police arrived at the scene. Dozens of officers entered the premises around 10 p.m., where they were met with gunfire and IEDs. Around thirty officers were injured. They were rushed to a nearby hospital, where officers Rabiul Karim and Salauddin Khan later died of their wounds. By this point, intense gunfire echoed around the neighbourhood. It ended abruptly as the police retreated, and the attack turned into a siege.

Siege

It was then around 10.30. Shishir recalled, 'I just heard full silence. Then the [terrorists] were maybe looking for people. Maybe at 10.30, 10.45, one terrorist tried to open the chiller. That time we held the door shut.' But that had tipped off the terrorists that there might be people inside, Shishir explained.

> I felt like I was going to have a heart attack. We were holding it closed for about two minutes, but the Japanese person and myself were [by this stage] very cold and our power was going less. That's why the terrorist people were able—maybe one or two minutes later—able to open the door. When it was opened, I saw that all guys have died, maybe twenty-five, all guests, where the Japanese were sitting, all people. That moment I realised they were finished. When he opened [the door] I saw the people, but also started to worry that I too would die.

The person on the other side of the door was Nibras. 'He said slowly, you come outside and sit, but I was already on the floor. All the dead people were on the floor.' Shishir lay on the ground in utter fear.

> The Japanese [man] was still in the chiller room and hadn't come out. And Nibras said [to me], 'What is your name?' I said Shishir, and he asked [what my work was]. I told him, 'Holey staff, pasta making.' I begged him, 'Please don't fire, I have a family'—like that I told him—then he said, 'You're staff?' I said yes. Then he said, 'You go to the hall where your colleagues are. Go and sit there.' At first I wasn't listening; I just was thinking 'don't kill me'. He said again, slowly, 'You go to where your colleagues are.' So I crawled towards where my colleagues were. I was crawling on top of the dead—the Japanese, the Italians—the blood was everywhere—my shirt, my pants, touching the blood.

As he crawled over the dead and dying, Shishir heard shots coming from the chiller room. 'I thought the Japanese guy had been shot,' he said. He looked back and saw:

> the Japanese guy was finished. … I was really afraid and sat with my colleagues, and a terrorist came down from the second floor. He looked at me … he was talking and was told that I had been inside the chiller. They were talking a bit of English but also another language that I did not understand; it was like Arabic but it wasn't Arabic.

Sat Prakash, the Indian man, spoke fluent Bengali, so was able to convince the terrorists that he was a local and survived the attack. Like almost all the hostages, he spent the night with his head on the table for hour after gruesome hour. He also recalled Shishir's companion's execution: 'They were asking the Japanese [man] whether he is alive. The Japanese [man] replied with yes. The guy shot him again. They, before shooting, asked us to cover our ears and to cover children's faces.'[5]

By this stage the electricity to the premises had been cut, so it was very dark, but the young men had rifled through the belongings of the dead and taken their phones. They used these to take photos of the corpses lying in pools of blood. They sent these to their accomplices by email and were talking on the phone. The attackers, amidst the dead bodies scattered on the floor, got a baker named Miraj Hossain and strapped explosives and a gas canister to his body. They tied him to a chair by the large glass windows on the first floor, to act as a human shield.

It was around this time, shortly after 11 p.m., that the attackers found out from news reports on the mobile phones that two of the police officers who had initially come to the rescue had died in hospital. 'See how blessed we are! We are alive inside and the OC [police officer in charge] is dead outside,' exclaimed Rohan. 'The police, BGB [Border Guards Bangladesh], RAB, all came to rescue you [hostages] but they have had to turn back. They have been forced to retreat. Allah has done this to ensure our mission is a success.'[6]

At some stage, Tarishi Jain, the young Indian student, texted her family: 'Terrorists have entered the restaurant. I am very afraid and not sure whether I will be able to come out alive. They are killing everyone here.'[7] Shishir does not recall or mention seeing the three students being discovered in the customers' bathroom, which was adjacent to the main dining room where the hostages were held. This would suggest that they were found and killed before Shishir himself was discovered at around 10.45. Shishir remembers:

I also saw some Indian people, Italian people, Japanese people dead. But … when I came [out of] the chiller and [was sitting with the staff at around] twelve o'clock night-time … [I saw] two Indian ladies and one Indian man [who had been outside], and at that time one Indian lady was not dead but had been shot. One lady [at] that time was not dead, and was moaning, and one terrorist came and said, 'Why are you not dead, how many times [do I] need to shoot?' [That was] around 12.30 time. Then [the terrorist] used a machete. Blood and meat went everywhere and I didn't look that time.

'So many times like that, so many times,' recalls Shishir, his previously stoic expression breaking, his voice wavering.

Tarishi was the only Indian woman on-site. There was one Sri Lankan woman there with her Sri Lankan husband; the couple survived. Faraaz Hossain, the young man with Tarishi and Abinta, could probably recite verses of the Quran, according to his family, who believe he could have survived by declaring and proving that he was a Muslim. However, it seems likely that the attackers became aware either that Tarishi was a Hindu Indian or of Abinta's American passport. It is unclear why all three students were not able to feign being Bangladeshi Muslims. It could well have been that the two female students' Western attire drew the terrorists' ire. The autopsies of the Italians paint a horrific picture: it was suggested by pathologists in Rome that all 'suffered a torturous death'.[8] By contrast, the majority of the seven slain Japanese were killed by gunshots. The attackers, it appeared from post-mortems, reserved the most medieval methods of killing for the women. Tarishi Jain was reportedly stabbed about forty times.[9]

When the attack began, British national Hasnat Karim was inside the restaurant with his wife and their two children. Outside in the gazebo were Tahmid Hasib Khan (who had only just returned to Dhaka from studying in Canada) and two of his female friends, Fairooz Maliha and Tahana Tasmia. In a very short video clip, shot from an adjacent building at the beginning of the siege, the three can be seen being ushered inside by the terrorists. Tahmid is heard saying, '*Bhaiya* [brother], please.'[10] The two women appear to be dressed in traditional Bangladeshi clothing and later told a court that they were at the restaurant to dine after an *iftar*—or meal to break the daily Ramadan fast—gathering at one of their homes. All seven people—Hasnat and his family and the trio of friends—were filmed leaving the compound the next morning. All the women have veils covering their hair. It was most probably these and other symbols of piety and perceived 'Bangladeshi-ness' that saved their lives.

Envy, Humiliation and Resentment

As discussed in the previous chapter, the place of gender in Islamist agitation is important. In many of the discussed cases, men have been threatened by women's empowerment, which is often seen as part of a Western corrupting conspiracy or malady. The diary of a young radical named Abdul Hadi, which was seized by police in 2017, is illuminating in this sense: 'In the name of equal rights, they want to bring women out of their homes, expose them … in this way, they want to harm Muslims.'[11]

Hadi railed against atheists and secularists as well, but his diary did not start with such violent, jihadist overtones. Hadi was seemingly wracked by poverty. His diary started in 2014 with a yearning for a better life, but amidst poems about seeking freedom, he bemoaned how 'All want happiness but only 10 per cent get it while 90 per cent are deprived of it.'

As it progresses towards the date of his arrest, Hadi's diary exhibits his increasing radicalisation: 'Jihad is power, jihad is freedom, jihad is a movement, jihad continues and will go on. Jihad will go on whenever necessary and will continue till *Qayamat* [the Day of Judgement].' The frustrated young man makes clear his sources of inspiration, saying:

> There will be an outburst of *mujahids* in Bangladesh too, and on that day, the dream of Shaiqul Hadith [*ameer* of Hefazat-e-Islam], Jasimuddin Rahmani [the detained leader of Ansarullah Bangla Team] and Jamaat-e-Islami Delwar Hossain Sayeedi [sentenced to life imprisonment on charges of committing genocide during the war of independence in 1971] will be accomplished. They won't be kept in the prisons then.[12]

Many of the themes that Hadi wrote about so candidly repeat themselves again and again—not only among young extremist Bangladeshis. The feelings and inferiority complex Hadi exhibits have been described by philosophers and psychologists as 'ressentiment': an existential resentment of other people who hold qualities, possessions or status one does not. As the German sociologist Max Scheler wrote:

> Envy does not strengthen the acquisitive urge; it weakens it. It leads to ressentiment when the coveted values are such as cannot be acquired and lie in the sphere in which we compare ourselves to others. The most powerless envy is also the most terrible. … This form of envy strips the opponent of his very existence, for this existence as such is felt to be … an unbearable humiliation.[13]

The sense of humiliation is a common trope in postcolonial Islamic thought. It often blends with leftist critiques of political economy to claim that there exists an anti-Islam conspiracy or that Islam is 'under attack' from some of the world's most powerful people or institutions. As discussed previously, these theories are sometimes not dissimilar to alt-right conspiracies, and ironically some of the supposed antagonists are the same: Jewish bankers, the American federal government or a 'globalist' elite. These forces are variously seen to be attacking Islam through defiling its traditions, in particular through such ideas as women's empowerment.

These feelings towards the world's elite were contextualised by contemporary thinker Pankaj Mishra, who wrote:

> Many people find it easy to aim their rage against an allegedly cosmopolitan and rootless cultural elite. Objects of hatred are needed more than ever before during times of crisis, and rich transnationals conveniently embody the vices of a desperately sought-after but infuriatingly unattainable modernity: money worship, lack of noble virtues such as patriotism. Thus, globalization, while promoting integration among shrewd elites, incites political and cultural sectarianism everywhere else, especially among people forced against their will into universal competition.[14]

Thus, Trump's Islamophobic voters are railing against the same somewhat ill-defined or indeterminate entities that Bangladeshi Hizb-ut-Tahrir members denounce. The reality, of course, is that there is indeed mushrooming inequality in most societies. But the causes of these are just as conveniently avoided by the 'defenders of Islam'—Hefazat-e-Islam—in Bangladesh as they are by the supporters of the English 'Defence' League. For thinkers such as Scheler, these emotions and the jump to defensiveness are particularly strong in the society that 'proclaims but does not meet equal rights.'[15] Members of the EDL and Hefazat both envy the status and power of 'the globalist elite'—a supposedly liberal educated class of people who permit and encourage such phenomena as immigration, women's empowerment or the Western decadence of Holey Bakery. The anxiety that inequality is rooted in the loss of male supremacy, or of white ethnic communities in European countries, is a driving reason for these 'defenders' to blame other groups, who seem to possess fortunes the sufferer does not.

Stockholm Syndrome?

At Holey Bakery, both Hasnat Karim and Tahmid Hasib Khan were filmed talking to the attackers, including on the roof of the building. In one shot, Tahmid is even seen holding a gun while chatting with the terrorists. Both men would, as a result, be detained after the attack. Tahmid was released in October.

Hasnat had for a time been a teacher at North South University, where a thriving network of Islamist radicals had developed, and could well have been part of that culture. He was reportedly a member or had at one time had connections with Hizb-ut-Tahrir, the transnational group of angry young Muslims who call themselves a political party as part of their campaign to bring about a caliphate. The group was proscribed in Bangladesh in 2009 by the Awami League but is very active in the UK, where Hasnat had completed both his undergraduate and graduate degrees. His time at university in the UK did not sound particularly rewarding. Hasnat had studied engineering at Queen Mary University of London, but after finishing had not found a job, leading his father to bring him back to Bangladesh, where he went on to work for the family company. He did not enjoy the work, so again returned to the UK and studied for a master's degree in Leeds, after which he finally returned to Bangladesh and got a job at North South University. His travails paint a picture of a long period of listlessness, throughout which his family supported him financially.

While the authorities may have had grounds for suspicion, Hasnat's detention was another case where justice was absent. He was denied consular visits and access to lawyers, and his assets were frozen. He was never charged with any crimes. His driving license was found on the body of one of the attackers; he had apparently handed it over during the ordeal. His family also claim that the attackers forced him to download specific apps, which were found on his phone. Hasnat and his family were reportedly allowed to use their phones on loudspeaker at various junctures throughout the night.

As with so many other cases, guilt or innocence is shrouded in unaccountability and the quagmire of Bangladesh's dysfunctional legal system. Hasnat was finally released from detention without trial from Kashimpur jail in August 2018, over two years after his initial arrest.[16]

An End in Sight

As the horrors unfolded inside the restaurant, the youngest staff member, 18-year-old Zakir Hossain Shaon, like the Argentine chef Diego Rossini managed to dash to the roof and jump to an adjacent property. He did so perhaps after hiding on the balcony that overlooked the lake. Eight other staff members were trembling in the bathroom outside. 'We could hear too much sound outside, too much crying, guns firing. It was too much hot inside the washroom—we all took our clothes off; it was very cramped and tense. We were trying to call [with phones]; everyone was crying, praying to God,' recalled Delwar Hossain, the assistant chef. They managed to send a photo out which made it onto Facebook. He told me what happened next:

> At about 2.30 a.m. a terrorist came to the door and said, 'Open the door.' But I wouldn't—no one would—so he said, 'If you don't open the door, I will fire.' So I opened the door, and he told everyone to put our hands up, and everyone came out. They asked us all, 'Are you Muslim?' Everyone said they were Muslim, even though three of us were Hindus. He said, 'Are there any foreigners in there?' and we said we had no foreigners. One [of the attackers] had a machete and one had a pistol; one of them was tall and one was dark. We were all scared and crying, and then they put us all back in the bathroom and locked it. Soon air became scarce so we turned the showers on; it was incredibly stifling.

It was around this time, 2.30 to 3 a.m., that Shishir was ordered by the attackers to prepare food in the kitchen. He went back into the kitchen while one of the attackers demanded other staff serve coffee and cheesecake. Shishir recalled that Rohan:

> asked me to come to the kitchen and asked me to make food. I showed him sea bass and shrimp, and I made the fish—fried, just with some butter and salt and paprika. I put [it] on a plate and came inside, and saw that we were four [staff] and there were [about] eight people with Hasnat. And [Rohan] said, 'It's Ramadan time so now you need to take breakfast, *sehri* [the pre-dawn meal that Muslims eat before fasting in Ramadan]. You take the *sehri* and you take *roja* [fast].' That food the terrorists didn't eat, and we couldn't eat, in a moment like that, so we just showed a little bit eat, then we took water and after [returned to] the same [sitting] position.

Hasnat's daughter complained that she didn't like fish; no one, it appeared, had an appetite, but the attackers insisted on the ritual meal. As the night wore on, Hasnat trod up and down to the roof with the attackers, where he smoked cigarettes as he chatted with them. It was while Shishir was cooking that Rohan asked him about his religion. He was lucky; despite being a Hindu he had many Muslim friends and could remember a few parts of the Quran, so he recited one of these and managed to save his life.

At around 6.30 a.m., Nibras gave Hasnat the keys to the gate and told him to go and unlock it, which he did before returning with the keys. Nibras ordered eight hostages to leave. A neighbour filmed this, and in the clip Hasnat can be seen ushering the group across the lawn towards safety. Shishir thought that this might mean the staff would also be able to leave, but they were not. Instead, all the restaurant workers were retrieved from the bathroom outside, and Miraj Hossain, who had been tied to the chair, was released. Nibras smiled and pointed at the dead, saying, 'Now you see dead people, you'll see us dead as well.'

The five terrorists had their backpacks on in the dining room. They lectured the staff about women's clothing and ancient books, before running out and trying to make it to a gate in the fence. Shishir told me that within moments:

> military people were firing … so we ran upstairs to the [upstairs] bakery [preparation] room, all staff, and [there was] firing all around. We thought we'd die, so we went upstairs; all thirteen people were on the ground. … [There was] firing and bombs, giving too much sound; we were too much afraid that at that time we would die. … The terrorists left because they thought they could escape by the [lake]. That's why they went to the left side; the right side had all military.

The five jihadists were little match for the military. Soon commandos stormed the premises and handcuffed all the staff. They went through them one by one, name-checking to make sure that they were actually staff. In the commando operation, pizza chef Saiful Islam Chowkidar was killed, most likely shot by commandos as they stormed the premises.

It was shortly thereafter that I arrived at the site. It was ferociously humid, and the nearby streets looked like the site of the D-Day landings. Multiple branches of the armed forces and security services were loitering and pacing—some were napping after the long siege; others were setting up impromptu desks from which to martial their troops. Snipers walked past from their posts on nearby buildings. A gaggle of foreign diplomats chatted to one another in various states of curiosity and stress. The American stood away from his European counterparts and angrily dismissed a curious correspondent. But it was from overhearing his loud, conspicuous clamour that I learned, and relayed to MSNBC, that an American national had been killed inside. The humid air was intermittently shaken by the sound of explosions as the security forces detonated the remaining IEDs they had found in clearance operations. It was a scene of utter chaos. Mobile internet in the area had been downed after the authorities realised that the terrorists had been uploading their gruesome photos. I recall seeing Shishir and his colleagues being driven away, handcuffed in the back of a minibus, still wearing their bloodstained chef's whites. The sight bored a hole of depressing confusion into any emerging narratives of what had taken place in the restaurant, which had been upturned into a vision of hell.

One person I did not see was the youngest person who worked at the restaurant. Zakir Hossain Shaon, the 18-year-old kitchen cleaner, had on that first day of July been elated that he had just been given an Eid bonus, and was excited to be heading back to his family the next day.[17] All being well, he should have been taking his hard-earned wages and bonus to his waiting family that morning, as I stood amidst a sea of journalists and camouflaged soldiers. Instead, Zakir spent most of the night in police custody. He was filmed by television news being taken away by police before 3 a.m. on 2 July, alive but bleeding from the chest, presumably from barbed wire injuries. On the morning of the third, his parents received a call from one of his colleagues saying he was at the Dhaka Medical College Hospital.

It was here that they found him, slipping in and out of consciousness. 'Every time he came to his senses he said one thing: "Don't hit me please, don't beat me any more. Let me go,"' Zakir's mother told the BBC. 'The police grabbed him, and they tortured him. They hit him on the head. They kicked him. They indiscriminately beat him.'[18] Zakir's body showed signs of torture. He died from his injuries in hospital on

8 July. He was the last person to die from one of the worst incidents of terrorist violence in Bangladesh. With bitter irony, the police most likely beat this victim of the attack to death.

There was little outcry over Zakir's death, and the press paid little attention to him. The young man's monthly wages would probably not have covered any one of the bills from the restaurant's tables that night. Internet campaigns flourished for the two detained men who had spent the night smoking and chatting with the wealthy terrorists. As far as I am aware, there was never much of a commemoration of Zakir's death; no campaign, or even so much as a Facebook page calling for 'justice for Zakir Shaon'. Dhaka, the third largest Facebook-using city on the planet, spent more time discussing the good looks of mass murderer Nibras, who spent that night delivering supposed moral lectures and hacking people to death because they wore the wrong clothes or could not recite a verse of a holy book.

9

POST MORTEM

Canadian national Tamim Chowdhury spent the night of 1 July in a flat not far from the Holey Bakery restaurant, in a new residential area known as Bashundhara. He took the attackers from this flat to the upmarket restaurant, probably by foot, leaving at around 5.30 p.m. The flat was owned by a senior member of staff from North South University, Gias Uddin Ahsan, a vice chancellor of the institution. The plotters had begun moving into the flat on 16 May that year.

Soon after the attack had commenced, a series of portraits of the attackers was released, which police believe had been taken in this same flat. These show the attackers in matching red-and-white *keffiyehs* (Arabic scarves), holding the same AK-22 and standing in front of a black ISIS banner. ISIS lost no time in taking credit for the barbarity and also spreading pictures of the victims of the Holey attack, lying in pools of blood in the restaurant. While Tamim was undoubtedly a key player in much of this, another of the masterminds behind the attack, which the attackers had termed 'Operation Ghazwat', after the *hadith* discussed in previous chapters, was a 22-year-old man named Nurul Islam, better known by his alias Marjan. It was he who had apparently set up the links for the horrific material to be uploaded securely during the night while the attack was underway. He had co-ordinated the attack, and had reportedly been heavily involved in training the attackers in the rural Gaibandha region in the north of the country.

Born to a poor, pious family in the Pabna region, Marjan was said to have been something of a child prodigy. From a rural village he went to Chittagong University, where he studied Arabic and quickly became involved with the Jamaat-e-Islami student wing, Islami Chhatra Shibir. From here he was able to meet members of the Jamaat-ul-Mujahideen Bangladesh (JMB), and it was this crucial relationship that enabled an aspirational group of members of the organisation to try and form what ISIS term a *wilayat*, or province, in Bangladesh. It was to an extent Marjan's brains and connections that assisted ISIS in its attempt to gain a foothold in the country.

Origins of Terror

In these personal stories, there are traces of several of the major debates about the nature of ISIS's presence in the country and the motivations of actors both in Bangladesh and elsewhere. As discussed previously, Bangladesh's government have often rather farcically denied the presence of ISIS in the country. The attack on the Holey restaurant struck at the heart of the Bangladeshi establishment and changed the complexion of militancy in the country. It also caused international observers to look more closely at Bangladesh. One who did so was Lieutenant General Terry Wolff, America's deputy special presidential envoy for the Global Coalition to Counter ISIL, who explained that:

> The question is, are [attacks] directed, inspired [by ISIS], or are they just local wannabes? In the history of these groups, again what we're seeing change is that a group like ISIS argues that its headquarters are in Raqqa or Mosul, that it's established a caliphate and that its interpretation of the faith is the only interpretation of the faith, and that it is looking to spread the caliphate to other locales, via the announced branches but also an undisclosed number of affiliates. Its expansion plan has been successful, reasonably successful, first and foremost by convincing other groups that are in some sort of competition with the government to join their cause.
>
> So, the ISIL element in Algeria was basically a former resistance movement that announced loyalty to Baghdadi. Of the seven or eight branches the only ISIL branch that was a new start was in Libya. The other seven—for example ISIL Sinai hijacked the ABM [Ansar Bait al-Maqdis]

movement. So, the big challenge out in Bangladesh or other locales is this: What does the country see? Is it the beginning of something more formal from ISIL central, or is it just some local resistance element that's picking up on the tenure and saying, 'I'm ISIL too,' or, 'I am Al-Qaeda too.'

This analysis demonstrates how movements that often start with very local, often politically inspired or even patronised, drivers can be subsumed by international groups.

Counter-offensive

In the months that followed the Holey attack, Bangladesh's security services made a series of raids and arrests. Tamim Chowdhury, they claim, was killed in a raid on a property in Narayanganj, just south of Dhaka, on 27 August 2016. This is almost certainly a fiction, like a good number of the official accounts of encounters in which suspects die. According to intelligence figures interviewed for this book, Tamim was secretly detained about a month earlier, and was most likely killed while in detention. Marjan's wife, who also happened to be his cousin, was detained in September 2016. In January 2017, Marjan himself, along with an accomplice named Saddam Hossain, was killed in a supposed gunfight with the police in the capital's Mohammadpur area. It was alleged that Hossain had been behind a number of the killings in northern Bangladesh, including that of Japanese national Kunio Hoshi.

The next major breakthrough by police related to 32-year-old Jahangir Alam, alias Rajiv Gandhi, who was detained on 13 January 2017. According to counter-terror police chief Monirul Islam, Jahangir was seen as the:

> most wanted in the Holey Bakery attack case and was a vital accused. … That is why it was imperative for us to capture him. … We finally succeeded in capturing him and in our custody he confessed everything: his involvement not only in this case, but in around twenty cases that occurred over the last one year, like killing, single killings in northern districts. … He was also involved in old JMB before the emergence of this new [ISIS-affiliated] faction and most of the active members, particularly leaders, were from old JMB. … They were involved with JMB or were JMB members or activists and later they differed in opinion

with the leaders of old JMB, so they came out and parted and formed this new faction.

Through Jahangir, one of the few leaders of the ISIS-affiliated militants to be caught alive, the new ISIS aspirants had a direct link to the JMB of old, which, after the demise of the BNP–Jamaat government and the capture and execution of its senior leaders, had become 'like a ship without a rudder', according to a Bangladesh intelligence figure.

Jahangir had been a cook for Abdul Awal, the son-in-law of JMB founder Abdur Rahman. Jahangir was responsible for supplying the two 'salt-of-the-earth' northern militants in the Holey attack: Ujjal and Payel. Jahangir had worked with Tamim, the quiet, estranged Canadian from a conservative family background who had felt existential angst in the West, and who had global connections, enabling him to develop links to ISIS. Tamim's primary contact with the group came from a similar background. Abu Terek Mohammad Tajuddin Kausar was a bright, computer science graduate. Like Marjan, he came from a poor family in Bangladesh, but had excelled at school. This initially won him a scholarship to a college in Dhaka, and later, in 2006, to the University of New South Wales in Australia. There, he had several IT jobs, married an Australian woman and had two children—all of which he gave up sometime around 2013.[1] He most probably met Tamim through the aforementioned Ex-cadets Islamic Learning Forum Facebook group.

Glimpses from the Grave

Through glimpses of these militant planners and what little we know about them, we see how the rump JMB joined up with the interconnected, globalised culture of ISIS. Soon after the attack on Holey, the ISIS publication *Rumiyah* published obituaries of the attackers, allegedly penned by Tamim.[2] These are fascinating in more ways than one. The article opens with the beaming portraits of the attackers that were published shortly after the attack took place, all taking it in turns to hold the same cheap AK-22 for the camera, wearing their matching black outfits and red-and-white *keffiyehs*.[3] They are described as *inghimasi*, a team of attackers who commit to causing maximum damage and do not intend to escape, but who do not seek

In addition, his relatives and associates began pressuring him to 'settle down' and get married. However, Allah protected him [Nibras] from falling into the various temptations of the *dunya* [temporal world].[6]

Nibras was most likely radicalised in Malaysia. It was perhaps there that he first felt some of the same anxieties that encourage Western jihadists to commit murderous acts. It was there that he became involved in 'contemporary jihadism', which French academic and jihadism expert Olivier Roy has called a 'youth movement that is not only constructed independently of parental religion and culture, but is also rooted in wider youth culture … they go to nightclubs, pick up girls, smoke and drink.'[7]

It was suggested that Nibras was introduced to a circle of Bangladeshi expatriates by fellow Monash student Andaleeb Ahmed, who knew Bangladeshi businessman Peyar Ahmed Akash.[8] Akash had fled Bangladesh in 2011 but was already an established political actor. He was arrested in 2005 but was bailed out of jail by the head of Jamaat in his Feni region, when the party was in power in coalition with the BNP. Akash set up a restaurant and manpower business in Malaysia, and at his restaurant allegedly held meetings and campaigned against the war crimes tribunals.[9] His restaurant 'became a gathering place for Jamaat leaders and supporters.'[10] On 2 September 2016 Akash was deported by Malaysia back to Bangladesh.[11] In Malaysia at this time there were a number of other Bangladeshi travellers who ran in the same circles. One was Tausif Hossain who, like Nibras and Andaleeb, attended the Australian Monash University in Malaysia. He was allegedly killed in the raid in Narayanganj in which authorities claimed the Canadian militant leader Tamim Chowdhury had been killed. Key attack planner and former North South University student Mohamed Basharuzzaman, who went by the alias Chocolate, also spent time in Malaysia.

In these profiles and lives we see both the common traits of a somewhat nihilistic international 'youth culture'—reflecting a certain unease, as described by Olivier Roy from his profiling of French jihadists—and also something distinctly Bangladeshi. Important actors like Payel and Jahangir were products of the Ahle Hadith madrassa and mosque network (which spawned JMB) when it had political patronage to blow themselves up as in the case of a classic suicide bombing. The eulogies of the attackers, as expected, glorify them as selfless heroes. They also clearly portray the division between the three upper-class recruits and the two JMB regulars from the north of the country, who were found by Marjan and Jahangir. The three rich kids are given the longest obituaries, and their obituaries appear first. Nibras and Rohan were evidently the most important and had the highest status, both within and outside of their jihadist cell. Mubasheer was clearly not very capable—his father once told press he was not bright—but *Rumiyah* still dedicated about four times the number of words to him than to the young man whose parents were farm labourers but who had nevertheless made it to college.

Rohan was named as the leader of the group. This is interesting for a number of reasons. His father, of course, was an Awami League politician; Rohan was relatively bright and capable, and by several accounts was pious for most of his life. As with young jihadists in the West, it is evident that he was also expressing a nihilistic rebellious anger. *Rumiyah* celebrated that he had 'once even [asked] the amir t allow him to go assassinate his own father, saying, "I know one pers who should be targeted, my *taghut* [tyrant] father. If you give permission, I will finish him."'[4]

Nibras, by contrast, can be said to be the only one who underwent a complete conversion, in that he went from revell a so-called secular, hedonistic lifestyle to murdering pregnant w in a restaurant because they did not know the Quran. As his *R* eulogy notes:

> he was known for his lavish lifestyle among his peers before]
> to his religion, he came to realize by the mercy of Allah tha
> guidance from Allah are the most important treasures for a
> this world and not appearance, wealth, educational back
> other material criteria.[5]

The obituary notes that Nibras had tried to travel to Syri had failed, and that he, like Rohan, was straining under far

Before he joined the Soldiers of the Khilafah in Bengal, hi wanted to hand him the reins of his garments business in Bangladesh. Others, including Holey attack planner Tanvir Kaderi, who supposedly killed himself in a police raid in Azimpur, Dhaka, were somewhere in between. Kaderi gave up a well-paid banking job and sold his car to donate to the jihadist cause. He brought his family along with him on his journey of radicalisation, through the final planning of the Holey Bakery attack to the raid where he died in September 2016. His son Tehreem's statement to police gives a glimpse of the final days in the life of an adolescent, trapped in his father's fantasies, which supposedly began after a trip to Saudi Arabia for the Hajj pilgrimage in 2014.

In the statement, Tehreem uses the aliases he knew the attackers by:

Tamim, [Basharuzzman] Chocolate, Marjan brought bags to our house. There were arms in those bags. Tamim, Raad [Nibras], Mamun [Rohan], Umar [Payel], Alif [Ujjal], and Shuvo [Mubasheer] lived in our Bashundhara house. They hardly went out of the house. They used to discuss inside a room closing the door. There were seven rooms with four bedrooms in our house. Five including Tamim stayed in one room. My father, brother and I stayed in drawing room. Shuvo's mother [Jahangir's wife] and my mother lived in one room. Of the five people, Alif [Ujjal] and Umar [Payel] told stories that they had carried out many operations. They told how they fled leaving the blood stained trousers after killing a Christian and a Hindu in Kushtia. They used to talk about jihad. They also told us about their trainings.[12]

On the night of the Holey attack, young Tehreem moved to another flat. He watched the horror unfold on television with his father, who spent the initial hours of the evening sweating over whether the attackers would be intercepted at a police checkpoint on their way. The security services might have anticipated an attack on that night, because, as Tamim wrote in *Rumiyah*, 'The night of the 27th of Ramadan was chosen [for the attack] because of the huge rewards that it could potentially bring to the *mujahid* brothers, as it may possibly be Laylat al-Qadr'—the holiest night of the year in Sunni Islam.

As Tehreem told the police:

My father asked us to pray so that they were not caught and could do a good operation. He asked us to seek mercy from Allah [*isteghfar*]. After a while we saw gun-fighting going on in Gulshan Holey Artisan.

Then we realized that the operation in Holey Artisan was going on. We watched news till the morning. Photos of participants were published in the morning. Dad told me that there was a very good operation and your brothers were martyred. Then we all said *Alhamdulillah* [praise be to God]. We came to know the names of the people who stayed in our house at Bashundhara after the pictures of the dead [attackers] were published in different media.[13]

Piety for Power

In the final reckoning, the Holey Bakery attack and the way it transpired show both a highly globalised ISIS presence in the country and, as Lieutenant General Terry Wolff described, a combination of local actors, as in almost every other province or country where ISIS has had an operational presence. This local presence is highly political. The recurrent links between some of the actors and Shibir, the Jamaat party's student wing, would suggest that in many ways, jihad is a reaction to supposedly secular governance and an attempt to mobilise disparate dissenters to foment regime change. Bangladesh's political rulers know this, having once been in the disenfranchised position of the opposition, in which they too faced harassment from the authorities, including the deeply politicised policing and judicial systems. They too once lacked access to crucial state resources and felt the need to win back power, whatever the cost.

In many ways, the binary arguments that the attacks were committed by either major international terror networks or by locally based actors miss the point. Practically, it is very difficult to operate or take over a territory solely through foreign force. Additionally, it is naïve and simplistic to claim, as former American ambassador William Milam has, that today's extremist murders and movements are entirely the result of the autocracy of the Awami League.[14] For a start, the movements in Bangladesh that gave rise to ISIS or Al-Qaeda had precursors that existed and indeed were sponsored by political actors in or from Bangladesh, many of whom were thrown up by the Cold War, including by the American-led anti-communist alliance. Indeed, the United States has in Bangladesh's short history supported dictators who have actively utilised and fostered the extremist culture that has now so bedevilled the American twenty-first century. Similarly, it was in a period of democracy under Khaleda Zia of the BNP that returnees from an American-sponsored war in Afghanistan formed organisations like JMB and Harkat-ul-Jihad al-Islami Bangladesh, which inspired today's generation of Islamist radicals.

It is also absurd to say that ISIS and Al-Qaeda had or have no presence in the country. This position, taken by the government of Bangladesh, most likely harmed the response to the threat. The United States government, for their part, knew of the presence of ISIS in Bangladesh from at least spring 2015, according to former officials interviewed for this book. This was months before Italian national Cesare Tavella was murdered in the first attack to be claimed by the group. There were serious differences of opinion within the upper echelons of the American government as to how to deal with this knowledge, and how to approach the Bangladeshi government. In the end, the US put no considerable pressure on Bangladesh to crack down on militancy, as many at the highest levels felt that Sheikh Hasina was using the militant attacks for her own political ends. They also believed that since there was such a range of opinions as to what the nature of the threat was, they should not provide much more counter-terror support.

This poses a huge question. While the realities of any terrorist challenge always have a local hue, threats today are usually much more globalised than in the past. As such, one would assume that responses, too, must be more global in character. Should rich nations withhold their support because of their justified fears that local entities might well use that support to suppress political opponents or to commit serious human rights abuses? After Holey, Western governments did ramp up counter-terror support for the Hasina government, which included training and resources. The Awami League government's autocratic lurches have been persistent and have worsened since the attack, as another disorderly election looms at the end of 2018. Dissent has been stamped out further; members of the opposition and participants in informal protests have been treated abysmally. The most egregious state actions have included forced disappearances and the blanket suppression of freedom of speech. When asked about radicalization of the desperately persecuted Rohingya minority, a senior member of Bangladesh's military intelligence complained to me about the lack of modern surveillance equipment compared to other nations' forces. As ever, surveillance is presented as a binary choice between security or liberty. The truth is probably worse: that government surveillance might be being used as much to suppress legitimate dissenting positions as to keep the public safe.

This is part of a process in which Bangladesh's government has ceded much ground to Islamists, largely because of political expediency. The use of religious rhetoric in 2013 was undoubtedly a political tactic by Jamaat to try to shield their convicted leaders from the judicial process of the International Crimes Tribunal. The BNP followed suit. Within the political context of Bangladesh, this was a winning formula that was calculated to be incendiary, and to stigmatise so as to shut down debate. The Awami League was forced to kow-tow to majoritarian forces of conservatism and, some would say, bigotry, in order to maintain stability and, most importantly, power.

It is without doubt that Bangladesh's Islamist extremists have political connections and fellow travellers and that they have most probably been encouraged and enabled by political actors. This is seldom not the case. In our interconnected, angry world, movements that may appear remote and localised to residents of affluent countries are also themselves highly connected to globalised sub-cultures, movements and feelings that reverberate across the internet.

ISIS and Al-Qaeda

Analysis of the connections developed by the two most prominent new strains of Islamist terror—ISIS and Al-Qaeda—is vital. ISIS followers and their support base from rump-JMB went for the more spectacular, headline-grabbing style of attack. Their connections were more international than regional, as they came from or had travelled to Europe, Canada, Australia, Japan, Malaysia and Syria. They chose their victims randomly, rather than targeting specific individuals for perceived crimes, and pursued a millenarian or fate-driven style of attack. There have seldom been times when Bangladesh has received as much media attention as the twenty-four hours following the attack on the Holey restaurant. In this sense, the attack was a success. It was successful as well in that it was choreographed with a view to creating a spectacle for the news media. It was one of the first attacks that ISIS claimed responsibility for while it was still under way. Furthermore, the terrorists disseminated shocking images from inside the restaurant while the attack was in process. This caused uproar, condemnation and a massive government crackdown.

Al-Qaeda, on the other hand, took a very different approach. The Al-Qaeda in the Indian Subcontinent (AQIS) subdivision, which emerged in 2014, was seen by many as a response to the growing global prominence of ISIS. In many ways, in Bangladesh, AQIS has been a roaring success. The group has never achieved 24-hour television coverage, but its successes have lasted. Like in the parable of the tortoise and the hare, AQIS has slowly but surely outpaced ISIS, by being in tune and reactive to domestic conservative sentiment and youth anger.

AQIS has a stronger local or regional vision. As a predominantly Pakistan-based entity, it puts regional imperatives front and centre. Its attacks are deliberate and targeted. While the choice of targets undoubtedly reflects the whims of well-heeled members within the network, the victims have also been eminently polarising figures. They tapped into widely held beliefs that had been laid down through decades of Cold War-inspired governance, pedagogy and resurgent Arab-inspired religious orthodoxy. Atheists and secular liberal bloggers challenged the self-styled personification of piety adopted by the Jamaat war criminals. By targeting these political dissidents, the attackers acted in concert—philosophically, politically and emotionally—with those on a broad sweep of Bangladesh's political right. The right had a major national newspaper to produce propaganda for them in the form of *Amar Desh*, which was to the BNP what Breitbart was for US President Trump around the time of his 2016 electoral victory. AQIS worked alongside, if not always in full agreement with, vast networks of madrassas belonging to the Hefazat movement, which both of the country's main political parties tried to co-opt or use. AQIS's targeting of LGBTQ+ activists played into a conservative ideology, as did the accusations levelled at these victims of being foreign agents. Crucially, these attacks forced government ministers to kowtow to the killers, both in terms of policy and public statements.

AQIS's statements did not just tap into public angst over issues relating to lifestyle or 'deviant' Muslims. By 2018, the group had issued public statements on the Rohingya refugees and the August student protests, which erupted after two students were killed on the road by reckless drivers. All of these themes, from the far-fetched linkages of homosexuality to America, to the more grounded complaints about the brutal treatment of the Rohingya, feed a sense of Muslim persecution and the need for order in a chaotic, immoral world.

It would be wrong to try to make sense of terror in Bangladesh only through comparison and analogy. But it would be even more erroneous to suggest that Bangladesh's experiences are aberrations and not linked to or symptomatic of more widely held psychological phenomena. Modern Bangladesh in many ways provides textbook breeding grounds for 'ressentiment'. It is a young political entity, now only four and a half decades old, and many of the terms of its constitution are not upheld. Promises of equality and justice go unmet, while corruption and inequality flourish.

Globalisation and Ressentiment

Bangladesh, like many other parts of the world, is experiencing demographic and economic changes, with rapid globalisation and population growth. As in other Muslim societies, religious trends and fashions now spread more quickly as a result of expanding interconnectivity. Pious one-upmanship is seen as a modern virtue. The growing consciousness of the lives of others in comparison to our own can be linked to the pace of economic change and globalisation. In quantitative studies, researchers at the Hebrew University in Jerusalem and at Turkey's Yasar University found that 'globalisation systematically predicts increases in religious legislation and religious discrimination towards minorities.'[15] They found that this specifically applied to economic globalisation as opposed to cultural or other forms of globalisation.

This analysis goes some way to explain the prominence of middle-class extremists in Bangladesh. Meanwhile in neighbouring Myanmar, the Rohingya Muslim minority became a target for fierce attack as soon as the country's economy began to open up in 2012. Simple though this explanation may be, it makes sense that material insecurity and rapid economic change lead to mass anxiety. As found by Max Scheler, within societies that promise social equality but fail to deliver it, men (and less often women) come to resent those whom they see as more successful, producing powerful emotions of envy and humiliation. This can be seen in the ideology expounded by attackers—in their search for 'freedom' through jihad, and their attraction to radical right-wing or Islamist politics, born of a desire for order.

One member of proscribed international movement Hizb-ut-Tahrir told me in Dhaka:

> People are growing fed up of democracy … there is a huge demand for political Islam in Muslim-dominated countries around the world, but the Western bloc, led by the US and its allies, is trying to destroy the idea of political Islam by recruiting some youth and motivating them into terrorism, so that people have a wrong understanding of what political Islam is, and to tarnish the image of Islam.

Pinning terrorism on 'the Western bloc' (with little evidence) helps to explain away complex anger and frustration by projecting it onto a vague, far-away global hegemon. At the same time, it reflects the repressed resentment and feelings of inadequacy thrown up by real global inequalities and centuries of injustice. After all, Muslim-majority countries, Bangladesh included, have suffered centuries of domination by Western nations. As the Turkish writer Orhan Pamuk reflected shortly after the 9/11 attacks:

> The western world is scarcely aware of this overwhelming humiliation experienced by most of the world's population. … It is neither Islam nor even poverty itself directly that succours terrorists whose ferocity and creativity are unprecedented in human history, but the crushing humiliation that has infected third world countries like cancer.[16]

In a very real sense, the effects of colonialism and subsequent Western interference or domination could be seen as responsible for this shared sense of humiliation across the rest of the world.

Arguably, these feelings of humiliation are not just confined to economically 'deprived' populations. Despite the simplistic narrative that Trump voters in the 2016 American election were poor or newly unemployed 'blue-collar workers'—code for less educated white males—they did not represent the most economically marginalised demographics.[17] Those populations were either disenfranchised or, more often, voted for the Democrats. In other words, populist ressentiment does not always surge from the straightforward economic conditions of its sufferers. Ressentiment did not seem to bedevil the 'swing state' rust-belt voters in the immediate wake of the global financial crisis, but rather two elections later. The emotion of ressentiment can be massaged and encouraged for political purpose. This is at play when one is told that one's community or identity is under threat, leading white evangelical Christians in America absurdly to 'see more discrimination against Christians than Muslims in the United States.'* In Bangladesh, meanwhile, there is a growing perception that Islam needs defending. This is despite the everyday persecution and diminishment of minority religious communities in Bangladesh, and the prejudicial dispensation of the law in favour of the majority group.

These myths, which play on the psychology of the individual, can be unleashed to serve the demagogue and the political opportunist. In this less-than-rational deployment, it helps if the perceived threat is only somewhat connected with reality. It can then never properly be proved to be false, its claims either being completely made up or perpetually expectant of a shadowy reality that never arrives. As Scheler puts it, 'Precisely because this kind of hostility is not caused by the "enemy's" actions and behaviour, it is deeper and more irreconcilable than any other.'[18]

Ironically enough, the concept of a pan-Islamic identity, which supposes that the humiliation of a Palestinian is shared by, say, an Indonesian, was fostered by the West itself. As Saudi Crown Prince Mohammad Bin Salman claimed in Washington, D.C. in 2018, his oil-rich kingdom spread Wahhabism at the behest of the West in order to push back against communism. In Bangladesh, as in many other parts of the world, the Saudi scheme has been central to the solidification of a pan-Islamic identity—one that is taking precedence over a Bengali or South Asian one. Thus, in many ways, the Cold War and Western nations' efforts, alongside allies such as Saudi Arabia, have created the conditions for radical terrorism both by inducing resentment through hegemonic domination, and by directly sponsoring the adoption of

* Ibid.

a homogenous Muslim identity, which has created a sense among otherwise unrelated people that another's persecution is theirs too, just because the victim happens to be a Muslim. This also points us to why political Islam is so potent. If 1.4 billion Muslims see their fates as linked, then of course that entity has the power to transform the world. Thus, it becomes clear how the notion of political Islam is precisely that: political. If Muslims in Bangladesh value or adhere to heterodox Bengali traditions, the unity of the Muslim world, or the *ummah*, is seen by some to evaporate, depriving Muslims of power. Forcing people at machete-point to believe or express a particular orthodoxy takes on a new meaning.

In sum, a number of concurrent trends and phenomena coalesce to cause extremism, which has the capability in rough political seas to upturn the messy but supposedly liberal character of Bangladesh since its inception as a nation state in 1971. In recent years, the guardians of the Bangladeshi state have accommodated more demands from radical groups as they seek to maintain their own power. If this goes on, politics in Bangladesh will undoubtedly continue to be shaped by the movements, people and ideas discussed in this book.

NOTES

INTRODUCTION

1. Edward Said, *Orientalism*, New York: Vintage Books, 1979, p. 10.

1. THE IDEA

1. Simon Dring, 'Tanks Crush Revolt in Pakistan', *The Daily Telegraph*, 30 March 1971. Accessible at http://www.docstrangelove.com/uploads/1971/foreign/19710330_dt_tanks_crush_revolt_in_pakistan.pdf
2. Shiraz Maher, *Salafi-Jihadism: The History of an Idea*, London: Hurst & Co., 2016, p. 145.
3. Ibid., p. 7.
4. Ibid., p. 181.
5. Karen Armstrong, *Fields of Blood: Religion and the History of Violence*, New York and Toronto: Knopf, 2014, p. 312.
6. The Muslim 500, http://themuslim500.com/profile/sayeedi-delwar-hossain
7. Ali Riaz, *Islamist Militancy in Bangladesh: A Complex Web*, New York: Routledge, 2008, p. 57.
8. A *waz mahfil* is a semi-musical public performance based on scripture.
9. Farahnaz Ispahani, *Purifying the Land of the Pure*, New York: Oxford University Press, 2015, p. 63.
10. Pakistan Bureau of Statistics, 'Population by Mother Tongue', 2006, http://www.pbs.gov.pk/sites/default/files/tables/POPULATION%20BY%20MOTHER%20TONGUE.pdf
11. Muhammad Ali Jinnah, quoted in Christophe Jaffrelot, *The Pakistan Paradox: Instability and Resilience*, London: Hurst & Co., 2015, p. 101.

12. On 15 August 1947, on the eve of independence, India's first prime minister, Jawaharlal Nehru, delivered a famous speech in Delhi: 'Long years ago we made a tryst with destiny, and now the time comes when we shall redeem our pledge, not wholly or in full measure, but very substantially. At the stroke of the midnight hour, when the world sleeps, India will awake to life and freedom.'

13. Salil Tripathi, *The Colonel Who Would Not Repent: The Bangladesh War and Its Unquiet Legacy*, New Haven: Yale University Press, 2016, p. 9.

14. 'By the turn of the nineteenth century,' notes Sushil Chaudhury, 'pro-Bengali views were being vigorously expressed.' As notions of Muslim-Indian identity were increasingly discussed in the region, so too was the assertion that the two identities Bengali and Muslim were not mutually exclusive. Sushil Chaudhury, 'Identity and Composite Culture: The Bengal Case', *Journal of the Asiatic Society of Bangladesh* 58, no. 1 (June 2013), pp. 1–25.

15. 'Pakistani and French Envoys Criticize UN Involvement in Bangladesh War Crimes Process', 12 May 2009, via Wikileaks, https://www.wikileaks.org/plusd/cables/09DHAKA474_a.hml

16. Sheikh Mujib had put forward a list of six demands in 1966. They were as follows: 1. For a federal Pakistan with universal adult franchise; 2. For the federal government to be tasked only with defense and foreign affairs, and for all other matters to be conducted by the federating states; 3. For distinct currencies for the respective wings, and/or independent central banks, and/or measures to prevent capital flight from east to west; 4. For the power of taxation and revenue collection to be held by the federating states; 5. For foreign exchange earnings to be held by the respective wings, and for the federating states to have the ability to build trading relations with foreign states; 6. For East Pakistan to have its own military or paramilitary and for the nation's navy to be headquartered in East Pakistan.

17. Tripathi, *The Colonel Who Would Not Repent*, p. 49.

18. Gary Bass, *The Blood Telegram: Nixon, Kissinger and a Forgotten Genocide*, London: Hurst & Co., 2014, p. 23.

19. S. Mahmud Ali, *Understanding Bangladesh*, London: Hurst & Co., 2010, p. 44.

20. Archer K. Blood, *The Cruel Birth of Bangladesh: Memoirs of an American Diplomat*, Dhaka: University Press Ltd, 2002, p. 115.

21. Bass, *The Blood Telegram*, p. 102.

22. Bass, *The Blood Telegram*, p. 24.

23. Blood, *The Cruel Birth of Bangladesh*, p. 116.

24. Central Intelligence Agency, 'Weekly Summary Special Report', 14 August 1970, p. 6, https://www.cia.gov/library/readingroom/docs/CIA-RDP85T00875R001500020039-8.pdf

25. Blood, *The Cruel Birth of Bangladesh*, p. 116.

26. Central Intelligence Agency, 'Weekly Summary Special Report', p. 5.

27. Ispahani, *Purifying the Land of the Pure*, p. 73.

28. Ibid.

29. Ibid.

30. Yahya Khan, radio broadcast, 2 March 1971, quoted in Sumit Ganguly, *Conflict Unending: India-Pakistan Tensions Since 1947*, New York: Columbia University Press, 2001, p. 59.

31. Blood, *The Cruel Birth of Bangladesh*, p. 155.

32. Sheikh Mujibur Rahman, speech on 7 March 1971, https://www.youtube.com/watch?v=rLol-VrOoB8

33. Ispahani, *Purifying the Land of the Pure*, p. 71.

34. Victor Mallet, 'Hindu minority become target of Bangladesh violence', *Financial Times*, 13 January 2014, https://www.ft.com/content/31cdd556-7c2d-11e3-9179-00144feabdc0

35. Dring, 'Tanks Crush Revolt in Pakistan'.

36. Ibid.

37. Malcolm W. Browne, 'Army Men in Pakistan See Heresy in Western-Style Education There', *The New York Times*, 13 May 1971, http://www.docstrangelove.com/uploads/1971/foreign/19710513_nyt_army_men_in_pakistan_see_heresy_in_western_style_education_there.pdf

38. 'Newsman Killed at the War's End', *The New York Times*, 5 May 1975, https://www.nytimes.com/1975/05/05/archives/newsman-killed-at-the-wars-end-french-photographer-was-hit-in-clash.html

39. Dring, 'Tanks Crush Revolt in Pakistan'.

40. Fray Sebastien Manrique, quoted in Richard M. Eaton, *The Rise of Islam on the Bengal Frontier, 1204–1760*, Berkeley: University of California Press, 1993, pp. 156, 177.

41. Blood, *The Cruel Birth of Bangladesh*, p. 196.

42. Ibid., p. 202.

43. Richard Sisson and Leo E. Rose, *War and Secession: Pakistan, India, and the Creation of Bangladesh*, Berkeley and Los Angeles: University of California Press, 1990, p. 154.

44. Yahya Khan, quoted in ibid.

45. Anthony Mascarenhas, 'Genocide', *The Sunday Times*, 13 June 1971, http://www.docstrangelove.com/uploads/1971/foreign/19710613_tst_genocide_center_page.pdf

46. 'Lie Worked Well', *The Daily Star*, 4 March 2013, http://www.thedailystar.net/news-detail-271242

47. Gary Bass, 'Bargaining Away Justice', *International Security* 41, no. 2 (Fall 2016), pp. 140–87.

48. Joseph Allchin, 'Explaining Bangladesh's Month of Massive Street Protests and Violence', Vice, 3 March 2013, https://www.vice.com/en_uk/article/ex5evj/explaining-Bangladeshs-month-of-massive-street-protests-and-violence

49. 'BNP cautiously welcomes Shahbagh protests', BDnews24, 12 February 2013, http://bdnews24.com/politics/2013/02/12/bnp-cautiously-welcomes-shahbagh-protests

50. 'The Final Sentence', *The Economist*, 13 September 2013, http://www.economist.com/blogs/banyan/2013/09/bangladesh-s-war-crimes-trials

51. Geeta Anand and Julfikar Ali Manik, 'Bangladesh Says It Now Knows Who's Killing the Bloggers', *The New York Times*, 8 June 2016, https://www.nytimes.com/2016/06/09/world/asia/bangladesh-killings-bloggers.html?_r=0

52. 'Out with a new trick?', *The Daily Star*, 20 February 2013, http://www.thedailystar.net/news-detail-269751

53. Ibid.

54. Prabir Barua Chowdhury and Farhana Mirza Barna, 'Khaleda slams Shahbagh youths', *The Daily Star*, 16 March 2013, https://www.thedailystar.net/news/khaleda-slams-shahbagh-youths

55. 'Widow of slain U.S.-Bangladeshi blogger lashes out at Dhaka', Reuters, 11 May 2015, http://www.reuters.com/article/us-usa-bangladesh-assassination-exclusiv-idUSKBN0NW04S20150511

56. 'Panel to check comments on Islam, Prophet,' BDnews24, 13 March 2013, http://bdnews24.com/bangladesh/2013/03/13/panel-to-check-comments-on-islam-prophet

57. 'Prime Minister Hasina says hurting religious sensitivities will not be accepted', BDnews24, 3 September 2015, http://bdnews24.com/bangladesh/2015/09/03/prime-minister-hasina-says-hurting-religious-sensitivities-will-not-be-accepted

2. 1975—ANNUS HORRIBILIS

1. Lawrence Lifschultz, *Bangladesh: The Unfinished Revolution*, London: Zed Press, 1979, p. 108.

2. Naomi Hossain, *Understanding Bangladesh's Unexpected Successes*, New York: Oxford University Press, 2017, p. 5.

3.   S. Mahmud Ali, *Understanding Bangladesh*, London: Hurst & Co., 2010, p. 107.
4.   Gary Bass, 'Bargaining Away Justice', *International Security* 41, no. 2 (Fall 2016), pp. 140–87.
5.   Ibid.
6.   Ibid.
7.   Talks between Secretary Kissinger and Prime Minister Mujib of Bangladesh, The Library of Congress, 30 October 1974.
8.   Salil Tripathi, *The Colonel Who Would Not Repent: The Bangladesh War and Its Unquiet Legacy*, New Haven: Yale University Press, 2016, p. 240.
9.   Ali, *Understanding Bangladesh*, p. 119.
10. Ibid.
11. 'A Just Cause Enjoys Abundant Support While An Unjust Cause Finds Little Support', *Peking Review* 51, 17 December 1971, p. 10, https://www.marxists.org/subject/china/peking-review/1971/PR1971-51.pdf
12. Ibid.
13. The Vietnamese invaded Cambodia in January 1979 to liberate the country from the clutches of the genocidal, Chinese-backed Khmer Rouge regime. Rather than welcoming the demise of the Khmer Rouge as a result of a neighbourly intervention by Vietnam, Western powers refused to recognise the pro-Vietnamese government in Phnom Penh, still vindictive that the Vietnamese had defeated the might of the United States. Instead, at the United Nations, they recognised the rump of Pol Pot's regime, which hid out on the Thailand–Cambodia border. This state of petty denial endured until 1991. William Shawcross' book *Sideshow* is well worth reading on the tragedy that that country endured. William Shawcross, *Sideshow: Kissinger, Nixon and the Destruction of Cambodia*, New York: Simon and Schuster, 1979.
14. Lifschultz, *Bangladesh*, p. 5.
15. Ali, *Understanding Bangladesh*, p. 120.
16. Abu Taher was determined not only to uphold the socialist elements of the newly independent state but also to instigate the revocation of colonial-era class hierarchy within the military. Abu Taher fell out with Mujib over Baksal and what he saw as unprincipled stances that the independence hero had taken.
17. 'High Court rules on "historic truth"', BDnews24, 21 June 2009, http://bdnews24.com/bangladesh/2009/06/21/high-court-rules-on-historical-truth
18. Ali, *Understanding Bangladesh*, p. 125.

19. 'Last Week in Bangladesh in Retrospect', 12 November 1975, via Wikileaks, https://wikileaks.org/plusd/cables/1975STATE267536_b.html

20. Ali, *Understanding Bangladesh*, p. 129.

21. 'Bangladesh: Leadership Troubles', 17 November 1975, via Wikileaks https://wikileaks.org/plusd/cables/1975DACCA05642_b.html

22. Lifschultz, *Bangladesh*, p. 51.

23. Ali Riaz, *Islamist Militancy in Bangladesh: A Complex Web*, New York: Routledge, 2008, p. 47.

24. Gary Bass, *The Blood Telegram: Nixon, Kissinger and a Forgotten Genocide*, London: Hurst & Co., 2014, p. 144.

25. 'Special Bangladesh Envoy to Pakistan', 25 November 1975, via Wikileaks, https://wikileaks.org/plusd/cables/1975ISLAMA10900_b.html

26. 'Trouble in Bangladesh: Quiet, Not Peace of Mind Prevails', 22 November 1975, via Wikileaks https://wikileaks.org/plusd/cables/1975DACCA05775_b.html

27. David Lewis, *Bangladesh: Politics, Economy and Civil Society*, Cambridge: Cambridge University Press, 2011.

28. Riaz, *Islamist Militancy in Bangladesh*, p. 37.

29. 'Never Trust a Non-Muslim [Anwar Awlaki]', YouTube, 10 January 2012, https://www.youtube.com/watch?v=TAOH1OXoy18

30. Jason Burke, *The New Threat from Islamic Militancy*, London: The Bodley Head, 2015, p. 114.

31. Scott Shane, 'The Lessons of Anwar al-Awlaki', *The New York Times*, 27 August 2015, https://www.nytimes.com/2015/08/30/magazine/the-lessons-of-anwar-al-awlaki.html?_r=0

32. Burke, *The New Threat from Islamic Militancy*, p. 114.

33. Shiraz Maher, *Salafi-Jihadism: The History of an Idea*, London: Hurst & Co., 2016, p. 35.

34. 'Another blogger stabbed at Pallabi', BDnews24, 7 March 2013, http://bdnews24.com/bangladesh/2013/03/07/another-blogger-stabbed-at-pallabi

35. 'Bangladesh: Beleaguered Bloggers', The International Federation of Journalists Asia-Pacific, 3 May 2016, https://samsn.ifj.org/bangladesh-beleaguered-bloggers; 'Panel to check comments on Islam, Prophet', BDnews24, 13 March 2013, http://bdnews24.com/bangladesh/2013/03/13/panel-to-check-comments-on-islam-prophet

36. Pulack Ghatack, 'Militants' hit-list preserved with police', *The Daily Observer*, 13 August 2015, http://www.observerbd.com/2015/08/13/104719.php

3. MOBILISATION

1. Empiricist philosophical movements are arguably more indigenous to the Indian subcontinent than Islam is. For more, see Charvaka and its philosophical origins, which began in the subcontinent about a thousand years prior to the birth of Islam in the Middle East.

2. Moinul Hoque Chowdhury, Reazul Bashar, Shaikh Abdullah and Golam Mujtaba, 'Govt must accede to our demands: Hifazat', BDnews24, 6 April 2013, http://bdnews24.com/bangladesh/2013/04/06/govt-must-accede-to-our-demands-hifazat

3. '18-party extends support to Islamists' demand', *The Daily Star*, 2 April 2013, http://www.thedailystar.net/news/18-party-extends-support-to-islamists-demand

4. Human Rights Watch, 'Blood on the Streets: The Use of Excessive Force During Bangladesh Protests', 1 August 2013, https://www.hrw.org/report/2013/08/01/blood-streets/use-excessive-force-during-bangladesh-protests#_ftn39

5. Jim Yardley and Julfikar Ali Manik, 'Anti-Blasphemy Protests in Bangladesh Turn Violent', *The New York Times*, 6 May 2013, http://www.nytimes.com/2013/05/07/world/asia/two-days-of-riots-in-bangladesh-turn-deadly.html?_r=0

6. Front Line Defenders, 'Ongoing Harassment of Adilur Rahman Khan', https://www.frontlinedefenders.org/en/case/ongoing-harassment-adilur-rahman-khan

7. 'MP George Galloway - Speaks at a protest against Mass killing of 1000s of Ulama in Bangladesh', YouTube, https://www.youtube.com/watch?v=7qpx6JGxzjo

8. UK Parliament, 'Alleged Massacre in Bangladesh, Early Day Motion 100', 15 May 2013, http://www.parliament.uk/edm/2013-14/100

9. Shakhawat Liton, 'BNP walks away from Sangsad', *The Daily Star*, 25 January 2012, https://www.thedailystar.net/news-detail-219808

10. Mushtaq H. Khan, 'Markets, States and Democracy: Patron-Client Networks and the Case for Democracy in Developing Countries', *Democratization* 12, no. 5 (2005), pp. 704–24.

11. 'I strongly oppose Hajj and Tablig Jamaat: Latif Siddiqui', *The Daily Observer*, 20 September 2014, http://www.observerbd.com/2014/09/29/46219.php

12. Ali Riaz, *Islamist Militancy in Bangladesh: A Complex Web*, New York: Routledge, 2008, p. 38.

13. Shah H. Imam, 'Sign of entente between AL and far-right?', *The Daily Star*, 8 March 2015.

14. http://www.ittefaq.com.bd/wholecountry/2016/03/16/59857.html
15. Riaz, *Islamist Militancy in Bangladesh*, p. 36.
16. Uttam Sengupta, 'Hifazat madrassa raided, bombs, explosives seized', BDnews24, 8 October 2013, http://bdnews24.com/bangladesh/2013/10/08/hifazat-madrasa-raided-bombs-explosives-seized
17. Arges Type HG 84 (Hand Grenade) Fragmentation Hand Grenade, via Militaryfactory.com, http://www.militaryfactory.com/smallarms/detail.asp?smallarms_id=141
18. 'Diplomatic Security Daily', 3 November 2008, via Wikileaks, https://wikileaks.org/plusd/cables/08STATE116943_a.html
19. 'Khaleda Zia Consolidates Leadership and BNP Adjusts to Life After Tarique Rahman', 27 October 2008, via wikileaks, https://wikileaks.org/plusd/cables/08DHAKA1120_a.html
20. Ashif Islam Shaon, 'Hasina escaped 4 assassination attempts in 25 years', *Dhaka Tribune*, 20 August 2014, https://www.dhakatribune.com/uncategorized/2014/08/20/hasina-escaped-4-assassination-attempts-in-25-years
21. Julfikar Ali Manik and Chaitanya Chandra Halder, 'Tarique okayed HUJI plot', *The Daily Star*, 22 August 2011, http://www.thedailystar.net/news-detail-199652
22. Kailash Sarkar, 'Huji's Hannan, Lashkar's Obaidullah old friends', *The Daily Star*, 22 July 2009, http://www.thedailystar.net/news-detail-98170
23. Manik and Halder, 'Tarique okayed HUJI plot'.
24. 'Senior Army Officer Briefs Embassy on Hasina Arrest', 19 July 2007, via Wikileaks, https://wikileaks.org/plusd/cables/07DHAKA1176_a.html
25. 'Ambassador Warns Bangladesh Intelligence Head to End Flirtation With Islamic Democratic Party', 17 November 2008, via Wikileaks, https://wikileaks.org/plusd/cables/08DHAKA1180_a.html
26. 'Senior Army Officer Briefs Embassy on Hasina Arrest'.
27. Ali Riaz, 'Islamist Parties, Elections and Democracy in Bangladesh', in Quinn Mecham and Julie Chernov Hwang (eds), *Islamist Parties and Political Normalization in the Muslim World*, Philadelphia: University of Pennsylvania Press, 2014, p. 167.
28. Ibid., p. 168.
29. Richard M. Eaton, *The Rise of Islam and the Bengal Frontier, 1204–1760*, Berkeley: University of California Press, 1993, p. 234.
30. Ibid., p. 292.
31. Ibid. p. 231.

32. Ibid. p. 267.

33. International Crisis Group, 'The Threat from Jamaat ul Mujahideen Bangladesh, Asia Report N°187', 1 March 2010, https://www.scribd.com/document/63908236/Jamaat-ul-Mujahideen

34. Ibid.

35. Eaton, *The Rise of Islam and the Bengal Frontier*, p. 50.

36. 'Bye Bye Bangla Bhai?,' 2 February 2005, via Wikileaks, https://wikileaks.org/plusd/cables/05DHAKA500_a.html

37. Julfikar Ali Manik, 'Bangla Bhai active for 6 yrs', *The Daily Star*, 13 May 2004, http://archive.thedailystar.net/2004/05/13/d4051301022.htm

38. Joseph Allchin and Matt Leone, 'Gaming in Dhaka', Polygon, 24 November 2014, https://www.polygon.com/features/2014/11/24/7258031/dhaka-bangladesh-video-games

39. Julfikar Ali Manik, 'Bangla Bhai's outfit has BNP men's blessing?', *The Daily Star*, 15 May 2004, http://archive.thedailystar.net/2004/05/15/d4051501022.htm

40. Julfikar Ali Manik, 'The Bangla Bhai Story', *The Daily Star*, 21 June 2007, http://archive.thedailystar.net/2007/06/21/d7062101011.htm

41. Riaz, *Islamist Militancy in Bangladesh*, p. 52.

42. Ibid., p. 127.

43. 'Jama'atul Mujahideen Bangladesh's "Three Tiers of Threat"', 13 February 2006, via Wikileaks, https://wikileaks.org/plusd/cables/06DHAKA768_a.html

44. In Bangladesh, family and inheritance law is dictated by a person's religion. Hindu and Muslim inheritance law prioritises male heirs.

45. 'No alliance with Hefajat: Quader', *The Daily Star*, 13 April 2017, http://www.thedailystar.net/country/no-alliance-hefazat-quader-1390792

46. 'PM Hasina says she too "dislikes" statue at Supreme Court', BDnews24, 11 April 2017, http://bdnews24.com/bangladesh/2017/04/11/pm-hasina-says-she-too-dislikes-statue-at-supreme-court

47. Chaitanya Chandra Halder and Shamim Ashraf, '2 Britons funded JMB to carry out bomb attacks', *The Daily Star*, 9 February 2006, http://archive.thedailystar.net/2006/02/09/d6020901044.htm

48. Probir, K. Sarker, 'First mass attack since 2005', *Dhaka Tribune*, 31 October 2015, https://www.dhakatribune.com/uncategorized/2015/10/31/first-mass-attack-since-2005

49. 'JMB Terrorist Investigation Marches On – Up to a Point', 3 May 2006, via Wikileaks, https://wikileaks.org/plusd/cables/06DHAKA2573_a.html

50. 'Bangladeshi Efforts to Bring JMB Bombers to Justice', 21 November 2005, via Wikileaks, https://wikileaks.org/plusd/cables/05DHAKA5650_a.html

51. 'Dissent From a Chief Zia Advisor', 15 December 2005, via Wikileaks, https://wikileaks.org/plusd/cables/05DHAKA6190_a.html

52. Tashrif Islam, 'JMB militants getting nomination for UP elections', Norrfika, 6 May 2016, http://www.norrfika.se/english/jmb-militants-getting-nomination-for-up-elections/

4. THE URBAN JIHAD

1. Douglas Murray, 'Where is the world's densest city?', *The Guardian*, 11 May 2017, https://www.theguardian.com/cities/2017/may/11/where-world-most-densely-populated-city

2. Ali Riaz, 'Who Are the Bangladeshi Islamists?', *Perspectives on Terrorism* 10, no. 1 (2016), http://www.terrorismanalysts.com/pt/index.php/pot/article/view/485

3. David Montero, 'Pakistani Militants Expand Abroad, Starting in Bangladesh', *The Christian Science Monitor*, 5 August 2010, http://www.csmonitor.com/World/Asia-South-Central/2010/0805/Pakistani-militants-expand-abroad-starting-in-Bangladesh

4. International Crisis Group, 'Mapping Bangladesh's Political Crisis, Asia Report N°264', 9 February 2015, https://d2071andvip0wj.cloudfront.net/264-mapping-bangladesh-s-political-crisis.pdf

5. Joseph Allchin, 'Whatever It Takes', *The Caravan*, 1 February 2014, http://www.caravanmagazine.in/letters/bangladesh-whatever-it-takes

6. Author's interview with senior BNP leader, on condition of anonymity.

7. Avijit Roy, 'The Virus of Faith', *Free Inquiry* 35, no. 3 (April/May 2015), https://www.centerforinquiry.net/uploads/attachments/Avijit-Roy-Final-Free-Inquiry.pdf

8. Ibid.

9. 'Farabi returns!', BDnews24, 26 August 2013, http://bdnews24.com/bangladesh/2013/08/26/farabi-returns

10. Front Line Defenders, 'Victim Blaming: Bangladesh's Failure to Protect Human Rights Defenders', November 2016, https://www.frontlinedefenders.org/sites/default/files/front_line_defenders_bangladesh_report_final_16_november_2016.pdf

11. Joshua Hammer, 'The Imperiled Bloggers of Bangladesh', *The New York Times*, 29 December 2015, https://www.nytimes.com/2016/01/03/magazine/the-price-of-secularism-in-bangladesh.html

12. Pew Research Center, 'Chapter 1: Beliefs About Sharia', 30 April 2013, http://www.pewforum.org/2013/04/30/the-worlds-muslims-religion-politics-society-beliefs-about-sharia/

13. 'Speaking against Jamaat tantamount to speaking against Islam', *The Daily Star*, 1 April 2005, http://archive.thedailystar.net/2005/04/01/d50401060668.htm

14. 'As-Saḥāb Media presents a new video message from al-Qā'idah's Dr. Ayman al-Ẓawāhirī: "Bangladesh: A Massacre Behind a Wall of Silence"', Jihadology.net, 14 January 2014, http://jihadology.net/2014/01/14/as-sa%E1%B8%A5ab-media-presents-a-new-video-message-from-al-qaidahs-dr-ayman-al-%E1%BA%93awahiri-bangladesh-a-massacre-behind-a-wall-of-silence/

15. Animesh Roul, 'Radical thinking—Transnational jihadists eye Bangladesh', *Jane's Intelligence Review*, 14 April 2014, https://janes.ihs.com/TerrorismInsurgencyCentre/Display/1708184

16. Raffaello Pantucci, 'Al-Awlaki Recruits Bangladeshi Militants for Strike on the United States', *Terrorism Monitor* 9, no. 7 (17 February 2011), https://jamestown.org/program/al-awlaki-recruits-bangladeshi-militants-for-strike-on-the-united-states/

17. Raffaello Pantucci, *'We Love Death As You Love Life': Britain's Suburban Terrorists*, London: Hurst and Co., 2015, p. 279.

18. Shariful Islam, 'Missing man now wanted', *The Daily Star*, 6 August 2016, http://www.thedailystar.net/frontpage/missing-man-now-wanted-1265359

19. Tehzeeb Karim, LinkedIn, https://www.linkedin.com/in/tehzeebk/?ppe=1

20. Tamanna Khan and Subir Das, 'Progressive force its prime target', *The Daily Star*, 14 August 2013, http://www.thedailystar.net/news/progressive-force-its-prime-target

21. Mosi Secret, '30-Year Prison Sentence in Plot to Bomb U.S. Bank', *The New York Times*, 9 August 2013, http://www.nytimes.com/2013/08/10/nyregion/30-year-sentence-for-man-who-tried-to-bomb-federal-reserve.html

22. Dean Nelson and David Bergman, 'New York Fed bomb plot: how Quazi Ahsan Nafis became radicalised', *The Telegraph*, 18 October 2012, http://www.telegraph.co.uk/news/worldnews/northamerica/usa/9617009/New-York-Fed-bomb-plot-how-Quazi-Ahsan-Nafis-became-radicalised.html

23. Nitin Gokhale, 'Bangladesh coup attempt: 5 members of banned Islamist outfit arrested', NDTV, 20 January 2012, http://www.ndtv.com/world-news/bangladesh-coup-attempt-5-members-of-banned-islamist-outfit-arrested-571152

24. 'Major Zia used UK mobile SIM to talk to officers', *The Daily Star*, 21 January 2012, http://www.thedailystar.net/news-detail-219282

25. Nuruzzaman Labu, 'Maj Zia was present when Avijit Roy was murdered', *Dhaka Tribune*, 7 November 2017, http://www.dhakatribune.com/bangladesh/crime/2017/11/07/maj-zia-present-avijit-roy-murdered/
26. David Bergman, 'Due Process and Bangladesh's Counter-Terrorism Measures', *The Wire*, 8 October 2016, https://thewire.in/71832/due-process-bangladeshs-counter-terrorism-measures/
27. Arifur Rahman Rabbi, 'Police: Sharif knew everything', *Dhaka Tribune*, 20 June 2016, http://www.dhakatribune.com/bangladesh/2016/06/20/police-sharif-knew-everything/
28. 'Prime Minister Concerned About Her Government's Future, Seeks USG Support', 12 March 2009, via Wikileaks, https://wikileaks.org/plusd/cables/09DHAKA263_a.html
29. Amy Kazmin and Joseph Allchin, 'Bangladesh to execute 152 found guilty of mutiny', *Financial Times*, 5 November 2013, https://www.ft.com/content/e013159c-45fd-11e3-b495-00144feabdc0
30. Victor Mallet, 'Bangladesh army funded to forget its role as neutral referee', *Financial Times*, 26 April 2015, https://www.ft.com/content/7baf6f5c-ea74-11e4-a701-00144feab7de
31. Hammer, 'The Imperiled Bloggers of Bangladesh'.
32. Julfikar Ali Manik and Ellen Barry, 'A Transgender Bangladeshi Changes Perceptions After Catching Murder Suspects', *The New York Times*, 2 April 2015, https://www.nytimes.com/2015/04/03/world/asia/an-act-of-courage-catches-murder-suspects-and-changes-perceptions-in-bangladesh.html
33. 'Remembering Ananta Bijoy: An unsung luminous soul', Mukto-Mona, 11 May 2017, http://enblog.mukto-mona.com/2017/05/11/remembering-ananta-bijoy-an-unsung-luminous-soul/
34. 'Swedish visa denied for murdered blogger Das', *The Local*, 13 May 2015, https://www.thelocal.se/20150513/sweden-slammed-for-denying-visa-to-murdered-blogger
35. 'Statement on the murder of "Niloy Neel"', Mukto-Mona, 7 August 2015, http://enblog.mukto-mona.com/2015/08/07/statement-on-the-murder-of-niloy-neel/
36. Praveen Swami, 'Head of al-Qaeda in Indian Subcontinent is from Uttar Pradesh', *The Indian Express*, 17 December 2015, http://indianexpress.com/article/india/india-news-india/head-of-al-qaeda-in-indian-subcontinent-is-from-up/
37. Asim Tanveer and Maria Golovnina, 'Al Qaeda's shadowy new "emir" in South Asia handed tough job', Reuters, 9 September 2014, http://www.reuters.com/article/us-southasia-alqaeda-insight-idUSKBN0H42DN20140909

38. C. Christine Fair, 'The Foreign Policy Essay: Al Qaeda's Re-launch in South Asia', Lawfare, 21 September 2014, https://www.lawfareblog.com/foreign-policy-essay-al-qaedas-re-launch-south-asia

39. Jeff Stein, 'Ayman al-Zawahiri: How a CIA Drone Strike Nearly Killed the Head of Al-Qaeda', Newsweek, 21 April 2017, http://www.newsweek.com/ayman-al-zawahiri-cia-donald-trump-drone-strike-osama-bin-laden-pakistan-587732

40. Praveen Swami, 'More Qaeda-Pak links: AQIS chief was at "ISI" PoK camp', The Indian Express, 13 March 2015, http://indianexpress.com/article/india/india-others/more-qaeda-pak-links-aqis-chief-was-at-isi-pok-camp/

41. Syed Tashfin Chowdhury, 'Al Qaeda Franchise in Bangladesh Claims Responsibility for Blogger's Murder', Vice, 4 May 2015, https://news.vice.com/article/al-qaeda-franchise-in-bangladesh-claims-responsibility-for-bloggers-murder

42. Benedict Wilkinson and Jack Barclay, The Language of Jihad: Narratives and Strategies of Al-Qa'ida in the Arabian Peninsula and UK Responses, London: Royal United Services Institute, 2011, https://rusi.org/sites/default/files/201201_whr_the_language_of_jihad_0.pdf

43. 'New statement from The Global Islamic Media Front and Anṣār Allah Bangla Team: "Glad Tidings: And Refuting the Lies of the Media"', Jihadology.net, 30 June 2015, http://jihadology.net/2015/06/30/new-statement-from-the-global-islamic-media-front-and-an%E1%B9%A3ar-allah-bangla-team-glad-tidings-and-refuting-the-lies-of-the-media/

44. Amy Kazmin and Joseph Allchin, 'Fears rise in Bangladesh after attack on secular forces', Financial Times, 1 November 2015, https://www.ft.com/content/a1cb09e0-8069-11e5-8095-ed1a37d1e096

45. 'Tutul: the Survivor—An interview with the target of a Bangladesh machete attack', International Humanist and Ethical Union, 4 April 2016, http://iheu.org/tutul-the-survivor-an-interview-with-the-target-of-a-bangladesh-machete-attack/

46. Raihan Abir, 'Another victim of state religion, free-thinker hacked to death by machete', Mukto-Mona, 7 April 2016, http://enblog.mukto-mona.com/2016/04/07/another-victim-of-state-religion-free-thinker-hacked-to-death-by-machete/

47. 'Bangladeshi secular bloggers should "control" their writings: Home Minister Asaduzzaman Khan', The Indian Express, 10 April 2016, http://indianexpress.com/article/world/world-news/bangladeshi-secular-bloggers-nazimuddin-samad-should-control-their-writings-home-minister-asaduzzaman-khan/

48. I. G. Napit, 'Se apagó el arcoíris en Bangladesh', *El País*, 9 May 2016, http://elpais.com/elpais/2016/05/06/planeta_futuro/1462532743_565781.html

49. Mohammad Jamil Khan, 'LGBT magazine Roopbaan editor hacked to death', *Dhaka Tribune*, 25 April 2016, http://archive.dhakatribune.com/bangladesh/2016/apr/25/dipu-monis-cousin-among-2-murdered-kalabagan

50. Arifur R. Rabbi, 'No investigator has contacted family in one year', *Dhaka Tribune*, 25 April 2017, http://www.dhakatribune.com/bangladesh/crime/2017/04/25/no-investigator-contacted-family-one-year/

51. 'Statement Regarding the Assassination of Xulhaz Mannan and Samir Mahbub Tonoy', via Jihadology, 4 May 2016, https://azelin.files.wordpress.com/2016/05/anscca3acc84r-al-islacc84m-bangladesh-22regarding-the-assassination-of-xulhaz-mannan-and-samir-mahbub-tonoy22.pdf

52. Ministry of Law, Justice and Parliamentary Affairs, Bangladesh, 'The Penal Code, 1860: Chapter XVI Of Offences Affecting The Human Body, Unnatural offences', http://bdlaws.minlaw.gov.bd/sections_detail.php?id=11&sections_id=3233

53. '"Writing for unnatural sex is a criminal offence"', *Dhaka Tribune*, 6 May 2016, https://www.dhakatribune.com/bangladesh/2016/05/06/writing-unnatural-sex-criminal-offence

54. 'Homosexuality is a criminal offence: Home Minister tells Nisha', News Bangladesh, 5 May 2016, http://www.newsbangladesh.com/english/details/14087

5. A DYSFUNCTIONAL NEIGHBOURHOOD

1. 'ULFA paid $99 mn bribe for arms' passage in Bangladesh', *The Hindustan Times*, 11 November 2010, http://www.hindustantimes.com/world/ulfa-paid-99-mn-bribe-for-arms-passage-in-bangladesh/story-kX8q5V34fAGRYEN4T2yk2O.html

2. Anthony Davis, 'New details emerge on Bangladesh arms haul', *Jane's Intelligence Review*, 1 August 2004.

3. Satish Kumar, ed., *India's National Security: Annual Review 2009*, New Delhi: Routledge, 19 June 2009.

4. Bertil Lintner, *Great Game East: India, China, and the Struggle for Asia's Most Volatile Frontier*, New Haven: Yale University Press, 2015, p. 146.

5. Ibid., p. 144.

6. 'Loyalty and Access Trump Titles in Influencing PM', 11 May 2005, via Wikileaks, https://wikileaks.org/plusd/cables/05DHAKA2243_a.html

7. 'Chittagong Candidates with Checkered Pasts Seek Redemption as Voters Remain Wary of Violence', 23 December 2008, via Wikileaks, https://wikileaks.org/plusd/cables/08DHAKA1334_a.html

8. International Crimes Tribunal-1, 'ICT-BD Case No. 01 of 2011 … The Chief Prosecutor Versus Delowar Hossain Sayeedi', 28 February 2013, p. 42, https://bangladeshtrialobserver.files.wordpress.com/2012/12/judgment-sayedee.pdf

9. Human Rights Watch, 'Bangladesh: Investigate Killing of Witness', 23 December 2013, https://www.hrw.org/news/2013/12/23/bangladesh-investigate-killing-witness

10. Human Rights Watch, 'India: Protect Bangladesh War Crimes Trial Witness', 16 May 2013, https://www.hrw.org/news/2013/05/16/india-protect-bangladesh-war-crimes-trial-witness

11. Seth Oldmixon, 'Escaping the Shadow of Pakistan', *Foreign Policy*, 10 March 2016, http://foreignpolicy.com/2016/03/10/escaping-the-shadow-of-pakistan/

12. David Bergman, '10 key concerns about the Salauddin Quader Chowdhury trial process', Bangladesh War Crimes Tribunal, 21 November 2015, http://bangladeshwarcrimes.blogspot.co.uk/2015/11/10-key-concerns-about-salauddin-quader.html

13. 'Ex Bangladesh army officer supervised offloading of illegal arms', Thaindian News, 4 June 2009, http://www.thaindian.com/newsportal/world-news/ex-bangladesh-army-officer-supervised-offloading-of-illegal-arms_100200575.html

14. Davis, 'New details emerge on Bangladesh arms haul'.

15. Lintner, *Great Game East*, p. 150.

16. C. Christine Fair, *Fighting to the End: The Pakistan Army's Way of War*, New York: Oxford University Press, 2014, p. 27.

17. Ibid., p. 226.

18. Stephen Tankel, *Storming the World Stage: The Story of Lashkar-e-Taiba*, London: Hurst & Co., 2011, p. 51.

19. Ibid.

20. Fair, *Fighting to the End*, p. 257.

21. Husain Haqqani, 'Prophecy & the Jihad in the Indian Subcontinent', The Hudson Institute, 27 March 2015, https://www.hudson.org/research/11167-prophecy-the-jihad-in-the-indian-subcontinent

22. Ibid.

23. Fair, *Fighting to the End*, p. 226.

24. Tankel, *Storming the World Stage*, p. 54.

25. Fair, *Fighting to the End*, p. 257.

26. Ibid., p. 260.

27. India had its only brush with non-elected government in the independent era between 1975 and 1977 under Indira Gandhi, but the country has otherwise had a much more enduring and persistent democratic culture than either Pakistan or Bangladesh.

28. Gary Bass, *The Blood Telegram: Nixon, Kissinger and a Forgotten Genocide*, London: Hurst & Co., 2014.

29. Karen De Young, 'Saudi prince denies Kushner is "in his pocket"', *The Washington Post*, 22 March 2018, https://www.washingtonpost.com/world/national-security/saudi-prince-denies-kushner-is-in-his-pocket/2018/03/22/701a9c9e-2e22-11e8-8688-e053ba58f1e4_story.html?utm_term=.0da27c0e8aaa

30. Oldmixon, 'Escaping the Shadow of Pakistan'.

31. 'Embraceable you', *The Economist*, 30 July 2011, http://www.economist.com/node/21524917

32. Joseph Allchin, 'Parochial Progress', *The New York Times*, 20 November 2013, http://www.nytimes.com/2013/11/21/opinion/parochial-progress.html

33. Gowher Rizvi (Bangladesh Prime Minister's International Affairs Advisor), Talking points for a seminar at the Bangladesh Enterprise Institute, ahead of the 2017 One Belt One Road summit in Beijing. Shared by email.

34. 'A Just Cause Enjoys Abundant Support While An Unjust Cause Finds Little Support', *Peking Review* 51, 17 December 1971, p. 10, https://www.marxists.org/subject/china/peking-review/1971/PR1971-51.pdf

35. Amnesty International, 'Caught Between Fear and Repression: Attacks on Freedom of Expression in Bangladesh', 8 May 2017, https://www.amnesty.org/en/documents/asa13/6114/2017/en/

36. 'Bangladesh and Pakistan: The table has been turned', *Dhaka Tribune*, 16 February 2016, https://www.dhakatribune.com/uncategorized/2016/02/16/bangladesh-and-pakistan-the-table-has-been-turned

37. 'Pakistan voices anguished concern at Dhaka hangings', *The Express Tribune*, 23 November 2015, https://tribune.com.pk/story/996561/flawed-war-crimes-trial-pakistan-voices-anguished-concern-at-dhaka-hangings/

38. Hummam Chowdhury was secretly detained in August 2016 and was not seen or heard from for seven months. See Human Rights Watch, 'Bangladesh: Man Released From Long Secret Detention', 2 March 2017, https://www.hrw.org/news/2017/03/02/bangladesh-man-released-long-secret-detention; 'SQ Chy, Mojaheed buried', New Age,

23 November 2015, http://newagebd.net/177941/sq-chy-mojaheed-buried/

39. Joshua Hammer, 'The Imperiled Bloggers of Bangladesh', *The New York Times*, 29 December 2015, https://www.nytimes.com/2016/01/03/magazine/the-price-of-secularism-in-bangladesh.html

40. 'Chittagong Candidates with Checkered Pasts Seek Redemption as Voters Remain Wary of Violence'.

41. 'Court refuses to put Barrister Shakila on new remand', *The Daily Star*, 19 October 2015, http://www.thedailystar.net/city/court-refuses-put-barrister-shakila-new-remand-159466

42. 'Pakistan withdraws official from High Commission in Dhaka', BDnews24, 3 February 2015, http://bdnews24.com/bangladesh/2015/02/03/pakistan-withdraws-official-from-high-commission-in-dhaka

43. 'Exclusive: Pakistan's ISI printing fake Indian currency in Dubai', India Today, 13 October 2015, http://indiatoday.intoday.in/story/exclusive-isi-sets-up-fake-indian-currency-printing-unit-in-dubai/1/497269.html

44. 'Bangladesh makes major haul of "fake rupees"', *The Daily Star*, 22 September 2015, http://www.thedailystar.net/backpage/major-haul-fake-rupees-146968

45. Vijaita Singh, 'NIA team for Bangladesh to probe fake currency case', *The Hindu*, 4 October 2015, http://www.thehindu.com/news/national/nia-team-for-bangladesh-to-probe-fake-currency-case/article7720759.ece

46. 'Tunda reveals links to fake notes kingpin', *The Hindustan Times*, 21 August 2013, http://www.hindustantimes.com/delhi-news/tunda-reveals-links-with-fake-notes-kingpin/story-IRibB7s110AXoWfaGojIqO.html

47. Sharmad Mahajan, 'India's fight against fake currency', *The Diplomat*, 15 November 2016, http://thediplomat.com/2016/11/indias-fight-against-fake-currency/

48. 'Diplomat recalled from Dhaka over "extremist link"', *Dawn*, 24 December 2015, https://www.dawn.com/news/1228505

6. THE ROHINGYA

1. 'The most persecuted group in Asia', *The Economist*, 13 June 2012, https://www.economist.com/blogs/banyan/2012/06/myanmars-minorities

2. Francis Wade, *Myanmar's Enemy Within: Buddhist Violence and the Making of a Muslim 'Other'*, London: Zed Books, 2017.

3. 'Arakan Rohingya National Organization Contacts With Al Qaeda And With Burmese Insurgent Groups On The Thai Border', 10 October 2002, via Wikileaks, https://wikileaks.org/plusd/cables/02RANGOON1310_a.html

4. 'Burma's Vast Internment Camp: Northern Rakhine State', 17 February 2006, via Wikileaks, https://wikileaks.org/plusd/cables/06RANGOON235_a.html

5. Fiona Macgregor and Shwe Yee Saw Myint, 'Foreign aid workers to be evacuated from Sittwe', *The Myanmar Times*, 27 March 2014, https://www.mmtimes.com/national-news/9978-foreigners-evacuated-from-sittwe-and-violent-tensions-erupt-in-rakhine-state.html

6. International Crisis Group, 'Myanmar's Rohingya Crisis Enters a Dangerous New Phase, Asia Report N°292', 7 December 2017, https://www.crisisgroup.org/asia/south-east-asia/myanmar/292-myanmars-rohingya-crisis-enters-dangerous-new-phase

7. Hannah Beech, 'Rohingya Militants Vow to Fight Myanmar Despite Disastrous Cost', *The New York Times*, 17 September 2017, https://www.nytimes.com/2017/09/17/world/asia/myanmar-rohingya-militants.html

8. Wa Lone, Kyaw Soe Oo, Simon Lewis and Antoni Slodkowsk, 'Massacre in Myanmar', Reuters, 8 February 2018, https://www.reuters.com/investigates/special-report/myanmar-rakhine-events/

9. Joseph Allchin, 'A history of "complete repression" in Arakan state', Democratic Voice of Burma, 29 October 2012, http://www.dvb.no/analysis/a-history-of-complete-repression-in-arakan/24496

10. 'Mosque Razed, Paramilitaries Trained', 28 July 2003, via Wikileaks, https://wikileaks.org/plusd/cables/03RANGOON897_a.html

11. 'YABA out of control', *The Daily Star*, 16 May 2018, https://www.thedailystar.net/frontpage/yaba-out-control-1576924

12. Ibid.

13. Zaw Htay, 16 May 2018, via Twitter, https://twitter.com/ZawHtayMyanmar/status/996626466816208898

14. Praveen Swami, 'To India's east an emerging sanctuary for Al Qaeda', *The Indian Express*, 6 January 2017, http://indianexpress.com/article/explained/in-fact-to-indias-east-an-emerging-sanctuary-for-al-qaeda-ahmad-farooq-india-pakistan-afghanistan-4460962/

15. International Crisis Group, 'Myanmar: A New Muslim Insurgency in Rakhine State, Asia Report N°283', 15 December 2016, https://d2071andvip0wj.cloudfront.net/283-myanmar-a-new-muslim-insurgency-in-rakhine-state.pdf

16. 'PM says Bangladesh cannot help Rohingya', Al Jazeera, 28 July 2012, https://www.aljazeera.com/news/asia/2012/07/201272718523671 1203.html
17. Mahadi Al Hasnat, 'Bangladesh govt bars 3 NGOs from Rohingya relief work over security concerns', *Dhaka Tribune*, 12 October 2017, https://www.dhakatribune.com/bangladesh/nation/2017/10/12/ bars-3-ngos-rohingya/

7. THE BLACK FLAGS

1. 'Jund At-Tawheed Wal Khilafah Announcement', https://archive.org/ details/JundAt-tawheedWalKhilafah
2. Amarnath Amarasingam, 'Searching for the shadowy Canadian leader of ISIS in Bangladesh', Jihadology.net, 2 August 2016, http://jihadology. net/2016/08/02/guest-post-searching-for-the-shadowy-canadian-leader-of-isis-in-bangladesh/
3. Alex Migdal, 'Bangladeshi terror group affiliated with IS reportedly led by a Canadian', *The Globe and Mail*, 2 July 2016, http://www. theglobeandmail.com/news/world/bangladeshi-terror-group-affiliated-with-is-reportedly-led-by-canadian/article30733718/
4. Ghaith Abdul-Ahad, 'Syria's al-Nusra Front – ruthless, organised and taking control', *The Guardian*, 10 July 2013, https://www.theguardian. com/world/2013/jul/10/syria-al-nusra-front-jihadi
5. Amarasignam, 'Searching for the shadowy Canadian leader of ISIS in Bangladesh'.
6. Julfikar Ali Manik and David Barstow, 'ISIS Says It Killed Italian Aid Worker in Bangladesh', *The New York Times*, 29 September 2015, https:// www.nytimes.com/2015/09/30/world/asia/-isis-bangladesh-cesare-tavella.html
7. Shiv Malik, Aisha Gani and Saad Hammadi, 'Briton arrested in Bangladesh "confessed to recruiting" for Isis', *The Guardian*, 29 September 2014, https://www.theguardian.com/world/2014/sep/29/briton-arrested-bangladesh-recruiting-islamic-state
8. Ellen Barry, 'Bangladesh Pushes Back as Warnings of ISIS Expansion Gather Steam', *The New York Times*, 30 October 2015, https://www. nytimes.com/2015/10/31/world/asia/bangladesh-isis-terrorism-warnings.html
9. Amanda Hodge, 'Security threats put Australian Bangladesh party on hold', *The Australian*, 30 September 2015, http://www.theaustralian.com.au/ national-affairs/foreign-affairs/security-threats-put-australian-bangladesh-party-on-hold/news-story/cddb61ed3d9cfcb4316208dd00105872

10. Bangladesh Awami League, 'PM Sheikh Hasina's address at 70th Session of UNGA', 4 October 2015, http://www.albd.org/articles/news/31157/PM-Sheikh-Hasina's-address-at-70th-Session-of-UNGA
11. Ibid.
12. 'BNP concerned over Australia's tour uncertainty', *Prothom Alo*, 28 September 2015, http://en.prothom-alo.com/bangladesh/news/80839/BNP-concerned-over-Australia-s-tour-uncertainty
13. Jesse Johnson, 'IS claims killing of Japanese in Bangladesh', *The Japan Times*, 4 October 2015, http://www.japantimes.co.jp/news/2015/10/04/national/islamic-state-claims-responsibility-killing-japanese-man-bangladesh/#.WR1ythPyvEY
14. Ashik Hossain and Shahjada Mia Azad, 'Japanese Kunio Hoshi converted to Islam three months before murder, locals claim', BDnews24, 5 October 2015, http://bdnews24.com/bangladesh/2015/10/05/japanese-kunio-hoshi-converted-to-islam-three-months-before-murder-locals-claim
15. 'Isis rivendica attentato al missionario italiano Parolari in Bangladesh. Arrestato politico locale', *Il Fatto Quotidiano*, 19 November 2015, http://www.ilfattoquotidiano.it/2015/11/19/isis-rivendica-attentato-al-missionario-italiano-parolari-bangladesh-arrestato-politico-locale/2234700/
16. Pew Research Center, 'Muslim Views on Suicide Bombing', 30 June 2014, http://www.pewglobal.org/2014/07/01/concerns-about-islamic-extremism-on-the-rise-in-middle-east/pg-2014-07-01-islamic-extremism-10/
17. C. Christine Fair, Ali Hamza, and Rebecca Heller, 'Who Supports Suicide Terrorism in Bangladesh? What the Data Say', 29 April 2017, via ResearchGate, https://www.researchgate.net/publication/316580206_Who_Supports_Suicide_Terrorism_in_Bangladesh_What_the_Data_Say
18. David Bergman and Muktadir Rashid, 'Tavella murder: Phone records support family claim of secret police detention', New Age, 24 November 2015, http://newagebd.net/178260/tavella-murder-phone-records-support-family-claim-of-secret-police-detention/
19. 'Foreigner killings: Bangladesh investigators focus on 2 names', *The Daily Star*, 28 October 2015, http://www.thedailystar.net/frontpage/two-names-focus-163366
20. Ibid.
21. Mohammad Jamil Khan and Arifur Rahman Rabbi, 'Dead Abdur Rahman is Abu Ibrahim al-Hanif', *Dhaka Tribune*, 21 October 2016, https://

www.dhakatribune.com/bangladesh/crime/2016/10/21/rab-dead-militant-abdur-rahman-new-jmb-chief/

22. 'Bangladesh court hands death sentence to five men for 2015 drive-by slaying of Japanese farmer', *The Japan Times*, 1 March 2017, http://www.japantimes.co.jp/news/2017/03/01/national/crime-legal/bangladesh-court-condemns-five-2015-drive-slaying-japanese-farmer/#.WSGPXBPyvEY

23. Iftekhar Iqbal, *The Bengal Delta: Ecology, State and Social Change, 1840–1943*, Basingstoke: Palgrave Macmillan, 2010, p. 68.

24. Ibid.

25. Ranajit Guha, *Elementary Aspects of Peasant Insurgency in Colonial India*, New York: Oxford University Press, 1983, p. 74.

26. Iqbal, *The Bengal Delta*, p. 68.

27. Ibid., p. 73.

28. 'Isis claims responsibility for killing of Hindu priest in Bangladesh', *The Guardian*, 21 February 2016, https://www.theguardian.com/world/2016/feb/21/isis-claim-responsibility-killing-hindu-priest-bangladesh

29. Mohammad Jamil Khan, 'DB: Indian national involved in Trishal police van attack', *Dhaka Tribune*, 15 November 2014, https://www.dhakatribune.com/uncategorized/2014/11/15/db-indian-national-involved-in-trishal-police-van-attack

30. 'JMB leader Mohammed Javed killed in "grenade explosion" a day after arrest', BDnews24, 6 October 2015, http://bdnews24.com/bangladesh/2015/10/06/jmb-leader-mohammed-javed-killed-in-grenade-explosion-a-day-after-arrest

31. '2 suspects in Mitu murder case killed', *Dhaka Tribune*, 10 July 2016, https://www.thedailystar.net/backpage/2-suspects-mitu-murder-case-killed-1251382

32. 'Another RU teacher killed brutally', *The Daily Star*, 23 April 2016, http://www.thedailystar.net/city/ru-teacher-knifed-death-1213369

33. Nuruzzaman Labu, *Holey Bakery: A Journalistic Investigation*, Dhaka: Annesha Prokashon, 2016, p. 212.

34. Nurruzaman Labu, 'Who brainwashed Nibras?', *Dhaka Tribune*, 2 July 2017, https://www.dhakatribune.com/bangladesh/crime/2017/07/02/poisoned-nibras-mind/

35. Labu, *Holey Bakery*, p. 212.

36. Ibid.

37. Zayadul Ahsan, 'Dhaka-Syria-Dhaka', *The Daily Star*, 3 February 2017, http://www.thedailystar.net/frontpage/dhaka-syria-dhaka-1355287

38. Dean Nelson and David Bergman, '"Terrorist volunteer" recruited by alleged British Isil agent was "death metal" rock singer', *The Telegraph*, 3 October 2014, http://www.telegraph.co.uk/news/worldnews/islamic-state/11138520/Terrorist-volunteer-recruited-by-alleged-British-Isil-agent-was-death-metal-rock-singer.html

39. Mohammad Jamil Khan, 'DB arrests suspected IS recruiter in Dhaka', *Dhaka Tribune*, 29 September 2014, https://www.dhakatribune.com/uncategorized/2014/09/29/db-arrests-suspected-is-recruiter-in-dhaka

40. Clare Semke, 'Jihadist dad from Portsmouth jailed for four years', *The News*, 5 December 2014, http://www.portsmouth.co.uk/news/crime/jihadist-dad-from-portsmouth-jailed-for-four-years-1-6458920

41. Joseph Allchin, 'This Girl Walked Through Fire So We Can Get Jeans for $9', Takepart.com, 16 December 2013, http://www.takepart.com/feature/2013/12/16/the-true-cost-of-cheap-fashion/

8. RAQQA, MEET DHAKA

1. Joseph Allchin, 'Bangladesh: infrastructure, corruption and the struggle to diversify', *The Financial Times*, 3 June 2014, https://www.ft.com/content/aba1b29c-f340-3a60-9339-caab4ed9ff5a

2. 'Bangladesh café siege: Chef's family waits for answers', BBC News, 1 September 2016, http://www.bbc.co.uk/news/world-asia-37232614

3. 'A survivor's statement', *Dhaka Tribune*, 12 August 2016, http://www.dhakatribune.com/bangladesh/2016/08/12/a-survivors-statement/

4. 'Sole Japanese survivor of Dhaka attack says he hid in cafe's garden', *The Japan Times*, 14 July 2016, http://www.japantimes.co.jp/news/2016/07/14/national/sole-japanese-survivor-dhaka-attack-says-hid-cafes-garden-shooting-started/#.WTAOhhPyvEY

5. 'A survivor's statement'.

6. 'Into the heart of darkness', *Dhaka Tribune*, 27 August 2016, https://www.dhakatribune.com/bangladesh/militancy/2018/07/01/into-the-heart-of-darkness-2

7. 'Not without my friends: How Faraaz Hossain refused to leave Tarishi Jain's side and died when he could live', India Today, 4 July 2016, http://indiatoday.intoday.in/story/not-without-my-friends-how-faraaz-hossain-refused-to-leave-tarishi-jains-side-and-died-when-he-could-live/1/707511.html

8. 'Gulshan attack: autopsy shows Italians were tortured', *Dhaka Tribune*, 9 July 2016, http://archive.dhakatribune.com/world/2016/jul/09/dhaka-attack-autopsy-finds-italian-victims-were-tortured

9. Ananya Roy, 'Dhaka café attack victims were brutally tortured, post-mortem reveals', *International Business Times*, 15 July 2016, http://www.ibtimes.co.uk/dhaka-cafe-terror-attack-victims-were-brutally-tortured-post-mortem-reports-reveal-1570779

10. 'Exclusive: Video footage of the inside of Holey Artisan Bakery premises', *Dhaka Tribune*, 4 August 2016, http://www.dhakatribune.com/videos/2016/08/04/twenty-seconds-terror/

11. M Abul Kalam Azad, 'Diary of a young radical', *The Daily Star*, 1 June 2018, https://www.thedailystar.net/star-weekend/spotlight/diary-young-radical-1584592

12. Ibid.

13. Max Scheler, *Ressentiment*, 1915, trans. Louis A. Coser, p. 9, http://www.mercaba.org/SANLUIS/Filosofia/autores/Contempor%C3%A1nea/Scheller/Ressentiment.pdf

14. Pankaj Mishra, *The Age of Anger: A History of the Present*, London: Allen Lane, 2017, p. 500.

15. Jeffrey K. Olick and Charles Demetriou, 'From Theodicy to *Ressentiment*: Trauma and the Ages of Compensation', in D. Bell (ed.), *Memory, Trauma and World Politics: Reflections on the Relationship Between Past and Present*, Basingstoke: Palgrave Macmillan, 2006, p. 80.

16. 'After 2 years, Hasnat freed', *The Daily Star*, 10 August 2018, https://www.thedailystar.net/news/city/dhaka-cafe-attack-hasnat-karim-walks-free-1618204

17. Linda Pressly, '"I escaped death by reciting from the Koran"', BBC News, 12 January 2017, http://www.bbc.co.uk/news/magazine-38459996

18. Ibid.

9. POST MORTEM

1. Greg Bearup and Mark Schliebs, 'Tajuddin, the terrorist husband she wishes she had never known', *The Australian*, 2 August 2016, http://www.theaustralian.com.au/in-depth/terror/tajuddin-the-terrorist-husband-she-wishes-she-had-never-known/news-story/ef011ca8023c6b060f61f414f6add33c

2. Tamim Chowdhury, 'The Shuhada of the Gulshan Attack', *Rumiyah* 2, 4 October 2016, p. 8, https://clarionproject.org/factsheets-files/Rumiyh-ISIS-Magazine-2nd-issue.pdf

3. Analysis of the photos shows that the assault rifle pictured has the same scratches in each image. It is believed that three AK-22s were deployed in the attack on Holey Bakery.

4. Chowdhury, 'The Shuhada of the Gulshan Attack', p. 8.

5. Ibid., p. 10.

6.   Ibid., p. 11.
7.   Olivier Roy, 'Who are the new jihadis?', *The Guardian*, 13 April 2017, https://www.theguardian.com/news/2017/apr/13/who-are-the-new-jihadis
8.   'Report: Feni's Akash planned terrorist attacks in Bangladesh', *Dhaka Tribune*, 23 September 2016, http://www.dhakatribune.com/bangladesh/crime/2016/09/23/report-fenis-akash-planned-terrorist-attacks-bangladesh/
9.   Large numbers of Bangladeshis travel as migrant labourers to the Gulf states, Singapore, and Malaysia.
10. Institute for Policy Analysis of Conflict, 'How South East Asian and Bangladeshi Extremism Intersect, IPAC Report No. 37', 8 May 2017, http://file.understandingconflict.org/file/2017/05/IPAC_Report_37.pdf
11. Shahriar Sharif, 'Deported Bangladeshi Met in Malaysia with Suspect in Dhaka Café Attack: Report', Benar News, 23 September 2016, http://www.benarnews.org/english/news/bengali/Paer-Ahmed-Akash-09232016185003.html
12. Nuruzzaman Labu, *Holey Bakery: A Journalistic Investigation*, Dhaka: Annesha Prokashon, 2016.
13. Ibid.
14. William B. Milam, 'The Real Source of Terror in Bangladesh', *The New York Times*, 19 May 2016, https://www.nytimes.com/2016/05/20/opinion/the-real-source-of-terror-in-bangladesh.html
15. Pazit Ben-Nun Bloom and Gizem Arikan, 'Globalisation has contributed to declining levels of religious freedom across the world', The London School of Economics blog, 15 July 2014, http://blogs.lse.ac.uk/politicsandpolicy/globalisation-religious-freedom/#Author
16. Orhan Pamuk, 'Listen to the damned', *The Guardian*, 29 September 2001, https://www.theguardian.com/world/2001/sep/29/afghanistan.terrorism7
17. Olga Khazan, 'Why did people vote for Trump?', *The Atlantic*, 23 April 2018, https://www.theatlantic.com/science/archive/2018/04/existential-anxiety-not-poverty-motivates-trump-support/558674/
18. Max Scheler, *Ressentiment*, 1915, trans. Louis A. Coser, p. 25, http://www.mercaba.org/SANLUIS/Filosofia/autores/Contempor%C3%A1nea/Scheller/Ressentiment.pdf

BIBLIOGRAPHY

Ali, S. Mahmud, *Understanding Bangladesh*, London: Hurst & Co., 2010.

Armstrong, Karen, *Fields of Blood: Religion and the History of Violence*, New York and Toronto: Knopf, 2014.

Bass, Gary, *The Blood Telegram: Nixon, Kissinger and a Forgotten Genocide*, London: Hurst & Co., 2014.

Bell, D. (ed.), *Memory, Trauma and World Politics: Reflections on the Relationship Between Past and Present*, Basingstoke: Palgrave Macmillan, 2006.

Blood, Archer K., *The Cruel Birth of Bangladesh: Memoirs of an American Diplomat*, Dhaka: University Press Ltd, 2002.

Burke, Jason, *The New Threat from Islamic Militancy*, London: The Bodley Head, 2015.

Eaton, Richard M., *The Rise of Islam on the Bengal Frontier, 1204–1760*, Berkeley: University of California Press, 1993.

Fair, C. Christine, *Fighting to the End: The Pakistan Army's Way of War*, New York: Oxford University Press, 2014.

Ganguly, Sumit, *Conflict Unending: India-Pakistan Tensions Since 1947*, New York: Columbia University Press, 2001.

Guha, Ranajit, *Elementary Aspects of Peasant Insurgency in Colonial India*, New York: Oxford University Press, 1983.

Hossain, Naomi, *Understanding Bangladesh's Unexpected Successes*, New York: Oxford University Press, 2017.

Iqbal, Iftekhar, *The Bengal Delta: Ecology, State and Social Change, 1840–1943*, Basingstoke: Palgrave Macmillan, 2010.

Ispahani, Farahnaz, *Purifying the Land of the Pure*, New York: Oxford University Press, 2015.

Jaffrelot, Christophe, *The Pakistan Paradox: Instability and Resilience*, London: Hurst & Co., 2015.

Labu, Nuruzzaman, *Holey Bakery: A Journalistic Investigation*, Dhaka: Annesha Prokashon, 2016.

Lewis, David, *Bangladesh: Politics, Economy and Civil Society*, Cambridge: Cambridge University Press, 2011.

Lifschultz, Lawrence, *Bangladesh: The Unfinished Revolution*, London: Zed Press, 1979.

Lintner, Bertil, *Great Game East: India, China, and the Struggle for Asia's Most Volatile Frontier*, New Haven: Yale University Press, 2015.

Maher, Shiraz, *Salafi-Jihadism: The History of an Idea*, London: Hurst & Co., 2016.

Mecham, Quinn and Julie Chernov Hwang (eds), *Islamist Parties and Political Normalization in the Muslim World*, Philadelphia: University of Pennsylvania Press, 2014.

Mishra, Pankaj, *The Age of Anger: A History of the Present*, London: Allen Lane, 2017.

Pantucci, Raffaello, *'We Love Death As You Love Life': Britain's Suburban Terrorists*, London: Hurst and Co., 2015.

Riaz, Ali, *Islamist Militancy in Bangladesh: A Complex Web*, New York: Routledge, 2008.

Said, Edward, *Orientalism*, New York: Vintage Books, 1979.

Shawcross, William, *Sideshow: Kissinger, Nixon and the Destruction of Cambodia*, New York: Simon and Schuster, 1979.

Sisson, Richard and Leo E. Rose, *War and Secession: Pakistan, India, and the Creation of Bangladesh*, Berkeley and Los Angeles: University of California Press, 1990.

Tankel, Stephen, *Storming the World Stage: The Story of Lashkar-e-Taiba*, London: Hurst & Co., 2011.

Tripathi, Salil, *The Colonel Who Would Not Repent: The Bangladesh War and Its Unquiet Legacy*, New Haven: Yale University Press, 2016.

Wade, Francis, *Myanmar's Enemy Within: Buddhist Violence and the Making of a Muslim 'Other'*, London: Zed Books, 2017.

INDEX

Abir, Raihan: *Philosophy of Disbelief*, 87–8, 104
Adnan, Asif: 159
Afghanistan: 13, 61, 131; borders of, 102; Operation Enduring Freedom (2001–14), 189; Soviet Invasion of (1979–89), 60–1, 69, 102, 121
Ahle Hadith movement: 69–71, 121; madrassas, 186
Ahmed, Andaleeb: 186
Ahmed, Ishraq: 97
Ahmed, Khondaker Mushtaq: 41; resignation of (1975), 41–2
Ahmed, Rafida Bonya: 89, 104; attack on (2015), 86–7
Ahsan, Gias Uddin: 181
Akash, Peyar Ahmed: background of, 186; death of (2016), 186
Akbar: adoption of proto-Hindu-Islamic calendar, 106; reign of, 105
Akhond, Ishrat: hostage in Holey Artisan Bakery Attack (2016), 166, 168
Aktar, Babul: family of, 155
Akther, Sonia: family of, 166
Alam, Jahangir (Rajiv Gandhi): 185; detaining of (2017), 183

Alam, Syed Wahidul: family of, 126
Alamgir, Mirza Fakhrul Islam: 53
Alcatel-Lucent: 158
Ali, S. Mahmud: 39
All India Muslim League: 12; formation of (1906), 12
Amanat (vessel): arms seized from (2004), 111
Amar Desh (newspaper): 32, 191
American International School: 146
Amin, A.T.M.: 64
animism: 66
Anjuman al-Bayyinat: 49
Ansarullah Bangla Team (ABT): 89, 94–5, 99, 101–3, 141; as Ansar al-Islam, 30, 101–4, 107–8, 155; claim of responsibility for attack on Avijit Roy and Rafida Bonya Ahmed (2015), 87–8; emergence of, 92–3; funding efforts of, 92–3, 127
d'Antona, Claudia: family of, 165; hostage in Holey Artisan Bakery Attack (2016), 165
Arab Spring: 27
Arabic (language): 131, 182
Arakan Army: 137